BRITAIN VOTES
6

BRITAIN VOTES

6

BRITISH PARLIAMENTARY ELECTION RESULTS 1997

Compiled and Edited by

COLIN RALLINGS AND MICHAEL THRASHER

Ashgate

Aldershot • Brookfield USA • Singapore • Sydney

Published by
Ashgate Publishing Limited
Gower House
Croft Road
Aldershot
Hants GU11 3HR
England

Ashgate Publishing Company
Old Post Road
Brookfield
Vermont 05036
USA

British Library Cataloguing in Publication Data
Rallings, Colin
  Britain votes
  6: British parliamentary election results 1997. -
  (Parliamentary research services)
  1.Great Britain. Parliament. House of Commons - Elections, 1997
  I.Title II.Thrasher, Michael
  324.9'41'0859

ISBN 1 84014 054 2

Printed in Great Britain by the Ipswich Book Company, Suffolk

CONTENTS

PREFACE

This is the sixth volume in a series of definitive reference books intended to provide an interim supplement to the series of volumes entitled *British Parliamentary Election Results*.

We took over this series from the late F.W.S. Craig. A number of changes to Craig's original format were introduced for *Britain Votes 5* and we have extended that process still further. The constituencies now only have a single identifying number. This identity number, commonly referred to as 'PA number', will also be used in most machine-readable data sets of the general election results.

The 1997 general election was fought on new constituency boundaries. Compared with the previous election in 1992 the number of constituencies was increased from 651 to 659. A total of only 165 seats were unchanged by the Boundary Commissioners. In order to make comparisons with the 1992 general election, therefore, it was necessary to compile an agreed set of 'notional results'. A media consortium comprising BBC, ITN, PA News and BSkyB commissioned us to prepare these notional results which were published in 1995 as *The Media Guide to the New Parliamentary Constituencies*. Where constituencies have new boundaries our calculations for party change are based on this earlier publication.

We have also increased further the number of Tables for this volume, reflecting our readers' favourable reaction to *Britain Votes 5*. In addition, the alphabetical index of candidates now also includes party affiliation.

A number of people have helped us considerably in compiling these results. First and foremost are the Returning Officers and their staffs who responded with such patience to our apparently endless requests for information. We should also like to thank those people from within the political parties who provided details about their candidates. Chris Long at ITN and Rob Clements of the Social and General Statistics Section of the House of Commons Library also supplied essential information. At Plymouth, Lawrence Ware constructed the computerised database of results while Alison Hale and Stephen Kelly ensured that election returns were collected, collated and processed.

As ever, we are happy to receive comments from readers either about any errors or with suggestions for possible improvements for future editions.

Colin Rallings and Michael Thrasher,
University of Plymouth,
August 1997

INTRODUCTORY NOTES

All constituencies in the United Kingdom are listed in alphabetical order following the practice of the Press Association. Thus Aberavon is number 1 and Yorkshire East number 659.

Under the name of each constituency are seven columns:

1a. Electors The estimated (†) or actual number of electors eligible to vote on May 1st 1997.

1b. 'Index of change' A general review of constituency boundaries was enacted before the 1997 general election. The 'index of change' provides a guide to how far the boundaries of a new constituency differ from that of the old constituency from which it was drawn. 'None' equals no change. The further the figure exceeds 0.0, the more the constituency has experienced boundary changes. A detailed definition of the 'index' and an explanation of how it is calculated can be found in C. Rallings and M. Thrasher (eds), *The Media Guide to the New Parliamentary Constituencies*(Plymouth: LGC Elections Centre, 1995).

2. Turnout The number of valid votes cast expressed as a percentage of the eligible electorate.

3. Candidate The surname and initials of the candidate. All women are listed as 'Ms.'; those candidates who were members of the 1992-97 Parliament are denoted by a *.

4. Party The party affiliation of the candidate.

5. Vote The number of votes polled by the candidate.

6. Share The number of votes polled by the candidate expressed as a percentage of the total valid votes cast. A * indicates a forfeited deposit.

7. Change The percentage change in the share of the vote for the party since the 1992 general election. In the case of constituencies with new boundaries, change is based on 'notional' results calculated as if those constituencies had been in existence in 1992. Detailed figures can be found in C.Rallings and M. Thrasher (eds), *The Media Guide to the New Parliamentary Constituencies* .

At the foot of each set of voting figures appears the majority of the successful candidate and this is also expressed as a percentage. (The rounding of percentages originally calculated to two decimal places sometimes results in the percentage majority figure differing by + or -0.1% from that obtained by subtracting the share of the first placed party from that of the second placed party.) The party which actually or 'notionally' won the seat at the 1992 general election is also noted.

BY ELECTIONS

The boundary changes came into effect with the dissolution of parliament. All by-elections in the 1992-97 Parliament were fought on the old boundaries and are NOT listed here. Detailed results of those by-elections can be found in *British Parliamentary Election Results 1983-97* (Aldershot: Ashgate, forthcoming). Table 4 in the current volume describes the subsequent fate of candidates elected at by-elections between 1992 and 1997.

CHANGE OF PARTY ALLEGIANCE

In a number of cases MPs changed their party allegiance following election. A.T. Howarth was elected as Conservative MP for Stratford-on-Avon, but subsequently took the Labour whip. He was elected Labour MP for Newport East in 1997. Ms. E. H. Nicholson, elected Conservative MP for Devon West and Torridge in 1992, and P. G. Thurnham, the 1992 Conservative victor in Bolton North East, both defected to the Liberal Democrats. Neither contested a seat at the 1997 election.

ELECTORATE STATISTICS

For this volume two different calculations have been used for electorate statistics. Where the electorate figure for a constituency is followed by a †, then it has been estimated from the statistics as first published by the Office for National Statistics, amended where necessary following information received from Returning Officers. For an explanation of the formula used to calculate the electorate on a given date, see F.W.S. Craig (ed), *British Electoral Facts, 1832-1987* (Aldershot: Dartmouth, 1989) p. xiii.

The increase in the availability of machine-readable electoral registers has meant that many Returning Officers were able to supply us with more exact counts of their electorates on the day of the election. Wherever possible we have used these, not least because in a number of constituencies the 'on the day' electorate differs quite sharply from that 'as first published' owing to a high incidence of late claims. Constituencies which fall into this category have NO † after their electorate.

FORFEITED DEPOSITS

A candidate forfeited a deposit of £500 if s/he was not elected and did not poll more than one-twentieth of the valid votes cast. For details about lost deposits see Table 37.

GENERAL ELECTION POLLING DATE

Polling took place on May 1st 1997.

SURNAMES AND INITIALS

The surnames and initials of candidates are based on returns made to the authors by Returning Officers. Only initials and titles which can be derived from these sources are listed.

VOTING STATISTICS

The number of votes cast for candidates are based on returns made to the authors by Returning Officers.

PARTY LABELS AND ABBREVIATIONS

Abbrev.	Party	Candidates
APNI	Alliance Party of Northern Ireland	17
BNP	British National Party	57
CD	Christian Democrat Party	2
Comm	Communist	3
Con	Conservative and Unionist Party	648
DUP	Democratic Unionist Party	9
Grn	Green Party	95
Hum	Humanist Party	2
Ind	Independent (when placed before a party label indicates an unofficial candidate)*	186
Lab†	Labour Party	639
LC	Legalise Cannabis	4
LD	Liberal Democratic Party	639
Lib	Liberal Party	55
MK	Mebyon Kernow	4
MRLP	Monster Raving Loony Party	24
Nat Dem	National Democrat	21
NF	National Front	6
NLP	Natural Law Party	197
PC	Plaid Cymru	40
PL	Pro-Life	56
Prog U	Progressive Unionist	3
Rainbow	Rainbow Dream Ticket	31
Ref	Referendum Party	547
SDLP	Social Democratic and Labour Party	18
SF	Sinn Fein	17
SL	Socialist Labour	64
SNP	Scottish National Party	72
Soc	Socialist	24
Speaker	Speaker seeking re-election	1
SSA	Scottish Socialist Alliance	16
UKI	UK Independence Party	193
UKU	UK Unionist Party	1
UU	Ulster Unionist Party	16
WP	Workers Party	8
WRP	Workers Revolutionary Party	9

*There has been growing controversy over the adoption by 'Independent' candidates of labels the same as or very similar to those used by the established political parties. Designations such as 'Local Conservative', 'Real Labour' or 'Liberal Democrat Alternative Candidate' -all of which occurred in 1997- clearly indicate a separation between the candidate and the political party. We have, however, noted 3 cases where it might be argued that there was an intention to mislead. R.J. Huggett, already well-known for his candidature as a 'Literal Democrat' in the Devon and Plymouth East Euro-constituency in 1994, legally stood as 'The Conservative Party Candidate' in Brighton Pavilion and as 'Liberal Democrat Top Choice for Parliament' in Winchester. D.K. Neal, presumably taking his cue from Huggett's 1994 venture, stood as 'The Conservatory Party Candidate' in Clwyd West. They are each listed as 'Ind' in the results section.

† A total of 26 Labour candidates, jointly sponsored by the Co-operative Party, are described in the results as 'Lab'. The following constituencies had Lab/Co-op candidates: Basildon; Brighton Pavilion; Bristol N.W.; Cardiff Central; Cardiff South & Penarth; Carrick, Cumnock and Doon Valley; Corby; Dumbarton; Edmonton; Feltham & Heston; Glasgow Pollok; Glasgow Rutherglen; Hemel Hempstead; Heywood & Middleton; Huddersfield; Ilford South; Islwyn; Kirkcaldy; Leicester N.W.; Liverpool Riverside; Loughborough; Paisley South; Plymouth Sutton; Stroud; Wolverhampton N.E.; Wolverhampton S.E.

The Result in Winchester

The general election result in Winchester was declared void by the High Court following an investigation into voting papers disqualified for want of the official mark. A new election was called for 20th November 1997. The result was as follows:

Winchester [633]

79,116	68.9	Oaten, M.	LD	37,006	68.0
		Malone, G.*	Con	15,450	28.4
44.3		Davies, P.	Lab	944	1.7*
		Page R.	Ref/UKI	521	1.0*
		Sutch D.	MRLP	316	0.6*
		Huggett, R.J.	Ind	59	0.1*
		Barry R.J. Ms.	NLP	48	0.1*
		Everest R.J.	Ind Con	40	0.1*
				———	——
1992: Con				21,556	39.6

All Tables in this book are based on the May 1st result.

PARLIAMENTARY CONSTITUENCY RESULTS

Aberavon [1]

50,031	71.9	Morris, J.*	Lab	25,650	71.3	+4.2
		McConville, R.L.	LD	4,079	11.3	-1.1
None		Harper, P.E.	Con	2,835	7.9	-6.0
		Cockwell, P.	PC	2,088	5.8	+1.0
		David, P.	Ref	970	2.7*	
		Beany, C.	Ind	341	0.9*	
1992: Lab				21,571	60.0	

Aberdeen Central [2]

54,390	65.5	Doran, F.	Lab	17,745	49.8	+6.7
		Wisely, J.G.A. Ms.	Con	6,944	19.5	-9.3
93.5		Topping, B.A.	SNP	5,767	16.2	-1.4
		Brown, J.D.	LD	4,714	13.2	+2.7
		Farquharson, J.S.	Ref	446	1.3*	
1992: Lab				10,801	30.3	

Aberdeen North [3]

54,331	70.7	Savidge, M.K.	Lab	18,389	47.9	+12.8
		Adam, B.J.	SNP	8,379	21.8	-0.7
87.7		Gifford, J.N.	Con	5,763	15.0	-3.6
		Rumbles, M.J.	LD	5,421	14.1	-9.7
		MacKenzie, A.W.E.	Ref	463	1.2*	
1992: Lab				10,010	26.1	

Aberdeen South [4]

60,566	72.8	Begg, A. Ms.	Lab	15,541	35.3	+11.4
		Stephen, N.R.	LD	12,176	27.6	+1.0
90.1		Robertson, R.S.*	Con	11,621	26.4	-11.0
		Towers, J.D.	SNP	4,299	9.8	-2.3
		Wharton, R.F.	Ref	425	1.0*	
1992: Con				3,365	7.6	

Aberdeenshire W & Kincardine [5]

59,123†	73.1	Smith, R.H.	LD	17,742	41.1	+6.4
		Kynoch, G.A.B.*	Con	15,080	34.9	-10.2
63.0		Mowatt, J.M. Ms.	SNP	5,649	13.1	+0.6
		Khan, Q.E.	Lab	3,923	9.1	+2.3
		Ball, S.L.	Ref	808	1.9*	
1992: Con				2,662	6.2	

Airdrie & Shotts [6]

57,673†	71.4	Liddell, H. Ms.*	Lab	25,460	61.8	-0.7
		Robertson, K.R.A.	SNP	10,048	24.4	+6.3
52.7		Brook, N.H.	Con	3,660	8.9	-6.0
		Wolseley, R.G.	LD	1,719	4.2*	-0.3
		Semple, C.	Ref	294	0.7*	
1992: Lab				15,412	37.4	

Aldershot [7]

76,499†	70.8	Howarth, J.G.D.	Con	23,119	42.7	-15.4
		Collett, A.P.	LD	16,498	30.5	+4.1
8.1		Bridgeman, T.D.	Lab	13,057	24.1	+10.3
		Howe, J.W.	UKI	794	1.5*	
		Pendragon, A.U.	Ind	361	0.7*	
		Stevens, D.M.	BNP	322	0.6*	
1992: Con				6,621	12.2	

Aldridge - Brownhills [8]

62,441†	74.3	Shepherd, R.C.S.*	Con	21,856	47.1	-7.2
		Toth, J.	Lab	19,330	41.7	+8.4
None		Downie, C.M. Ms.	LD	5,184	11.2	-1.2
1992: Con				2,526	5.4	

Altrincham & Sale West [9]

70,625†	73.3	Brady, G.	Con	22,348	43.2	-11.3
		Baugh, J.E. Ms.	Lab	20,843	40.3	+13.8
52.7		Ramsbottom, M.S.	LD	6,535	12.6	-5.8
		Landes, A.L.	Ref	1,348	2.6*	
		Stephens, J.P.	PL	313	0.6*	
		Mrozinski, R.A.	UKI	270	0.5*	
		Renwick, J.C.	NLP	125	0.2*	
1992: Con				1,505	2.9	

Alyn & Deeside [10]

58,091†	72.2	Jones, S.B.*	Lab	25,955	61.9	+11.0
		Roberts, T.P.	Con	9,552	22.8	-14.1
6.0		Burnham, E. Ms.	LD	4,076	9.7	-0.0
		Jones, M.J.D.	Ref	1,627	3.9*	
		Hills, S. Ms.	PC	738	1.8*	+0.6
1992: Lab				16,403	39.1	

Amber Valley [11]

72,116†	76.0	Mallaber, C.J. Ms.	Lab	29,943	54.7	+10.3
		Oppenheim, P.A.C.L.*	Con	18,330	33.5	-13.0
2.7		Shelley, R.P.	LD	4,219	7.7	-1.4
		McGibbon, I.E. Ms.	Ref	2,283	4.2*	
1992: Con				11,613	21.2	

Angus [12]

59,708†	72.1	Welsh, A.P.*	SNP	20,792	48.3	+9.1
		Leslie, S.A.A.	Con	10,603	24.6	-13.5
22.9		Taylor, C.D. Ms.	Lab	6,733	15.6	+2.7
		Speirs, R.B.	LD	4,065	9.4	+0.6
		Taylor, B.A.	Ref	883	2.0*	
1992: SNP				10,189	23.7	

Antrim East [13]

59,032	58.2	Beggs, R.*	UU	13,318	38.8	-4.8
		Neeson, S.	APNI	6,929	20.2	-5.0
21.8		McKee, J.	DUP	6,682	19.5	-3.2
		Dick, T.S.	Con	2,334	6.8	-1.1
		Donaldson, B.	Prog U	1,751	5.1	
		O'Connor, D.G.	SDLP	1,576	4.6*	
		Mason, R.L.	Ind	1,145	3.3*	
		McAuley, C. Ms.	SF	543	1.6*	
		McCann, M. Ms.	NLP	69	0.2*	
1992: UU				6,389	18.6	

Antrim North [14]

72,491	63.7	Paisley, I.R.K.*	DUP	21,495	46.5	-4.3
		Leslie, J.S.	UU	10,921	23.6	+5.6
None		Farren, S.N.	SDLP	7,333	15.9	+1.6
		McCarry, J.K.	SF	2,896	6.3	+2.1
		Alderdice, D.K.	APNI	2,845	6.2	-1.4
		Hinds, B.A.T. Ms.	Ind	580	1.3*	
		Wright, J.D.O.	NLP	116	0.3*	
1992: DUP				10,574	22.9	

Antrim South [15]

69,512	57.8	Forsythe, C.*	UU	23,108	57.5	-13.9
		McClelland, D.	SDLP	6,497	16.2	+2.6
4.7		Ford, D.R.J.	APNI	4,668	11.6	+0.7
		Smyth, H.	Prog U	3,490	8.7	
		Cushinan, H.J.	SF	2,229	5.5	+2.5
		Briggs, B.A. Ms.	NLP	203	0.5*	
1992: UU				16,611	41.3	

Argyll & Bute [16]

48,983	72.9	Michie, R. Ms.*	LD	14,359	40.2	+5.3
		MacCormick, N.	SNP	8,278	23.2	-0.6
None		Leishman, R.M.	Con	6,774	19.0	-8.8
		Syed, A.	Lab	5,596	15.7	+2.1
		Stewart, M.A.S.G.	Ref	713	2.0*	
1992: LD				6,081	17.0	

Arundel & South Downs [17]

68,010†	75.5	Flight, H.E.	Con	27,251	53.1	-9.7
		Goss, J.M.	LD	13,216	25.7	+0.6
104.7		Black, R.	Lab	9,376	18.3	+8.9
		Herbert, J.T.	UKI	1,494	2.9*	
1992: Con				14,035	27.3	

Ashfield [18]

72,299	70.0	Hoon, G.W.*	Lab	32,979	65.2	+10.3
		Simmonds, M.J.M.	Con	10,251	20.3	-12.4
0.1		Smith, J.W.E.	LD	4,882	9.6	-2.9
		Betts, M.I.	Ref	1,896	3.7*	
		Belshaw, S.E.	BNP	595	1.2*	
1992: Lab				22,728	44.9	

Ashford [19]

74,512†	74.2	Green, D.H.	Con	22,899	41.4	-13.2
		Ennals, J.R.	Lab	17,544	31.7	+11.7
None		Williams, J.	LD	10,901	19.7	-4.3
		Cruden, C.L.	Ref	3,201	5.8	
		Boden, R.T.	Grn	660	1.2*	
		Tyrrell, S.D.L.	NLP	89	0.2*	
1992: Con				5,355	9.7	

Ashton under Lyne [20]

72,308†	65.4	Sheldon, R.E.*	Lab	31,919	67.5	+10.5
		Mayson, R.J.	Con	8,954	18.9	-9.8
52.3		Pickstone, T.D.	LD	4,603	9.7	-2.2
		Clapham, L.E. Ms.	Ref	1,346	2.8*	
		Cymbal, P.	MRLP	458	1.0*	
1992: Lab				22,965	48.6	

Aylesbury [21]

79,047†	72.8	Lidington, D.*	Con	25,426	44.2	-13.1
		Bowles, S. Ms.	LD	17,007	29.5	+1.8
4.0		Langridge, R.	Lab	12,759	22.2	+8.7
		John, M.	Ref	2,196	3.8*	
		Sheaff, L.	NLP	166	0.3*	
1992: Con				8,419	14.6	

Ayr [22]

55,925†	80.0	Osborne, S. Ms.	Lab	21,679	48.4	+5.8
		Gallie, P.*	Con	15,136	33.8	-4.6
16.6		Blackford, I.	SNP	5,625	12.6	+1.4
		Hamblen, C.A. Ms.	LD	2,116	4.7*	-2.7
		Enos, J.C.	Ref	200	0.4*	
1992: Lab				6,543	14.6	

Banbury [23]

77,797†	75.1	Baldry, A.B.*	Con	25,076	42.9	-11.9
		Peperell, H.Y. Ms.	Lab	20,339	34.8	+7.9
3.8		Bearder, C.Z. Ms.	LD	9,761	16.7	-1.1
		Ager, J.W.	Ref	2,245	3.8*	
		Cotton, B.M.	Grn	530	0.9*	
		King, L. Ms.	UKI	364	0.6*	
		Pearson, I.	NLP	131	0.2*	
1992: Con				4,737	8.1	

Banff & Buchan [24]

58,493†	68.7	Salmond, A.E.A.*	SNP	22,409	55.8	+4.9
		Frain Bell, W.	Con	9,564	23.8	-10.9
11.6		Harris, M. Ms.	Lab	4,747	11.8	+3.2
		Fletcher, N.D.	LD	2,398	6.0	+0.1
		Buchan, A.S.	Ref	1,060	2.6*	
1992: SNP				12,845	32.0	

Barking [25]

53,458	61.7	Hodge, M.E. Ms.*	Lab	21,698	65.8	+13.6
		Langford, K.R.	Con	5,802	17.6	-16.3
10.6		Marsh, M.J.P.	LD	3,128	9.5	-4.4
		Taylor, C.E.	Ref	1,283	3.9*	
		Tolman, M.C.	BNP	894	2.7*	
		Mearns, D.F.	PL	159	0.5*	
1992: Lab				15,896	48.2	

Barnsley Central [26]

61,160	59.7	Illsley, E.E.*	Lab	28,090	77.0	+6.2
		Gutteridge, S.P.	Con	3,589	9.8	-8.7
14.3		Finlay, D.	LD	3,481	9.5	-1.2
		Walsh, J.J.	Ref	1,325	3.6*	
1992: Lab				24,501	67.2	

Barnsley East & Mexborough [27]

68,105	63.6	Ennis, J.*	Lab	31,699	73.1	+0.2
		Ellison, J.E. Ms.	Con	4,936	11.4	-6.0
56.6		Willis, D.J.	LD	4,489	10.4	+0.6
		Capstick, W.K.	SL	1,213	2.8*	
		Miles, A.J.	Ref	797	1.8*	
		Hyland, J.E. Ms.	Ind	201	0.5*	
1992: Lab				26,763	61.8	

Barnsley West & Penistone [28]

64,912	65.0	Clapham, M.*	Lab	25,017	59.3	+1.0
		Watkins, P.A.	Con	7,750	18.4	-9.7
None		Knight, W.I. Ms.	LD	7,613	18.0	+6.4
		Miles, J. Ms.	Ref	1,828	4.3*	
1992: Lab				17,267	40.9	

Barrow & Furness [29]

67,007	72.0	Hutton, J.M.P.*	Lab	27,630	57.3	+9.5
		Hunt, R.	Con	13,133	27.2	-14.1
None		Metcalfe, A. A. Ms.	LD	4,264	8.8	-2.1
		Hamezeian, J.	Ind	1,995	4.1*	
		Mitchell, D.Y.	Ref	1,208	2.5*	
1992: Lab				14,497	30.1	

Basildon [30]

73,714	72.0	Smith, A.E. Ms.	Lab	29,646	55.8	+15.1
		Baron, J.C.	Con	16,366	30.8	-14.3
68.1		Granshaw, L. Ms.	LD	4,608	8.7	-5.5
		Robinson, C.B.	Ref	2,462	4.6*	
1992: Con				13,280	25.0	

Basingstoke [31]

77,063	74.1	Hunter, A.R.F.*	Con	24,751	43.3	-10.2
		Lickley, N.J.D.	Lab	22,354	39.1	+14.0
9.5		Rimmer, M.E.	LD	9,714	17.0	-3.4
		Selim, E.M.O.	Ind	310	0.5*	
1992: Con				2,397	4.2	

Bassetlaw [32]

68,101†	70.5	Ashton, J.W.*	Lab	29,298	61.0	+7.7
		Cleasby, M.A.	Con	11,950	24.9	-10.1
0.0		Kerrigan, S.D.M.	LD	4,915	10.2	-1.4
		Graham, R.	Ref	1,838	3.8*	
1992: Lab				17,348	36.1	

Bath [33]

70,975	76.1	Foster, D.M.E.*	LD	26,169	48.5	+1.6
		McNair, A. Ms.	Con	16,850	31.2	-12.2
11.2		Bush, T.	Lab	8,828	16.4	+8.2
		Cook, A.P.	Ref	1,192	2.2*	
		Scrase, R.J.	Grn	580	1.1*	
		Sandell, P.G.	UKI	315	0.6*	
		Pullen, N.A.	NLP	55	0.1*	
1992: LD				9,319	17.3	

Batley & Spen [34]

64,202	73.2	Wood, M.R.	Lab	23,213	49.4	+6.4
		Peacock, E.J. Ms.*	Con	17,072	36.4	-8.3
16.3		Pinnock, K.M. Ms.	LD	4,133	8.8	-2.5
		Wood, E.O.C.	Ref	1,691	3.6*	
		Smith, R.A.	BNP	472	1.0*	
		Lord, C.R.	Grn	384	0.8*	
1992: Con				6,141	13.1	

Battersea [35]

66,895	70.9	Linton, J.M.	Lab	24,047	50.7	+9.5
		Bowis, J.C.*	Con	18,687	39.4	-11.0
0.3		Keaveney, P.C. Ms.	LD	3,482	7.3	+0.3
		Slater, M.W.	Ref	804	1.7*	
		Banks, A.	UKI	250	0.5*	
		Marshall, J.	Rainbow	127	0.3*	
1992: Con				5,360	11.3	

Beaconsfield [36]

68,959†	72.8	Grieve, D.C.R.	Con	24,709	49.2	-14.5
		Mapp, P.G.D.	LD	10,722	21.4	+1.9
3.3		Hudson, A.S.	Lab	10,063	20.0	+6.4
		Lloyd, H.A.	Ref	2,197	4.4*	
		Story, C.E.H.	Ind Con	1,434	2.9*	
		Cooke, C.W.R.	UKI	451	0.9*	
		Duval, G.S. Ms.	PL	286	0.6*	
		Dyball, T.W.S.	NLP	193	0.4*	
		Matthews, R.R.	Ind	146	0.3*	
1992: Con				13,987	27.9	

Beckenham [37]

73,126	74.3	Merchant, P.R.G.*	Con	23,084	42.5	-17.7
		Hughes, R.N.	Lab	18,131	33.4	+12.2
24.8		Vetterlein, R.E. Ms.	LD	9,858	18.1	+1.4
		Mead, L.F.	Ref	1,663	3.1*	
		Rimmer, P.H.	Lib	720	1.3*	
		Pratt, C.N.	UKI	506	0.9*	
		McAuley, J.C.	NF	388	0.7*	
1992: Con				4,953	9.1	

Bedford [38]

66,560†	73.5	Hall, P.	Lab	24,774	50.6	+14.2
		Blackman, R.J.	Con	16,474	33.7	-11.8
47.4		Noyce, C.D.	LD	6,044	12.3	-4.1
		Conquest, P.C.	Ref	1,503	3.1*	
		Saunders, P.A. Ms.	NLP	149	0.3*	
1992: Con				8,300	17.0	

Bedfordshire Mid [39]

66,521†	78.9	Sayeed, J.	Con	24,176	46.0	-16.4
		Mallett, N.	Lab	17,086	32.5	+12.7
99.4		Hill, T.J.	LD	8,823	16.8	+1.0
		Marler, S.C. Ms.	Ref	2,257	4.3*	
		Lorys, M.J.	NLP	174	0.3*	
1992: Con				7,090	13.5	

Bedfordshire North East [40]

65,308†	77.2	Lyell, N.W.*	Con	22,311	44.3	-15.0
		Lehal, J.	Lab	16,428	32.6	+12.6
78.2		Bristow, P.J.	LD	7,179	14.2	-4.3
		Taylor, J.C.	Ref	2,490	4.9*	
		Foley, F.L.	Ind Con	1,842	3.7*	
		Bence, B.H.	NLP	138	0.3*	
1992: Con				5,883	11.7	

Bedfordshire South West [41]

69,781†	75.8	Madel, W.D.*	Con	21,534	40.7	-15.5
		Date, A.R.	Lab	21,402	40.5	+14.7
13.0		Owen, S.H.M.	LD	7,559	14.3	-2.3
		Hill, R. Ms.	Ref	1,761	3.3*	
		Wise, T.H.	UKI	446	0.8*	
		Le Carpentier, A.	NLP	162	0.3*	
1992: Con				132	0.2	

Belfast East [42]

61,837	63.1	Robinson, P.*	DUP	16,640	42.6	-11.8
		Empey, R.	UU	9,886	25.3	+25.3
22.3		Hendron, J.	APNI	9,288	23.8	-3.5
		Dines, S.E. Ms.	Con	928	2.4*	-7.7
		Corr, D.	SF	810	2.1*	+0.4
		Lewsley, P. Ms.	SDLP	629	1.6*	
		Dougan, A.D.	Ind	541	1.4*	
		Bell, J.	WP	237	0.6*	
		Collins, D.H.	NLP	70	0.2*	
1992: DUP				6,754	17.3	

Belfast North [43]

64,645	64.1	Walker, C.*	UU	21,478	51.8	+0.1
		Maginness, A.	SDLP	8,454	20.4	+2.1
24.4		Kelly, G.	SF	8,375	20.2	+8.9
		Campbell, T.	APNI	2,221	5.4	-2.4
		Emerson, P.	Grn	539	1.3*	
		Treanor, P.G.	WP	297	0.7*	
		Gribben, A.H. Ms.	NLP	88	0.2*	
1992: UU				13,024	31.4	

Belfast South [44]

63,633	62.0	Smyth, W.M.*	UU	14,201	36.0	-16.7
		McDonnell, A.	SDLP	9,601	24.3	+10.1
26.3		Ervine, D.	Prog U	5,687	14.4	
		McBride, S.	APNI	5,112	12.9	-2.7
		Hayes, S.	SF	2,019	5.1	+2.6
		Campbell, A. Ms.	Ind	1,204	3.0*	
		Boal, M.M. Ms.	Con	962	2.4*	-9.2
		Cusack, N.	Ind Lab	292	0.7*	
		Lynn, P.J.	WP	286	0.7*	
		Anderson, J.M.	NLP	120	0.3*	
1992: UU				4,600	11.7	

Belfast West [45]

61,920	74.1	Adams, G.	SF	25,662	55.9	+13.9
		Hendron, J.G.*	SDLP	17,753	38.7	-5.5
21.3		Parkinson, F.	UU	1,556	3.4*	-8.2
		Lowry, J.	WP	721	1.6*	
		Kennedy, L.	Ind	102	0.2*	
		Daly, M. Ms.	NLP	91	0.2*	
1992: SDLP				7,909	17.2	

Berwick-upon-Tweed [46]

56,878	73.5	Beith, A.J.*	LD	19,007	45.5	+1.1
		Brannen, P.	Lab	10,965	26.2	+3.4
None		Herbert, N.	Con	10,056	24.1	-8.7
		Lambton, E.R.	Ref	1,423	3.4*	
		Dodds, I.C.	UKI	352	0.8*	
1992: LD				8,042	19.2	

Bethnal Green & Bow [47]

74,146†	60.3	King, O.T. Ms.	Lab	20,697	46.3	-7.2
		Choudhury, K.H.	Con	9,412	21.1	+4.7
25.9		Nurul Islam, S.	LD	5,361	12.0	-13.8
		King, D.M.	BNP	3,350	7.5	
		Milson, T.B.	Lib	2,963	6.6	
		Osman, S.	Ind Lab	1,117	2.5*	
		Petter, S.	Grn	812	1.8*	
		Abdullah, M.	Ref	557	1.2*	
		Hamid, A.	SL	413	0.9*	
1992: Lab				11,285	25.3	

Beverley & Holderness [48]

72,049	72.9	Cran, J.D.*	Con	21,629	41.2	-13.3
		O'Neill, N.J.	Lab	20,418	38.9	+18.8
89.5		Melling, J.M.	LD	9,689	18.4	-6.9
		Barley, D.	UKI	695	1.3*	
		Withers, S.H.	NLP	111	0.2*	
1992: Con				1,211	2.3	

Bexhill & Battle [49]

65,803	74.5	Wardle, C.F.*	Con	23,570	48.1	-12.2
		Field, K.M. Ms.	LD	12,470	25.5	-3.4
0.1		Beckwith, R.D.	Lab	8,866	18.1	+8.7
		Thompson, V. Ms.	Ref	3,302	6.7	
		Pankhurst, J.D.	UKI	786	1.6*	
1992: Con				11,100	22.7	

Bexleyheath & Crayford [50]

63,373	76.1	Beard, C.N.	Lab	21,942	45.5	+14.2
		Evennett, D.A.*	Con	18,527	38.4	-15.8
74.6		Montford, F.J. Ms.	LD	5,391	11.2	-3.2
		Thomas, B.R.	Ref	1,551	3.2*	
		Smith, P. Ms.	BNP	429	0.9*	
		Jenner, W.J.	UKI	383	0.8*	
1992: Con				3,415	7.1	

Billericay [51]

76,304	72.6	Gorman, T.E. Ms.*	Con	22,033	39.8	-17.9
		Richards, P.A.	Lab	20,677	37.3	+17.3
57.9		Williams, G.	LD	8,763	15.8	-6.5
		Hughes, B.R.J.O.	Ind Con	3,377	6.1	
		Buchanan, J.R.	PL	570	1.0*	
1992: Con				1,356	2.4	

Birkenhead [52]

59,630	65.9	Field, F.*	Lab	27,825	70.8	+7.1
		Crosby, A.J.	Con	5,982	15.2	-9.9
None		Wood, R.J.	LD	3,548	9.0	-0.6
		Cullen, M.	SL	1,168	3.0*	
		Evans, R.P.	Ref	800	2.0*	
1992: Lab				21,843	55.5	

Birmingham Edgbaston [53]

70,310	68.9	Stuart, G.G. Ms.	Lab	23,554	48.6	+9.3
		Marshall, A.	Con	18,712	38.6	-10.7
32.2		Gallagher, J.Y.	LD	4,691	9.7	-0.5
		Oakton, J.P.	Ref	1,065	2.2*	
		Campbell, D.L.	BNP	443	0.9*	
1992: Con				4,842	10.0	

Birmingham Erdington [54]

66,431	60.8	Corbett, R.*	Lab	23,764	58.8	+5.5
		Tompkins, A.C.	Con	11,107	27.5	-9.0
39.7		Garrett, I.A.G.	LD	4,112	10.2	-0.1
		Cable, G.	Ref	1,424	3.5*	
1992: Lab				12,657	31.3	

Birmingham Hall Green [55]

58,783	71.1	McCabe, S.J.	Lab	22,372	53.5	+15.2
		Hargreaves, A.R.*	Con	13,952	33.4	-12.7
None		Dow, C.A.	LD	4,034	9.6	-6.0
		Bennett, P.R.	Ref	1,461	3.5*	
1992: Con				8,420	20.1	

Birmingham Hodge Hill [56]

56,082	60.9	Davis, T.A.G.*	Lab	22,398	65.6	+12.0
		Grant, E.A.G.	Con	8,198	24.0	-12.3
None		Thomas, H.A.	LD	2,891	8.5	-0.7
		Johnson, P.F.	UKI	660	1.9*	
1992: Lab				14,200	41.6	

Birmingham Ladywood [57]

70,126	54.2	Short, C. Ms.*	Lab	28,134	74.1	+2.7
		Vara, S.L.	Con	5,052	13.3	-7.1
95.2		Marwa, S.	LD	3,020	8.0	-0.2
		Gurney, R.A. Ms.	Ref	1,086	2.9*	
		Carmichael, A.	Nat Dem	685	1.8*	
1992: Lab				23,082	60.8	

Birmingham Northfield [58]

56,866	68.3	Burden, R.H.*	Lab	22,316	57.4	+11.5
		Blumenthal, A.	Con	10,873	28.0	-14.5
24.0		Ashall, M.R.	LD	4,078	10.5	-1.1
		Gent, J.D.W.	Ref	1,243	3.2*	
		Axon, K.A.	BNP	337	0.9*	
1992: Lab				11,443	29.5	

Birmingham Perry Barr [59]

71,150	64.5	Rooker, J.W.*	Lab	28,921	63.0	+11.1
		Dunnett, A.P.	Con	9,964	21.7	-15.6
56.0		Hassall, R.G.	LD	4,523	9.9	-0.9
		Mahmood, S.	Ref	843	1.8*	
		Baxter, W.A.	Lib	718	1.6*	
		Windridge, L.	BNP	544	1.2*	
		Panesar, A.S.	Ind	374	0.8*	
1992: Lab				18,957	41.3	

Birmingham Selly Oak [60]

72,136	70.1	Jones, L.M. Ms.*	Lab	28,121	55.6	+9.6
		Greene, G.G.	Con	14,033	27.8	-14.5
None		Osborne, D.	LD	6,121	12.1	+1.8
		Marshall, L.T.	Ref	1,520	3.0*	
		Gardner, G.T.	PL	417	0.8*	
		Sherriff-Knowles, P.	MRLP	253	0.5*	
		Meads, H.S.	NLP	85	0.2*	
1992: Lab				14,088	27.9	

Birmingham Sparkbrook & Small Heath [61]

73,215	57.0	Godsiff, R.D.*	Lab	26,841	64.3	+1.2
		Hardeman, K.G.	Con	7,315	17.5	-8.1
40.3		Harmer, R.K.	LD	3,889	9.3	+1.4
		Clawley, A.	Grn	959	2.3*
		Dooley, R.A.	Ref	737	1.8*
		Patel, P.	Ind	538	1.3*
		Syed, R.M.	Ind	513	1.2*
		Bi, S. Ms.	Ind	490	1.2*
		Wren, C.D.	SL	483	1.2*
1992: Lab				19,526	46.8

Birmingham Yardley [62]

53,151	71.1	Morris, E. Ms.*	Lab	17,778	47.0	+12.2
		Hemming, J.A.M.	LD	12,463	33.0	+2.8
None		Jobson, A.M. Ms.	Con	6,736	17.8	-16.7
		Livingston, D.K.	Ref	646	1.7*
		Ware, A.J.	UKI	164	0.4*
1992: Lab				5,315	14.1

Bishop Auckland [63]

67,294	68.4	Foster, D.*	Lab	30,359	65.9	+18.3
		Fergus, J.H. Ms.	Con	9,295	20.2	-12.6
47.7		Ashworth, L.	LD	4,293	9.3	-10.2
		Blacker, D.S.W.	Ref	2,104	4.6*
1992: Lab				21,064	45.7

Blaby [64]

70,471†	76.0	Robathan, A.R.G.*	Con	24,564	45.8	-11.0
		Willmott, R.	Lab	18,090	33.8	+12.0
18.3		Welsh, G.L.	LD	8,001	14.9	-5.1
		Harrison, R.C.	Ref	2,018	3.8*
		Peacock, J.A.	BNP	523	1.0*
		Stokes, T.M.	Ind	397	0.7*
1992: Con				6,474	12.1

Blackburn [65]

73,132	64.9	Straw, J.W.*	Lab	26,141	55.0	+6.6
		Sidhu, S.K. Ms.	Con	11,690	24.6	-12.9
None		Fenn, S.J.	LD	4,990	10.5	-1.0
		Bradshaw, D.P.	Ref	1,892	4.0*	
		Wingfield, T.D. Ms.	Nat Dem	671	1.4*	
		Drummond, H.M. Ms.	SL	635	1.3*	
		Field, R.R.C.	Grn	608	1.3*	
		Carmichael-Grimshaw, M.Baroness	Ind	506	1.1*	
		Batchelor, W.J.	Ind	362	0.8*	
1992: Lab				14,451	30.4	

Blackpool North & Fleetwood [66]

75,097†	71.6	Humble, J. Ms.	Lab	28,051	52.2	+14.6
		Elletson, H.D.H.*	Con	19,105	35.5	-14.2
98.8		Hill, B. Ms.	LD	4,600	8.6	-3.4
		Stacey, K. Ms.	Ref	1,704	3.2*	
		Ellis, J.T.	BNP	288	0.5*	
1992: Con				8,946	16.6	

Blackpool South [67]

75,861†	67.7	Marsden, G.	Lab	29,282	57.0	+13.6
		Booth, G.R.	Con	17,666	34.4	-9.7
35.0		Holt, D. Ms.	LD	4,392	8.6	-3.6
1992: Con				11,616	22.6	

Blaenau Gwent [68]

54,815	72.3	Smith, L.T.*	Lab	31,493	79.5	+0.5
		Layton, G. Ms.	LD	3,458	8.7	+2.3
None		Williams, M.A. Ms.	Con	2,607	6.6	-3.2
		Criddle, J.B.	PC	2,072	5.2	+0.4
1992: Lab				28,035	70.7	

Blaydon [69]

64,699†	71.0	McWilliam, J.D.*	Lab	27,535	60.0	+7.3
		Maughan, P.J.	LD	10,930	23.8	+3.1
None		Watson, M.A.	Con	6,048	13.2	-13.5
		Rook, R.J.	Ind Lab	1,412	3.1*	
1992: Lab				16,605	36.2	

Blyth Valley [70]

61,761†	68.8	Campbell, R.*	Lab	27,276	64.2	+14.3
		Lamb, A.J.	LD	9,540	22.5	-11.1
None		Musgrave, B.A.S. Ms.	Con	5,666	13.3	-2.3
1992: Lab				17,736	41.7	

Bognor Regis & Littlehampton [71]

66,736†	69.6	Gibb, N.J.	Con	20,537	44.2	-12.6
		Nash, R.A.	Lab	13,216	28.5	+15.0
17.9		Walsh, J.M.M.	LD	11,153	24.0	-2.7
		Stride, G.T.	UKI	1,537	3.3*	
1992: Con				7,321	15.8	

Bolsover [72]

66,547	71.2	Skinner, D.E.*	Lab	35,073	74.0	+9.5
		Harwood, R.J.	Con	7,924	16.7	-8.6
0.1		Cox, I.G.	LD	4,417	9.3	-0.9
1992: Lab				27,149	57.3	

Bolton North East [73]

67,996†	72.4	Crausby, D.A.	Lab	27,621	56.1	+8.7
		Wilson, R.O.B.	Con	14,952	30.4	-11.7
16.3		Critchley, E.M.R.	LD	4,862	9.9	-0.2
		Staniforth, D.A.	Ref	1,096	2.2*	
		Kelly, W.	SL	676	1.4*	
1992: Lab				12,669	25.7	

Bolton South East [74]

66,542†	65.1	Iddon, B.	Lab	29,856	68.9	+14.6
		Carter, R.P.	Con	8,545	19.7	-9.0
0.2		Harasiwka, F.	LD	3,805	8.8	-1.8
		Pickering, W.A.	Ref	973	2.2*	
		Walch, L.J.	NLP	170	0.4*	
1992: Lab				21,311	49.2	

Bolton West [75]

63,607†	77.3	Kelly, R.M. Ms.	Lab	24,342	49.5	+10.4
		Sackville, T.G.*	Con	17,270	35.1	-12.2
13.4		Ronson, B.O. Ms.	LD	5,309	10.8	-2.4
		Kelly, D. Ms.	SL	1,374	2.8*	
		Frankl-Slater, G.P. Ms.	Ref	865	1.8*	
1992: Con				7,072	14.4	

Bootle [76]

57,284†	66.7	Benton, J.E.*	Lab	31,668	82.9	+6.3
		Mathews, R.O.	Con	3,247	8.5	-5.6
13.2		Reid, K.J.C.	LD	2,191	5.7	-0.7
		Elliott, J.	Ref	571	1.5*	
		Glover, P.	Soc	420	1.1*	
		Cohen, S.J.	NLP	126	0.3*	
1992: Lab				28,421	74.4	

Boston & Skegness [77]

67,623†	68.9	Body, R.B.F.S.*	Con	19,750	42.4	-8.4
		McCauley, P.J.	Lab	19,103	41.0	+12.8
72.8		Dodsworth, J.L.	LD	7,721	16.6	-4.4
1992: Con				647	1.4	

Bosworth [78]

68,249†	76.4	Tredinnick, D.A.S.*	Con	21,189	40.6	-11.0
		Furlong, A.C.	Lab	20,162	38.7	+12.3
17.7		Ellis, J.M.H.	LD	9,281	17.8	-2.9
		Halborg, S.	Ref	1,521	2.9*	
1992: Con				1,027	2.0	

Bournemouth East [79]

61,858	70.2	Atkinson, D.A.*	Con	17,997	41.4	-14.0
		Eyre, D.	LD	13,655	31.4	+0.4
16.8		Stevens, J.L. Ms.	Lab	9,181	21.1	+8.3
		Musgrave-Scott, A.	Ref	1,808	4.2*	
		Benney, K.F.	UKI	791	1.8*	
1992: Con				4,342	10.0	

Bournemouth West [80]

62,032	66.2	Butterfill, J.V.*	Con	17,115	41.7	-10.8
		Dover, J. Ms.	LD	11,405	27.8	+0.3
50.2		Gritt, D.	Lab	10,093	24.6	+5.1
		Mills, R.W.	Ref	1,910	4.7*	
		Tooley, L.M. Ms.	UKI	281	0.7*	
		Morse, J.	BNP	165	0.4*	
		Springham, A.	NLP	103	0.3*	
1992: Con				5,710	13.9	

Bracknell [81]

79,292†	74.5	Mackay, A.J.*	Con	27,983	47.4	-13.0
		Snelgrove, A.C. Ms.	Lab	17,596	29.8	+9.5
51.5		Hilliar, A.R.	LD	9,122	15.4	-3.9
		Tompkins, J.W.	Ind Lab	1,909	3.2*	
		Cairns, W.	Ref	1,636	2.8*	
		Boxall, L.J.A.	UKI	569	1.0*	
		Roberts, D.M. Ms.	PL	276	0.5*	
1992: Con				10,387	17.6	

Bradford North [82]

66,228†	63.3	Rooney, T.H.*	Lab	23,493	56.1	+8.2
		Skinner, E.G.	Con	10,723	25.6	-6.6
None		Browne, T.A.S.	LD	6,083	14.5	-4.1
		Wheatley, H.	Ref	1,227	2.9*	
		Beckett, W.	MRLP	369	0.9*	
1992: Lab				12,770	30.5	

Bradford South [83]

68,391†	65.9	Sutcliffe, G.*	Lab	25,558	56.7	+9.1
		Hawkesworth, A.G. Ms.	Con	12,622	28.0	-10.4
None		Wilson-Fletcher, A.C.E.	LD	5,093	11.3	-2.4
		Kershaw, M. Ms.	Ref	1,785	4.0*	
1992: Lab				12,936	28.7	

Bradford West [84]

71,961†	63.3	Singh, M.	Lab	18,932	41.5	-11.7
		Riaz, M.	Con	15,055	33.0	-0.8
None		Wright, H. Ms.	LD	6,737	14.8	+4.3
		Khan, A.R.	SL	1,551	3.4*	
		Royston, C.A.	Ref	1,348	3.0*	
		Robinson, J.E.	Grn	861	1.9*	
		Osborn, G.A.	BNP	839	1.8*	
		Shah, S.	Soc	245	0.5*	
1992: Lab				3,877	8.5	

Braintree [85]

73,032†	76.1	Hurst, A.A.	Lab	23,729	42.7	+15.3
		Newton, A.H.*	Con	22,278	40.1	-10.5
22.6		Ellis, T.K.	LD	6,418	11.5	-9.2
		Westcott, N.P.	Ref	2,165	3.9*	
		Abbott, J.E.	Grn	712	1.3*	
		Nolan, M.A.	Ind	274	0.5*	
1992: Con				1,451	2.6	

Brecon & Radnorshire [86]

52,142†	82.2	Livsey, R.A.L.	LD	17,516	40.8	+5.1
		Evans, J.P.*	Con	12,419	29.0	-7.1
None		Mann, C.J.	Lab	11,424	26.6	+0.4
		Phillips, E.F. Ms.	Ref	900	2.1*	
		Cornelius, S.	PC	622	1.5*	+0.5
1992: Con				5,097	11.9	

Brent East [87]

53,548†	65.9	Livingstone, K.R.*	Lab	23,748	67.3	+14.5
		Francois, M.G.	Con	7,866	22.3	-14.3
0.3		Hunter, I.M.C.	LD	2,751	7.8	-1.1
		Keable, S.E.	SL	466	1.3*	
		Shanks, A.J.	PL	218	0.6*	
		Warrilow, C.M. Ms.	Rainbow	120	0.3*	
		Jenkins, D.	NLP	103	0.3*	
1992: Lab				15,882	45.0	

Brent North [88]

54,149†	70.5	Gardiner, B.S.	Lab	19,343	50.7	+20.4
		Boyson, R.*	Con	15,324	40.1	-17.3
16.0		Lorber, P.	LD	3,104	8.1	-2.5
		Davids, T.	NLP	204	0.5*	
		Clark, G.F.	Rainbow	199	0.5*	
1992: Con				4,019	10.5	

Brent South [89]

53,505†	64.5	Boateng, P.Y.*	Lab	25,180	73.0	+15.4
		Jackson, S.J.	Con	5,489	15.9	-15.2
16.0		Brazil, J.C.M.	LD	2,670	7.7	-1.7
		Phythian, J.S. Ms.	Ref	497	1.4*	
		Edler, D.P.P.	Grn	389	1.1*	
		Howard, C.P.	Rainbow	175	0.5*	
		Mahaldar, A. Ms.	NLP	98	0.3*	
1992: Lab				19,691	57.1	

Brentford & Isleworth [90]

80,722†	69.5	Keen, A. Ms.	Lab	32,249	57.4	+14.7
		Deva, N.J.A.*	Con	17,825	31.8	-13.9
15.2		Hartwell, G.G.	LD	4,613	8.2	-1.9
		Bradley, J.W.	Grn	687	1.2*	
		Simmerson, B. Ms.	UKI	614	1.1*	
		Ahmed, M.	NLP	147	0.3*	
1992: Con				14,424	25.7	

Brentwood & Ongar [91]

66,181	76.6	Pickles, E.J.*	Con	23,031	45.4	-12.2
		Bottomley, E.T. Ms.	LD	13,341	26.3	-4.2
0.1		Young, M.C.	Lab	11,231	22.1	+11.2
		Kilmartin, A. Ms.	Ref	2,658	5.2	
		Mills, D.C.	UKI	465	0.9*	
1992: Con				9,690	19.1	

Bridgend [92]

59,826†	72.3	Griffiths, W.*	Lab	25,115	58.1	+6.8
		Davies, D.T.C.	Con	9,867	22.8	-12.9
None		McKinlay, A.	LD	4,968	11.5	+1.2
		Greaves, D.T.	Ref	1,662	3.8*	
		Watkins, D.R.	PC	1,649	3.8*	+1.0
1992: Lab				15,248	35.2	

Bridgwater [93]

73,412	74.4	King, T.J.*	Con	20,174	36.9	-9.8
		Hoban, M.F.	LD	18,378	33.6	+4.0
None		Lavers, R.J.	Lab	13,519	24.8	+3.0
		Evens, F. Ms.	Ref	2,551	4.7*	
1992: Con				1,796	3.3	

Brigg & Goole [94]

64,073	73.0	Cawsey, I.A.	Lab	23,493	50.2	+14.5
		Stewart, D.M.	Con	17,104	36.5	-13.3
86.1		Hardy, M. Ms.	LD	4,692	10.0	-4.5
		Rigby, D.M.	Ref	1,513	3.2*	
1992: Con				6,389	13.7	

Brighton Kemptown [95]

65,319	70.6	Turner, D.S.	Lab	21,479	46.6	+14.0
		Bowden, A. Sir*	Con	17,945	38.9	-13.9
41.0		Gray, C.J.	LD	4,478	9.7	-4.2
		Inman, D.C.	Ref	1,526	3.3*	
		Williams, H. Ms.	SL	316	0.7*	
		Bowler, J.J.	NLP	172	0.4*	
		Newman, L.	MRLP	123	0.3*	
		Darlow, R.	Rainbow	93	0.2*	
1992: Con				3,534	7.7	

Brighton Pavilion [96]

66,720	73.4	Lepper, D.	Lab	26,737	54.6	+14.4
		Spencer, D.H. Sir*	Con	13,556	27.7	-17.6
13.8		Blanshard, K.C.	LD	4,644	9.5	-2.9
		Stocken, P.A.	Ref	1,304	2.7*	
		West, P.R.W.	Grn	1,249	2.6*	
		Huggett, R.J.	Ind	1,098	2.2*	
		Stevens, F.M.	UKI	179	0.4*	
		Dobbs, B.	Ind	125	0.3*	
		Card, A.J.R.	Rainbow	59	0.1*	
1992: Con				13,181	26.9	

Bristol East [97]

69,118	69.7	Corston, J. Ms.*	Lab	27,418	56.9	+9.6
		Vaizey, E.	Con	11,259	23.4	-14.2
43.2		Tyzack, P.L.	LD	7,121	14.8	+0.0
		Philp, G.H.	Ref	1,479	3.1*	
		Williams, P.F.	SL	766	1.6*	
		McLaggan, J.H.N.	NLP	158	0.3*	
1992: Lab				16,159	33.5	

Bristol North West [98]

73,133	75.5	Naysmith, J.D.	Lab	27,575	49.9	+4.7
		Stern, M.C.*	Con	16,193	29.3	-9.5
22.9		Parry, I.H.	LD	7,263	13.1	-1.7
		Horton, C.E.	Ind Lab	1,718	3.1*	
		Quintanilla, J.L.	Ref	1,609	2.9*	
		Shorter, G.B.	SL	482	0.9*	
		Parnell, S.L.	BNP	265	0.5*	
		Leighton, T.G.	NLP	140	0.3*	
1992: Lab				11,382	20.6	

Bristol South [99]

72,493	68.8	Primarolo, D. Ms.*	Lab	29,890	59.9	+12.7
		Roe, M.	Con	10,562	21.2	-12.0
16.0		Williams, S.R.	LD	6,691	13.4	-4.5
		Guy, D.W.	Ref	1,486	3.0*	
		Boxall, J.H.	Grn	722	1.4*	
		Marshall, I.P.	Soc	355	0.7*	
		Taylor, L.P.	Ind	153	0.3*	
1992: Lab				19,328	38.8	

Bristol West [100]

85,275	73.5	Davey, V. Ms.	Lab	22,068	35.2	+11.9
		Waldegrave, W.A.*	Con	20,575	32.8	-12.3
11.8		Boney, C.R.	LD	17,551	28.0	-1.2
		Beauchamp, R.E.M. Lady	Ref	1,304	2.1*	
		Quinnell, J.M.	Grn	852	1.4*	
		Nurse, R.C.M.T.	SL	244	0.4*	
		Brierley, J.J.	NLP	47	0.1*	
1992: Con				1,493	2.4	

Bromley & Chislehurst [101]

71,210	74.1	Forth, E.*	Con	24,428	46.3	-15.6
		Yeldham, R.J.	Lab	13,310	25.2	+8.0
82.0		Booth, P.J.H.	LD	12,530	23.8	+5.9
		Bryant, R.M.	UKI	1,176	2.2*	
		Speed, F.M. Ms.	Grn	640	1.2*	
		Stoneman, M.R.	NF	369	0.7*	
		Aitman, G.	Lib	285	0.5*	
1992: Con				11,118	21.1	

Bromsgrove [102]

67,744†	77.1	Kirkbride, J. Ms.	Con	24,620	47.1	-6.9
		McDonald, P.M.	Lab	19,775	37.8	+7.2
0.2		Davy, J.M. Ms.	LD	6,200	11.9	-1.9
		Winsor, D. Ms.	Ref	1,411	2.7*	
		Wetton, B.G. Ms.	UKI	251	0.5*	
1992: Con				4,845	9.3	

Broxbourne [103]

66,817	70.3	Roe, M.A. Ms.*	Con	22,952	48.9	-13.4
		Coleman, B.J.	Lab	16,299	34.7	+13.3
8.7		Davies, J.M. Ms.	LD	5,310	11.3	-4.7
		Millward, D.S.	Ref	1,633	3.5*	
		Bruce, D.J.	BNP	610	1.3*	
		Cheetham, B.A.	Ind	172	0.4*	
1992: Con				6,653	14.2	

Broxtowe [104]

74,264†	78.3	Palmer, N.D.	Lab	27,343	47.0	+12.3
		Lester, J.T. Sir*	Con	21,768	37.4	-13.5
0.2		Miller, T.P.	LD	6,934	11.9	-1.8
		Tucker, C.R.	Ref	2,092	3.6*	
1992: Con				5,575	9.6	

Buckingham [105]

62,945†	78.5	Bercow, J.S.	Con	24,594	49.8	-12.5
		Lehmann, R.C.	Lab	12,208	24.7	+8.7
5.7		Stuart, N.	LD	12,175	24.6	+3.8
		Clements, G.	NLP	421	0.9*	
1992: Con				12,386	25.1	

Burnley [106]

67,582†	66.9	Pike, P.L.*	Lab	26,210	57.9	+4.9
		Wiggin, W.D.	Con	9,148	20.2	-10.4
None		Birtwistle, G.	LD	7,877	17.4	+1.0
		Oakley, R.J.	Ref	2,010	4.4*	
1992: Lab				17,062	37.7	

Burton [107]

72,638	75.0	Dean, J.E.A. Ms.	Lab	27,810	51.0	+9.8
		Lawrence, I.J.*	Con	21,480	39.4	-8.8
4.9		Fletcher, D.A.	LD	4,617	8.5	-2.1
		Sharp, K.	Nat Dem	604	1.1*	
1992: Con				6,330	11.6	

Bury North [108]

70,717†	77.8	Chaytor, D.M.	Lab	28,523	51.8	+10.2
		Burt, A.J.H.*	Con	20,657	37.5	-12.1
None		Kenyon, N.A.	LD	4,536	8.2	-0.3
		Hallewell, R.S.	Ref	1,337	2.4*	
1992: Con				7,866	14.3	

Bury South [109]

66,797†	75.4	Lewis, I.	Lab	28,658	56.9	+12.2
		Sumberg, D.A.G.*	Con	16,277	32.3	-13.7
0.4		D'Albert, V.D.	LD	4,227	8.4	-0.6
		Slater, B.H.	Ref	1,216	2.4*	
1992: Con				12,381	24.6	

Bury St Edmunds [110]

74,017†	75.0	Ruffley, D.L.	Con	21,290	38.3	-7.6
		Ereira, M.A.	Lab	20,922	37.7	+11.7
96.9		Cooper, D.A.	LD	10,102	18.2	-8.7
		McWhirter, I.C.H.	Ref	2,939	5.3	
		Lillis, J.B. Ms.	NLP	272	0.5*	
1992: Con				368	0.7	

Caernarfon [111]

46,815†	73.7	Wigley, D.*	PC	17,616	51.0	-8.0
		Williams, E.W.	Lab	10,167	29.5	+13.9
None		Williams, E.	Con	4,230	12.3	-6.9
		MacQueen, J.M. Ms.	LD	1,686	4.9*	-0.9
		Collins, C.	Ref	811	2.4*	
1992: PC				7,449	21.6	

Caerphilly [112]

64,621†	70.1	Davies, R.*	Lab	30,697	67.8	+4.2
		Harris, H.R.	Con	4,858	10.7	-7.4
None		Whittle, L.G.	PC	4,383	9.7	+0.0
		Ferguson, A.D.	LD	3,724	8.2	-0.3
		Morgan, M.E.	Ref	1,337	3.0*	
		Williams, C.M. Ms.	PL	270	0.6*	
1992: Lab				25,839	57.1	

Caithness, Sutherland & Easter Ross [113]

41,652†	70.0	Maclennan, R.A.R.*	LD	10,381	35.6	-8.8
		Hendry, J.M.	Lab	8,122	27.8	+12.2
32.5		Harper, E.J.	SNP	6,710	23.0	+4.6
		Miers, T.D.P.C.	Con	3,148	10.8	-10.8
		Ryder, C.M. Ms.	Ref	369	1.3*	
		Martin, J.	Grn	230	0.8*	
		Carr, M.B.N.	UKI	212	0.7*	
1992: LD				2,259	7.7	

Calder Valley [114]

74,901†	75.4	McCafferty, C. Ms.	Lab	26,050	46.1	+8.7
		Thompson, D.*	Con	19,795	35.1	-10.4
None		Pearson, S.J.	LD	8,322	14.7	-1.4
		Mellor, A.	Ref	1,380	2.4*	
		Smith, V.P. Ms.	Grn	488	0.9*	
		Jackson, C.M.	BNP	431	0.8*	
1992: Con				6,255	11.1	

Camberwell & Peckham [115]

51,313	55.3	Harman, H. Ms.*	Lab	19,734	69.5	+9.2
		Humphreys, K.	Con	3,283	11.6	-12.2
34.6		Williams, N.	LD	3,198	11.3	-3.8
		China, N.	Ref	692	2.4*	
		Ruddock, A. Ms.	SL	685	2.4*	
		Williams, G.	Lib	443	1.6*	
		Barker, J.	Soc	233	0.8*	
		Eames, C.	WRP	106	0.4*	
1992: Lab				16,451	58.0	

Cambridge [116]

71,812	71.5	Campbell, A. Ms.*	Lab	27,436	53.4	+13.8
		Platt, D.W.	Con	13,299	25.9	-12.6
None		Heathcock, G.J.	LD	8,287	16.1	-3.7
		Burrows, W.J.S.	Ref	1,262	2.5*	
		Wright, M.E. Ms.	Grn	654	1.3*	
		Johnstone, A. Ms.	PL	191	0.4*	
		Athow, R.J.	WRP	107	0.2*	
		Gladwin, M.L.P. Ms.	NLP	103	0.2*	
1992: Lab				14,137	27.5	

Cambridgeshire North East [117]

76,353†	72.6	Moss, M.D.*	Con	23,855	43.0	-10.5
		Bucknor, V.M. Ms.	Lab	18,754	33.8	+20.2
8.3		Nash, A.J.	LD	9,070	16.4	-14.6
		Bacon, M.W.	Ref	2,636	4.8*	
		Bennett, C.J.	SL	851	1.5*	
		Leighton, L.K.C.	NLP	259	0.5*	
1992: Con				5,101	9.2	

Cambridgeshire North West [118]

65,791†	74.2	Mawhinney, B.S.*	Con	23,488	48.1	-14.2
		Steptoe, L.A.	Lab	15,734	32.2	+6.3
88.4		McCoy, B.D. Ms.	LD	7,388	15.1	+6.4
		Watt, A.R.	Ref	1,939	4.0*	
		Wyatt, W.G.	UKI	269	0.6*	
1992: Con				7,754	15.9	

Cambridgeshire South [119]

70,557†	76.1	Lansley, A.D.	Con	22,572	42.0	-16.5
		Quinlan, J.A.	LD	13,860	25.8	+1.0
49.0		Gray, T.	Lab	13,485	25.1	+9.8
		Page, R.	Ref	3,300	6.1	
		Norman, D.A.	UKI	298	0.6*	
		Chalmers, F.	NLP	168	0.3*	
1992: Con				8,712	16.2	

Cambridgeshire South East [120]

76,393	74.4	Paice, J.E.T.*	Con	24,397	42.9	-14.5
		Collinson, R.F.	Lab	15,048	26.5	+7.0
23.3		Brinton, S.V. Ms.	LD	14,246	25.1	+3.9
		Howlett, J.E.	Ref	2,838	5.0*	
		Lam, K.H.L.	Ind	167	0.3*	
		While, P.H.	NLP	111	0.2*	
1992: Con				9,349	16.5	

Cannock Chase [121]

70,784	74.0	Wright, A.W.*	Lab	28,705	54.8	+5.8
		Backhouse, J.E.	Con	14,227	27.2	-11.0
0.0		Kirby, R.D.	LD	4,537	8.7	-3.5
		Froggatt, J.P.	Ref	1,663	3.2*	
		Hurley, W.J.	Ind Lab	1,615	3.1*	
		Conroy, M.	SL	1,120	2.1*	
		Hartshorn, M.	MRLP	499	1.0*	
1992: Lab				14,478	27.6	

Canterbury [122]

74,684	72.5	Brazier, J.W.H.*	Con	20,913	38.6	-11.8
		Hall, C.H. Ms.	Lab	16,949	31.3	+15.9
4.2		Vye, M.J.	LD	12,854	23.8	-8.8
		Osborne, J.F.	Ref	2,460	4.5*	
		Meaden, G.J.	Grn	588	1.1*	
		Moore, J.D.	UKI	281	0.5*	
		Pringle, A.J.	NLP	64	0.1*	
1992: Con				3,964	7.3	

Cardiff Central [123]

60,393	70.0	Jones, J.O.*	Lab	18,464	43.7	+1.7
		Randerson, J.E. Ms.	LD	10,541	24.9	+3.6
None		Melding, D.R.M.	Con	8,470	20.0	-13.9
		Burns, T.J.	SL	2,230	5.3	
		Vernon, W.A.	PC	1,504	3.6*	+1.8
		Lloyd, N.L.	Ref	760	1.8*	
		James, C.	MRLP	204	0.5*	
		Hobbs, A.R.	NLP	80	0.2*	
1992: Lab				7,923	18.8	

Cardiff North [124]

60,468	80.2	Morgan, J. Ms.	Lab	24,460	50.4	+11.5
		Jones, G.H.*	Con	16,334	33.7	-11.5
None		Rowland, R.P.J.	LD	5,294	10.9	-2.7
		Palfrey, C.F.	PC	1,201	2.5*	+0.6
		Litchfield, E.J.W.	Ref	1,199	2.5*	
1992: Con				8,126	16.8	

Cardiff South & Penarth [125]

62,138	68.3	Michael, A.E.*	Lab	22,647	53.4	-2.2
		Roberts, C.E. Ms.	Con	8,786	20.7	-12.9
None		Wakefield, S.J.	LD	3,964	9.3	+1.5
		Foreman, J.	Ind Lab	3,942	9.3	
		Haswell, D.B.L.	PC	1,356	3.2*	+1.6
		Morgan, P.S.E.	Ref	1,211	2.9*	
		Shepherd, M.K.	Soc	344	0.8*	
		Caves, B. Ms.	NLP	170	0.4*	
1992: Lab				13,861	32.7	

Cardiff West [126]

58,244	69.2	Morgan, H.R.*	Lab	24,297	60.3	+7.1
		Hoare, S.J.	Con	8,669	21.5	-11.4
0.8		Gasson, J. Ms.	LD	4,366	10.8	-0.1
		Carr, G.A. Ms.	PC	1,949	4.8*	+2.3
		Johns, T.	Ref	996	2.5*	
1992: Lab				15,628	38.8	

Carlisle [127]

59,917†	72.8	Martlew, E.A.*	Lab	25,031	57.4	+12.1
		Lawrence, R.T.	Con	12,641	29.0	-12.3
9.2		Mayho, C.A.	LD	4,576	10.5	-2.5
		Fraser, A.J.	Ref	1,233	2.8*	
		Stevens, W.	NLP	126	0.3*	
1992: Lab				12,390	28.4	

Carmarthen East & Dinefwr [128]

53,121	78.6	Williams, A.W.*	Lab	17,907	42.9	+1.4
		Thomas, H.R.G.	PC	14,457	34.6	+5.6
39.6		Hayward, E.R.	Con	5,022	12.0	-8.3
		Hughes, J.M. Ms.	LD	3,150	7.5	-1.6
		Humphreys-Evans, W.I.	Ref	1,196	2.9*	
1992: Lab				3,450	8.3	

Carmarthen West & Pembrokeshire South [129]

55,724†	76.5	Ainger, N.R.*	Lab	20,956	49.1	+10.6
		Williams, O.J.	Con	11,335	26.6	-8.9
84.9		Llewellyn, D.J.R.	PC	5,402	12.7	-2.4
		Evans, K.J.	LD	3,516	8.2	-2.6
		Poirrier, J.A. Ms.	Ref	1,432	3.4*	
1992: Lab				9,621	22.6	

Carrick, Cumnock & Doon Valley [130]

65,593†	75.0	Foulkes, G.*	Lab	29,398	59.8	+5.7
		Marshall, A.J.	Con	8,336	17.0	-8.7
19.7		Hutchison, C. Ms.	SNP	8,190	16.7	+1.6
		Young, D.G.	LD	2,613	5.3	+0.1
		Higgins, J.K.	Ref	634	1.3*	
1992: Lab				21,062	42.8	

Carshalton & Wallington [131]

66,064	73.3	Brake, T.A.	LD	18,490	38.2	+7.3
		Forman, F.N.*	Con	16,223	33.5	-16.2
None		Theobald, A.C.	Lab	11,565	23.9	+6.2
		Storey, J.E.C.	Ref	1,289	2.7*	
		Hickson, P.H.	Grn	377	0.8*	
		Ritchie, G.N.	BNP	261	0.5*	
		Povey, L.B.	UKI	218	0.5*	
1992: Con				2,267	4.7	

Castle Point [132]

67,324†	72.1	Butler, C.M. Ms.	Lab	20,605	42.4	+18.4
		Spink, R.M.*	Con	19,462	40.1	-15.5
None		Baker, M.D.	LD	4,477	9.2	-9.9
		Maulkin, H.A.	Ref	2,700	5.6	
		Kendall, L.D.M. Ms.	Ind	1,301	2.7*	
1992: Con				1,143	2.4	

Ceredigion [133]

54,378†	73.9	Dafis, C.G.*	PC	16,728	41.6	+10.7
		Harris, R.G.	Lab	9,767	24.3	+5.7
19.6		Davies, D.M.B.	LD	6,616	16.5	-10.0
		Aubel, F.F.E.	Con	5,983	14.9	-9.1
		Leaney, C.L.J.	Ref	1,092	2.7*	
1992: PC				6,961	17.3	

Charnwood [134]

73,034†	76.9	Dorrell, S.J.*	Con	26,110	46.5	-14.1
		Knaggs, D.J.	Lab	20,210	36.0	+14.4
133.1		Wilson, R.M.	LD	7,224	12.9	-5.0
		Meechan, H.L.	Ref	2,104	3.7*	
		Palmer, M.	BNP	525	0.9*	
1992: Con				5,900	10.5	

Chatham & Aylesford [135]

69,644	70.6	Shaw, J.R.	Lab	21,191	43.1	+16.4
		Knox-Johnston, R.A.	Con	18,401	37.4	-13.8
74.8		Murray, R.J.	LD	7,389	15.0	-6.2
		Riddle, K.A.	Ref	1,538	3.1*	
		Harding, A.J.	UKI	493	1.0*	
		Martel, T.D.J.	NLP	149	0.3*	
1992: Con				2,790	5.7	

Cheadle [136]

67,853†	77.3	Day, S.R.*	Con	22,944	43.7	-13.9
		Calton, P. Ms.	LD	19,755	37.7	+8.1
2.2		Diggett, P.G.	Lab	8,253	15.7	+3.3
		Brook, A.S.P.	Ref	1,511	2.9*	
1992: Con				3,189	6.1	

Chelmsford West [137]

76,271†	76.8	Burns, S.H.M.*	Con	23,781	40.6	-14.2
		Bracken, M.W.	LD	17,090	29.2	+0.2
45.1		Chad, R.K.	Lab	15,436	26.4	+11.2
		Smith, T.C.	Ref	1,536	2.6*	
		Rumens, G.	Grn	411	0.7*	
		Levin, M.	UKI	323	0.6*	
1992: Con				6,691	11.4	

Cheltenham [138]

67,950†	74.0	Jones, N.D.*	LD	24,877	49.5	+1.8
		Todman, W.J.	Con	18,232	36.2	-7.9
15.8		Leach, B.	Lab	5,100	10.1	+3.4
		Powell, A.F. Ms.	Ref	1,065	2.1*	
		Hanks, K.R.S.	MRLP	375	0.7*	
		Cook, G.	UKI	302	0.6*	
		Harriss, A. Ms.	PL	245	0.5*	
		Brighouse, S.B. Ms.	NLP	107	0.2*	
1992: LD				6,645	13.2	

Chesham & Amersham [139]

70,029†	74.5	Gillan, C.E.K. Ms.*	Con	26,298	50.4	-13.0
		Brand, M.E.	LD	12,439	23.8	-0.7
4.5		Farrelly, C.P.	Lab	10,240	19.6	+9.3
		Andrews, P.A.	Ref	2,528	4.8*	
		Shilson, C.	UKI	618	1.2*	
		Godfrey, H.R.A.	NLP	74	0.1*	
1992: Con				13,859	26.6	

City of Chester [140]

71,730†	78.4	Russell, C.M. Ms.	Lab	29,806	53.0	+12.4
		Brandreth, G.D.*	Con	19,253	34.2	-10.5
7.6		Simpson, D.P.	LD	5,353	9.5	-4.1
		Mullen, R.F.A.	Ref	1,487	2.6*	
		Sanderson, I.	MRLP	204	0.4*	
		Johnson, W.G.	Ind	154	0.3*	
1992: Con				10,553	18.8	

Chesterfield [141]

72,472†	70.9	Benn, A.N.W.*	Lab	26,105	50.8	+3.5
		Rogers, A.H.	LD	20,330	39.6	+3.8
None		Potter, M.J.K.	Con	4,752	9.2	-7.7
		Scarth, N.	Ind	202	0.4*	
1992: Lab				5,775	11.2	

Chichester [142]

74,812†	74.6	Tyrie, A.G.	Con	25,895	46.4	-12.9
		Gardiner, P.F.	LD	16,161	29.0	+2.4
7.6		Smith, C.	Lab	9,605	17.2	+5.9
		Denny, D.E.	Ref	3,318	5.9	
		Rix, J.G.R.	UKI	800	1.4*	
1992: Con				9,734	17.5	

Chingford & Woodford Green [143]

62,904†	70.7	Duncan Smith, G.I.*	Con	21,109	47.5	-13.9
		Hutchinson, T.J.	Lab	15,395	34.6	+13.7
42.3		Seeff, G.M.	LD	6,885	15.5	+1.2
		Gould, A.	BNP	1,059	2.4*	
1992: Con				5,714	12.9	

Chipping Barnet [144]

69,088	71.7	Chapman, S.B.*	Con	21,317	43.0	-13.6
		Cooke, G.N.	Lab	20,282	40.9	+14.7
19.3		Hooker, S.J.	LD	6,121	12.3	-3.7
		Ribekow, V.G.	Ref	1,190	2.4*	
		Miskin, B.L.	MRLP	253	0.5*	
		Scallan, B.D.	PL	243	0.5*	
		Derksen, D. Ms.	NLP	159	0.3*	
1992: Con				1,035	2.1	

Chorley [145]

74,615	77.3	Hoyle, L.	Lab	30,607	53.0	+11.4
		Dover, D.R.*	Con	20,737	35.9	-9.9
7.0		Jones, S.N.	LD	4,900	8.5	-3.5
		Heaton, A.C.	Ref	1,319	2.3*	
		Leadbetter, P.D.N.	NLP	143	0.2*	
1992: Con				9,870	17.1	

Christchurch [146]

71,566	78.5	Chope, C.R.	Con	26,095	46.4	-17.3
		Maddock, D.M. Ms.*	LD	23,930	42.6	+19.2
4.7		Mannan, C.	Lab	3,884	6.9	-5.2
		Spencer, R.A.	Ref	1,684	3.0*	
		Dickinson, R.H.	UKI	606	1.1*	
1992: Con				2,165	3.9	

Cities of London & Westminster [147]

74,035	54.2	Brooke, P.L.*	Con	18,981	47.3	-12.0
		Green, K. Ms.	Lab	14,100	35.1	+11.0
19.8		Dumigan, M.C.	LD	4,933	12.3	-1.8
		Walters, A. Sir	Ref	1,161	2.9*	
		Wharton, P.M. Ms.	Ind	266	0.7*	
		Merton, C.R.	UKI	215	0.5*	
		Johnson, R.P.	NLP	176	0.4*	
		Walsh, N.T	MRLP	138	0.3*	
		Webster, G.C.	Ind	112	0.3*	
		Sadowitz, J.	Rainbow	73	0.2*	
1992: Con				4,881	12.2	

Cleethorpes [148]

68,763†	73.4	McIsaac, S. Ms.	Lab	26,058	51.6	+15.7
		Brown, M.R.*	Con	16,882	33.4	-14.5
17.3		Melton, K.M.	LD	5,746	11.4	-3.3
		Berry, J.C.	Ref	1,787	3.5*	
1992: Con				9,176	18.2	

Clwyd South [149]

53,495†	73.6	Jones, M.D.*	Lab	22,901	58.1	+8.4
		Johnson, A.B.de F.	Con	9,091	23.1	-7.2
67.8		Chadwick, A.	LD	3,684	9.4	-1.7
		Williams, G.V.	PC	2,500	6.3	-1.6
		Lewis, A.	Ref	1,207	3.1*	
1992: Lab				13,810	35.1	

Clwyd West [150]

53,467†	75.3	Thomas, G.	Lab	14,918	37.1	+6.2
		Richards, R.*	Con	13,070	32.5	-16.0
65.5		Williams, E.W.	PC	5,421	13.5	+8.9
		Williams, W.G.	LD	5,151	12.8	-2.9
		Bennett-Collins, H. Ms.	Ref	1,114	2.8*	
		Neal, D.K.	Ind	583	1.4*	
1992: Con				1,848	4.6	

Clydebank & Milngavie [151]

52,092†	75.0	Worthington, A.*	Lab	21,583	55.2	+5.0
		Yuill, J.W.	SNP	8,263	21.1	+2.7
7.1		Morgan, N.E. Ms.	Con	4,885	12.5	-9.0
		Moody, K.W.	LD	4,086	10.5	+0.9
		Sanderson, J.	Ref	269	0.7*	
1992: Lab				13,320	34.1	

Clydesdale [152]

63,428†	71.6	Hood, J.*	Lab	23,859	52.5	+7.9
		Doig, A.	SNP	10,050	22.1	-0.9
None		Izatt, M.A.	Con	7,396	16.3	-7.1
		Grieve, S.M. Ms.	LD	3,796	8.4	+0.1
		Smith, K.	BNP	311	0.7*	
1992: Lab				13,809	30.4	

Coatbridge & Chryston [153]

52,024†	72.3	Clarke, T.*	Lab	25,694	68.3	+6.5
		Nugent, B.	SNP	6,402	17.0	+0.3
25.5		Wauchope, P.A.C.	Con	3,216	8.6	-7.0
		Daly, M.E. Ms.	LD	2,048	5.4	-0.5
		Bowsley, B.	Ref	249	0.7*	
1992: Lab				19,292	51.3	

Colchester [154]

74,743†	69.6	Russell, R.E.	LD	17,886	34.4	+1.7
		Shakespeare, S.A.	Con	16,305	31.4	-10.7
80.9		Green, R.A.	Lab	15,891	30.6	+6.5
		Hazell, J.B.	Ref	1,776	3.4*	
		Basker, L. Ms.	NLP	148	0.3*	
1992: Con				1,581	3.0	

Colne Valley [155]

73,347	76.9	Mountford, K.C.J. Ms.	Lab	23,285	41.3	+11.5
		Riddick, G.E.G.*	Con	18,445	32.7	-9.3
None		Priestley, N.J.	LD	12,755	22.6	-4.4
		Brooke, A.J.	SL	759	1.3*	
		Cooper, A.V.	Grn	493	0.9*	
		Nunn, J.D.	UKI	478	0.8*	
		Staniforth, M.E. Ms.	MRLP	196	0.3*	
1992: Con				4,840	8.6	

Congleton [156]

68,873†	77.6	Winterton, J.A. Ms.*	Con	22,012	41.2	-7.3
		Walmsley, J.M. Ms.	LD	15,882	29.7	-2.0
6.6		Scholey, F.H.E. Ms.	Lab	14,713	27.5	+8.4
		Lockett, J.B.	UKI	811	1.5*	
1992: Con				6,130	11.5	

Conwy [157]

55,092†	75.4	Williams, B.H. Ms.	Lab	14,561	35.0	+9.3
		Roberts, J.R.	LD	12,965	31.2	-0.2
None		Jones, D.I.	Con	10,085	24.3	-9.5
		Davies, R.V.	PC	2,844	6.8	-0.5
		Barham, A.C.	Ref	760	1.8*	
		Bradley, R.B.	Ind LD	250	0.6*	
		Hughes, D.E.	NLP	95	0.2*	
1992: Con				1,596	3.8	

Copeland [158]

54,263†	76.3	Cunningham, J.A.*	Lab	24,077	58.2	+9.5
		Cumpsty, A.	Con	12,081	29.2	-14.2
None		Putnam, R.C.	LD	3,814	9.2	+1.6
		Johnston, C.	Ref	1,036	2.5*	
		Hanratty, G.	PL	389	0.9*	
1992: Lab				11,996	29.0	

Corby [159]

69,446†	77.7	Hope, P.I.	Lab	29,888	55.4	+11.5
		Powell, W.R.*	Con	18,028	33.4	-11.1
None		Hankinson, I.	LD	4,045	7.5	-2.7
		Riley-Smith, S.D.C.	Ref	1,356	2.5*	
		Gillman, I.F.	UKI	507	0.9*	
		Bence, J.R. Ms.	NLP	133	0.2*	
1992: Con				11,860	22.0	

Cornwall North [160]

80,076†	73.0	Tyler, P.A.*	LD	31,100	53.2	+5.8
		Linacre, N.G.T.	Con	17,253	29.5	-14.8
None		Lindo, A.E. Ms.	Lab	5,523	9.4	+2.9
		Odam, F.A. Ms.	Ref	3,636	6.2	
		Bolitho, J.E.	MK	645	1.1*	
		Winfield, R.	Lib	186	0.3*	
		Cresswell, N.J.	NLP	152	0.3*	
1992: LD				13,847	23.7	

Cornwall South East [161]

75,825†	75.7	Breed, C.E.	LD	27,044	47.1	+9.0
		Lightfoot, W.	Con	20,564	35.8	-15.1
None		Kirk, D. Ms.	Lab	7,358	12.8	+3.6
		Wonnacott, J.A.	UKI	1,428	2.5*	
		Dunbar, P.A.R.	MK	573	1.0*	
		Weights, B.	Lib	268	0.5*	
		Hartley, M.K.F. Ms.	NLP	197	0.3*	
1992: Con				6,480	11.3	

Cotswold [162]

67,590	75.6	Clifton-Brown, G.R.*	Con	23,698	46.4	-8.0
		Gayler, D.R.	LD	11,733	23.0	-10.4
55.4		Elwell, D.	Lab	11,608	22.7	+11.8
		Lowe, R.J.G.	Ref	3,393	6.6	
		Michael, V. Ms.	Grn	560	1.1*	
		Brighouse, H.W.	NLP	129	0.3*	
1992: Con				11,965	23.4	

Coventry North East [163]

74,173†	64.8	Ainsworth, R.W.*	Lab	31,856	66.2	+16.6
		Burnett, M.J.	Con	9,287	19.3	-8.7
18.7		Sewards, G.B.	LD	3,866	8.0	-2.5
		Brown, N.E.	Lib	1,181	2.5*	
		Hurrell, R.	Ref	1,125	2.3*	
		Khamis, H.W.	SL	597	1.2*	
		Sidwell, C.J.	Rainbow	173	0.4*	
1992: Lab				22,569	46.9	

Coventry North West [164]

76,845†	70.7	Robinson, G.*	Lab	30,901	56.9	+5.6
		Bartlett, P.	Con	14,300	26.3	-10.6
54.9		Penlington, G.N.	LD	5,690	10.5	-1.3
		Butler, D.S.	Ref	1,269	2.3*	
		Spencer, D.C.	SL	940	1.7*	
		Wheway, R.	Lib	687	1.3*	
		Mills, P.L.	PL	359	0.7*	
		Francis, L.G.	Rainbow	176	0.3*	
1992: Lab				16,601	30.6	

Coventry South [165]

72,967†	68.7	Cunningham, J.D.*	Lab	25,511	50.9	+16.2
		Ivey, P.C.	Con	14,558	29.0	-10.8
99.0		MacDonald, G.F.	LD	4,617	9.2	-0.0
		Nellist, D.J.	Soc	3,262	6.5	
		Garratt, P.J.	Ref	943	1.9*	
		Jenking, R.E.	Lib	725	1.4*	
		Astbury, J.	BNP	328	0.7*	
		Bradshaw, A. Ms.	Rainbow	180	0.4*	
1992: Con				10,953	21.9	

Crawley [166]

69,194	72.9	Moffatt, L.J. Ms.	Lab	27,750	55.0	+14.7
		Crabb, J.A. Ms.	Con	16,043	31.8	-12.1
15.8		De Souza, H.	LD	4,141	8.2	-6.3
		Walters, R.G.	Ref	1,931	3.8*	
		Saunders, E.J.	UKI	322	0.6*	
		Kahn, A.	Ind	230	0.5*	
1992: Con				11,707	23.2	

Crewe & Nantwich [167]

68,472	73.9	Dunwoody, G.P. Ms.*	Lab	29,460	58.2	+10.6
		Loveridge, M.W.	Con	13,662	27.0	-11.9
21.2		Cannon, D.J.	LD	5,940	11.7	-0.8
		Astbury, P.	Ref	1,543	3.0*	
1992: Lab				15,798	31.2	

Crosby [168]

57,190†	77.2	Curtis-Tansley, C. Ms.	Lab	22,549	51.1	+22.4
		Thornton, M.*	Con	15,367	34.8	-13.9
51.8		McVey, P.J.	LD	5,080	11.5	-8.5
		Gauld, J.A.	Ref	813	1.8*	
		Marks, J.A.	Lib	233	0.5*	
		Hite, W.R.	NLP	99	0.2*	
1992: Con				7,182	16.3	

Croydon Central [169]

80,152†	69.6	Davies, G.R.	Lab	25,432	45.6	+14.1
		Congdon, D.L.*	Con	21,535	38.6	-16.9
87.9		Schlich, G.W.	LD	6,061	10.9	-2.1
		Cook, C.E.	Ref	1,886	3.4*	
		Barnsley, M.S.G.G.	Grn	595	1.1*	
		Woollcott, J.L.A.	UKI	290	0.5*	
1992: Con				3,897	7.0	

Croydon North [170]

77,063†	68.2	Wicks, M.H.*	Lab	32,672	62.2	+17.8
		Martin, I.R.	Con	14,274	27.2	-17.5
45.2		Morris, M.	LD	4,066	7.7	-3.2
		Billis, R.W.	Ref	1,155	2.2*	
		Feisenberger, J.R.	UKI	396	0.8*	
1992: Con				18,398	35.0	

Croydon South [171]

73,787†	73.5	Ottaway, R.G.J.*	Con	25,649	47.3	-14.3
		Burling, C.E.	Lab	13,719	25.3	+9.0
16.5		Gauge, S.H.	LD	11,441	21.1	-0.5
		Barber, A.H.	Ref	2,631	4.9*	
		Ferguson, P.C.	BNP	354	0.7*	
		Harker, A.G.	UKI	309	0.6*	
		Samuel, M.R.L.	Ind	96	0.2*	
1992: Con				11,930	22.0	

Cumbernauld & Kilsyth [172]

48,032†	75.0	McKenna, R. Ms.	Lab	21,141	58.7	+4.7
		Barrie, C.	SNP	10,013	27.8	-1.2
None		Sewell, I.J.	Con	2,441	6.8	-4.5
		Biggam, J.S.	LD	1,368	3.8*	-2.0
		Kara, J. Ms.	PL	609	1.7*	
		McEwan, K.	SSA	345	1.0*	
		Cook, P. Ms.	Ref	107	0.3*	
1992: Lab				11,128	30.9	

Cunninghame North [173]

55,526†	74.1	Wilson, B.D.H.*	Lab	20,686	50.3	+9.3
		Mitchell, M. Ms.	Con	9,647	23.5	-10.7
None		Nicoll, K. Ms.	SNP	7,584	18.4	+0.2
		Freel, K. Ms.	LD	2,271	5.5	-1.2
		McDaid, L.A.M. Ms.	SL	501	1.2*	
		Winton, I.D.	Ref	440	1.1*	
1992: Lab				11,039	26.8	

Cunninghame South [174]

49,543†	71.5	Donohoe, B.H.*	Lab	22,233	62.7	+9.8
		Burgess, M. Ms.	SNP	7,364	20.8	-3.4
None		Paterson, P.M. Ms.	Con	3,571	10.1	-6.2
		Watson, E.	LD	1,604	4.5*	-1.7
		Edwin, K.	SL	494	1.4*	
		Martlew, A.	Ref	178	0.5*	
1992: Lab				14,869	42.0	

Cynon Valley [175]

48,286†	69.2	Clwyd, A. Ms.*	Lab	23,307	69.7	+0.6
		Davies, T.A.R.	PC	3,552	10.6	-0.4
None		Price, H.	LD	3,459	10.3	+3.3
		Smith, A.M.	Con	2,260	6.8	-6.1
		John, G.	Ref	844	2.5*	
1992: Lab				19,755	59.1	

Dagenham [176]

58,232	62.1	Church, J.A. Ms.*	Lab	23,759	65.7	+14.0
		Fairrie, J.P.J.	Con	6,705	18.5	-18.3
2.9		Dobrashian, T.	LD	2,704	7.5	-4.0
		Kraft, S.	Ref	1,411	3.9*	
		Binding, W.	BNP	900	2.5*	
		Dawson, R.H.	Ind	349	1.0*	
		Hipperson, M.B.	Nat Dem	183	0.5*	
		Goble, K.A. Ms.	PL	152	0.4*	
1992: Lab				17,054	47.2	

Darlington [177]

65,169	73.9	Milburn, A.*	Lab	29,658	61.6	+13.5
		Scrope, P.G.	Con	13,633	28.3	-14.7
None		Boxell, L.	LD	3,483	7.2	-1.1
		Blakey, M.A.	Ref	1,399	2.9*	
1992: Lab				16,025	33.3	

Dartford [178]

69,726†	74.6	Stoate, H.G.A.	Lab	25,278	48.6	+12.4
		Dunn, R.J.*	Con	20,950	40.3	-10.6
7.9		Webb, D.J. Ms.	LD	4,872	9.4	-2.8
		McHale, P.	BNP	424	0.8*	
		Homden, P.A.	Ind	287	0.6*	
		Pollitt, J.W.	CD	228	0.4*	
1992: Con				4,328	8.3	

Daventry [179]

80,750	76.5	Boswell, T.E.*	Con	28,615	46.3	-11.4
		Ritchie, K.G.H.	Lab	21,237	34.4	+10.5
14.1		Gordon, J.K.	LD	9,233	15.0	-2.7
		Russocki, B.A. de B. Ms.	Ref	2,018	3.3*	
		Mahoney, B.J.	UKI	443	0.7*	
		France, R.B.	NLP	204	0.3*	
1992: Con				7,378	11.9	

Delyn [180]

53,693†	75.9	Hanson, D.G.*	Lab	23,300	57.2	+10.3
		Lumley, K.E. Ms.	Con	10,607	26.0	-13.6
20.3		Lloyd, D.P.	LD	4,160	10.2	-0.8
		Drake, A.	PC	1,558	3.8*	+1.3
		Soutter, E.H. Ms.	Ref	1,117	2.7*	
1992: Lab				12,693	31.2	

Denton & Reddish [181]

68,866†	66.9	Bennett, A.F.*	Lab	30,137	65.4	+12.4
		Nutt, B.E. Ms.	Con	9,826	21.3	-12.5
24.8		Donaldson, I.C.	LD	6,121	13.3	+3.3
1992: Lab				20,311	44.1	

Derby North [182]

75,880	74.0	Laxton, R.	Lab	29,844	53.2	+12.3
		Knight, G.*	Con	19,229	34.3	-14.2
None		Charlesworth, R.A.	LD	5,059	9.0	-0.5
		Reynolds, P.W.H.	Ref	1,816	3.2*	
		Waters, J.H.M. Ms.	PL	195	0.3*	
1992: Con				10,615	18.9	

Derby South [183]

76,157	68.0	Beckett, M.M. Ms.*	Lab	29,154	56.3	+8.0
		Arain, J.	Con	13,048	25.2	-15.7
12.5		Beckett, J.W.R.	LD	7,438	14.4	+3.5
		Browne, J.K.	Ref	1,862	3.6*	
		Evans, R.	Nat Dem	317	0.6*	
1992: Lab				16,106	31.1	

Derbyshire North East [184]

71,653†	72.5	Barnes, H.*	Lab	31,425	60.5	+11.6
		Elliott, S.	Con	13,104	25.2	-13.0
None		Hardy, S.P.	LD	7,450	14.3	+1.4
1992: Lab				18,321	35.2	

Derbyshire South [185]

76,672†	78.2	Todd, M.W.	Lab	32,709	54.5	+10.5
		Currie, E. Ms.*	Con	18,742	31.3	-15.9
10.2		Renold, R.C.	LD	5,408	9.0	+0.7
		North, R.A.E.	Ref	2,491	4.2*	
		Crompton, I.E.	UKI	617	1.0*	
1992: Con				13,967	23.3	

Derbyshire West [186]

72,716†	78.2	McLoughlin, P.A.*	Con	23,945	42.1	-12.1
		Clamp, S.J.	Lab	19,060	33.5	+11.2
2.6		Seeley, C.R.	LD	9,940	17.5	-6.0
		Gouriet, J.P.	Ref	2,499	4.4*	
		Meynell, G.	Ind Grn	593	1.0*	
		Price, H.G.K.	UKI	484	0.9*	
		Delves, N.C.E.	MRLP	281	0.5*	
		Kyslun, M.	Ind	81	0.1*	
1992: Con				4,885	8.6	

Devizes [187]

80,383†	74.7	Ancram, M.A.*	Con	25,710	42.8	-10.1
		Vickers, A.J.M.	LD	15,928	26.5	-5.9
71.3		Jeffrey, F.	Lab	14,551	24.2	+12.2
		Goldsmith, J.O.	Ref	3,021	5.0	
		Oram, S.	UKI	622	1.0*	
		Haysom, S.A.	NLP	204	0.3*	
1992: Con				9,782	16.3	

Devon East [188]

69,146	76.0	Emery, P.*	Con	22,797	43.4	-9.2
		Trethewey, R.H. Ms.	LD	15,303	29.1	+2.0
14.7		Siantonas, A.	Lab	9,292	17.7	+5.5
		Dixon, W.G.	Ref	3,200	6.1	
		Halliwell, G.J.	Lib	1,363	2.6*	
		Giffard, C.A.	UKI	459	0.9*	
		Needs, G.A.	Nat Dem	131	0.2*	
1992: Con				7,494	14.3	

Devon North [189]

70,521	77.7	Harvey, N.B.*	LD	27,824	50.8	+3.7
		Ashworth, R.J.	Con	21,643	39.5	-6.2
0.1		Brenton, E.A. Ms.	Lab	5,347	9.8	+3.9
1992: LD				6,181	11.3	

Devon South West [190]

69,293†	76.2	Streeter, G.N.*	Con	22,659	42.9	-14.7
		Mavin, C.J.	Lab	15,262	28.9	+13.1
78.6		Baldry, K.J.	LD	12,542	23.8	-1.8
		Sadler, R.	Ref	1,668	3.2*	
		King, H.M.L. Ms.	UKI	491	0.9*	
		Hyde, J.C.	NLP	159	0.3*	
1992: Con				7,397	14.0	

Devon West & Torridge [191]

75,919†	77.9	Burnett, J.P.A.	LD	24,744	41.8	+0.1
		Liddell-Grainger, I.R.P.	Con	22,787	38.5	-8.6
3.7		Brenton, D.G.	Lab	7,319	12.4	+2.9
		Lea, R.	Ref	1,946	3.3*	
		Jackson, M.J.	UKI	1,841	3.1*	
		Pithouse, M.B.	Lib	508	0.9*	
1992: Con				1,957	3.3	

Dewsbury [192]

61,519	70.0	Taylor, W.A. Ms.*	Lab	21,286	49.4	+2.1
		McCormick, P.M.	Con	12,963	30.1	-9.9
51.1		Hill, K.	LD	4,422	10.3	+0.4
		Taylor, F. Ms.	BNP	2,232	5.2	
		Goff, W.S. Ms.	Ref	1,019	2.4*	
		Daniel, D.	Ind Lab	770	1.8*	
		McCourtie, I.M.	Grn	383	0.9*	
1992: Lab				8,323	19.3	

Don Valley [193]

65,643†	66.4	Flint, C.L. Ms.	Lab	25,376	58.3	+7.7
		Gledhill, C.H. Ms.	Con	10,717	24.6	-12.2
44.5		Johnston, P.	LD	4,238	9.7	-1.4
		Davis, P.R.	Ref	1,379	3.2*	
		Ball, N.	SL	1,024	2.4*	
		Platt, T.S.	Grn	493	1.1*	
		Johnson, C.D. Ms.	PL	330	0.8*	
1992: Lab				14,659	33.7	

Doncaster Central [194]

67,965†	63.9	Winterton, R. Ms.	Lab	26,961	62.1	+7.7
		Turtle, D.C.	Con	9,105	21.0	-12.5
None		Tarry, S.P.	LD	4,091	9.4	-2.4
		Cliff, M.J.	Ref	1,273	2.9*	
		Kenny, M.A.	SL	854	2.0*	
		Redden, J.F.	PL	694	1.6*	
		Davies, P.	UKI	462	1.1*	
1992: Lab				17,856	41.1	

Doncaster North [195]

63,019†	63.3	Hughes, K.M.*	Lab	27,843	69.8	+5.4
		Kennerley, P.D.	Con	5,906	14.8	-7.5
15.1		Cook, M.R.	LD	3,369	8.4	-4.8
		Thornton, R.W.	Ref	1,589	4.0*	
		Swan, N.M.	Ind	1,181	3.0*	
1992: Lab				21,937	55.0	

Dorset Mid & Poole North [196]

67,357	75.3	Fraser, C.J.	Con	20,632	40.7	-9.4
		Leaman, A.J.	LD	19,951	39.3	+1.4
120.1		Collis, D.C.	Lab	8,014	15.8	+3.9
		Nabarro, D.J.N.	Ref	2,136	4.2*	
1992: Con				681	1.3	

Dorset North [197]

68,923†	76.3	Walter, R.J.	Con	23,294	44.3	-12.2
		Yates, P.G. Ms.	LD	20,548	39.1	+1.6
24.2		Fitzmaurice, J.F.	Lab	5,380	10.2	+4.2
		Evans, M.J. Ms.	Ref	2,564	4.9*	
		Wheeler, D.J.C.	UKI	801	1.5*	
1992: Con				2,746	5.2	

Dorset South [198]

66,493†	74.0	Bruce, I.C.*	Con	17,755	36.1	-14.8
		Knight, J.	Lab	17,678	35.9	+15.1
11.1		Plummer, M.I.	LD	9,936	20.2	-6.4
		McAndrew, P.C.	Ref	2,791	5.7	
		Shakesby, M.L.	UKI	861	1.8*	
		Napper, G.T.H.	NLP	161	0.3*	
1992: Con				77	0.2	

Dorset West [199]

70,369†	76.1	Letwin, O.	Con	22,036	41.1	-9.7
		Legg, R.A.S.	LD	20,196	37.7	+1.5
0.0		Bygrave, R.J.	Lab	9,491	17.7	+4.8
		Jenkins, P.	UKI	1,590	3.0*	
		Griffiths, M.R.F.	NLP	239	0.4*	
1992: Con				1,840	3.4	

Dover [200]

68,713	78.9	Prosser, G.M.	Lab	29,535	54.5	+11.9
		Shaw, D.L.*	Con	17,796	32.8	-11.3
0.2		Corney, M.B.	LD	4,302	7.9	-2.9
		Anderson, S.L. Ms.	Ref	2,124	3.9*	
		Hyde, C.D.	UKI	443	0.8*	
1992: Con				11,739	21.7	

Down North [201]

63,101	57.9	McCartney, R.L.*	UKU	12,817	35.1	+35.1
		McFarland, A.R.	UU	11,368	31.1	+31.1
31.3		Napier, O.J.	APNI	7,554	20.7	+5.0
		Fee, A.L.	Con	1,810	5.0*	-29.7
		Farrell, M.J. Ms.	SDLP	1,602	4.4*	+4.4
		Morrice, J. Ms.	Ind	1,240	3.4*	
		Mullins, T.	NLP	108	0.3*	
		Mooney, R.G.	Ind	57	0.2*	
1992: UPUP				1,449	4.0	

Down South [202]

69,977	70.7	McGrady, E.*	SDLP	26,181	52.9	-3.2
		Nesbitt, D.	UU	16,248	32.8	-2.6
16.4		Murphy, M.	SF	5,127	10.4	+6.8
		Crozier, J.S.	APNI	1,711	3.5*	+1.0
		McKeon, R. Ms.	NLP	219	0.4*	
1992: SDLP				9,933	20.1	

Dudley North [203]

68,886	69.4	Cranston, R.F.	Lab	24,471	51.2	+5.7
		MacNamara, C.V.F.	Con	15,014	31.4	-12.3
69.2		Lewis, G.P.	LD	3,939	8.2	-1.5
		Atherton, M.	SL	2,155	4.5*	
		Bavester, S.D.	Ref	1,201	2.5*	
		Cartwright, G.E.	NF	559	1.2*	
		Darby, S.	Nat Dem	469	1.0*	
1992: Lab				9,457	19.8	

Dudley South [204]

66,793	71.7	Pearson, I.P.*	Lab	27,124	56.6	+9.6
		Simpson, G.M.	Con	14,097	29.4	-12.5
62.1		Burt, R.G.	LD	5,214	10.9	-0.2
		Birch, C.	Ref	1,467	3.1*	
1992: Lab				13,027	27.2	

Dulwich & West Norwood [205]

70,203†	65.0	Jowell, T.J.H.D. Ms.*	Lab	27,807	61.0	+14.6
		Gough, R.	Con	11,038	24.2	-18.6
73.2		Kramer, S. Ms.	LD	4,916	10.8	+1.0
		Coles, B.	Ref	897	2.0*	
		Goldie, G.M.A.	Lib	587	1.3*	
		Goodman, D.	Rainbow	173	0.4*	
		Pike, E.C.	UKI	159	0.3*	
		Rizz, C.	Ind	38	0.1*	
1992: Lab				16,769	36.8	

Dumbarton [206]

56,229†	73.4	McFall, J.*	Lab	20,470	49.6	+6.0
		Mackechnie, B.	SNP	9,587	23.2	+4.8
None		Ramsay, P.J.	Con	7,283	17.6	-12.1
		Reid, A.	LD	3,144	7.6	-0.1
		Robertson, L.A.	SSA	283	0.7*	
		Dempster, G.J.	Ref	255	0.6*	
		Lancaster, R.D.	UKI	242	0.6*	
1992: Lab				10,883	26.4	

Dumfries [207]

62,759†	78.9	Brown, R.L.	Lab	23,528	47.5	+17.9
		Stevenson, S.J.S.	Con	13,885	28.0	-15.1
2.4		Higgins, R.J.	SNP	5,977	12.1	-2.7
		Wallace, N.C.	LD	5,487	11.1	-0.6
		Parker, D.F.	Ref	533	1.1*	
		Hunter, E. Ms.	NLP	117	0.2*	
1992: Con				9,643	19.5	

Dundee East [208]

58,487	69.3	McAllion, J.*	Lab	20,718	51.1	+6.8
		Robison, S.M. Ms.	SNP	10,757	26.5	-5.5
11.5		Mackie, B.D.	Con	6,397	15.8	-2.7
		Saluja, G.S.	LD	1,677	4.1*	-0.2
		Galloway, T.	Ref	601	1.5*	
		Duke, H.	SSA	232	0.6*	
		MacKenzie, E.S. Ms.	NLP	146	0.4*	
1992: Lab				9,961	24.6	

Dundee West [209]

57,434	67.6	Ross, E.*	Lab	20,875	53.8	+6.1
		Dorward, J.C.	SNP	9,016	23.2	-1.3
9.2		Powrie, N.I.C.	Con	5,105	13.2	-5.7
		Dick, E.G. Ms.	LD	2,972	7.7	+0.2
		Ward, M.M. Ms.	SSA	428	1.1*	
		MacMillan, J.R.	Ref	411	1.1*	
1992: Lab				11,859	30.6	

Dunfermline East [210]

52,133	70.2	Brown, G.*	Lab	24,441	66.8	+3.9
		Ramage, J.J.	SNP	5,690	15.6	+0.8
3.7		Mitchell, I.G.	Con	3,656	10.0	-6.3
		Tolson, J.	LD	2,164	5.9	-0.2
		Dunsmore, T.	Ref	632	1.7*	
1992: Lab				18,751	51.3	

Dunfermline West [211]

52,538	69.3	Squire, R.A. Ms.*	Lab	19,338	53.1	+11.6
		Lloyd, J.	SNP	6,984	19.2	-0.7
3.5		Harris, E.B.A. Ms.	LD	4,963	13.6	-2.0
		Newton, K.A.	Con	4,606	12.6	-10.4
		Bain, J.	Ref	543	1.5*	
1992: Lab				12,354	33.9	

Durham North [212]

68,135	69.2	Radice, G.H.*	Lab	33,142	70.3	+10.4
		Hardy, M.T.	Con	6,843	14.5	-10.3
9.5		Moore, B.D.	LD	5,225	11.1	-4.2
		Parkin, I.A.C.	Ref	1,958	4.2*	
1992: Lab				26,299	55.8	

Durham North West [213]

67,390	68.7	Armstrong, H.J. Ms.*	Lab	31,855	68.8	+10.7
		St John Howe, L. Ms.	Con	7,101	15.3	-12.0
10.2		Gillings, A.T.	LD	4,991	10.8	-3.9
		Atkinson, R.E.B.	Ref	2,372	5.1	
1992: Lab				24,754	53.4	

City of Durham [214]

69,417	70.8	Steinberg, G.N.*	Lab	31,102	63.3	+10.0
		Chalk, R.E.O.	Con	8,598	17.5	-6.2
None		Martin, N.	LD	7,499	15.3	-6.2
		Robson, M.G. Ms.	Ref	1,723	3.5*	
		Kember, P.A.	NLP	213	0.4*	
1992: Lab				22,504	45.8	

Ealing Acton & Shepherd's Bush [215]

72,078†	66.7	Soley, C.S.*	Lab	28,052	58.4	+12.0
		Yerolemou, B.C. Ms.	Con	12,402	25.8	-13.6
74.8		Mitchell, A.D.	LD	5,163	10.7	-1.3
		Winn, C.W.H.	Ref	637	1.3*	
		Gilbert, J.	SL	635	1.3*	
		Gomm, J.D.	UKI	385	0.8*	
		Danon, P.F.E.	PL	265	0.6*	
		Beasley, C.G.	Ind	209	0.4*	
		Edwards, W.T.	Ind	163	0.3*	
		Turner, K.A.	NLP	150	0.3*	
1992: Lab				15,650	32.6	

Ealing North [216]

78,144†	71.3	Pound, S.P.	Lab	29,904	53.7	+17.9
		Greenway, H.*	Con	20,744	37.2	-14.2
16.1		Gupta, A.K.	LD	3,887	7.0	-3.8
		Slysz, G.M.	UKI	689	1.2*	
		Siebe, A.I. Ms.	Grn	502	0.9*	
1992: Con				9,160	16.4	

Ealing Southall [217]

81,704†	66.9	Khabra, P.S.*	Lab	32,791	60.0	+14.7
		Penrose, J.D.	Con	11,368	20.8	-15.5
13.2		Thomson, N.F. Ms.	LD	5,687	10.4	+2.3
		Brar, H.	SL	2,107	3.9*	
		Goodwin, N.	Grn	934	1.7*	
		Cherry, D.B.	Ref	854	1.6*	
		Klepacka, K.M. Ms.	PL	473	0.9*	
		Mead, R.G.C.	UKI	428	0.8*	
1992: Lab				21,423	39.2	

Easington [218]

62,518†	67.0	Cummings, J.S.*	Lab	33,600	80.2	+7.5
		Hollands, J.D.	Con	3,588	8.6	-8.1
None		Heppell, J.P.	LD	3,025	7.2	-3.4
		Pulfrey, R.B.	Ref	1,179	2.8*	
		Colborn, S.P.	Soc	503	1.2*	
1992: Lab				30,012	71.6	

East Ham [219]

66,111†	60.3	Timms, S.C.*	Lab	25,779	64.6	+10.7
		Bray, A.L. Ms.	Con	6,421	16.1	-15.9
19.8		Khan, I.	SL	2,697	6.8	
		Sole, M.J.	LD	2,599	6.5	-7.5
		Smith, C.	BNP	1,258	3.2*	
		McCann, J.E. Ms.	Ref	845	2.1*	
		Hardy, G.G.	Nat Dem	290	0.7*	
1992: Lab				19,358	48.5	

East Kilbride [220]

65,229†	74.8	Ingram, A.P.*	Lab	27,584	56.5	+9.2
		Gebbie, G.C.	SNP	10,200	20.9	-2.7
2.0		Herbertson, C.T.	Con	5,863	12.0	-6.6
		Philbrick, K. Ms.	LD	3,527	7.2	-3.2
		Deighan, J.	PL	1,170	2.4*	
		Gray, J. Ms.	Ref	306	0.6*	
		Gilmour, E.C.	NLP	146	0.3*	
1992: Lab				17,384	35.6	

East Lothian [221]

57,489	75.5	Home Robertson, J.D.*	Lab	22,881	52.7	+7.2
		Fraser, M.M.	Con	8,660	19.9	-10.2
16.7		McCarthy, D.R.	SNP	6,825	15.7	+2.4
		MacAskill, A. Ms.	LD	4,575	10.5	-0.5
		Nash, N.S.	Ref	491	1.1*	
1992: Lab				14,221	32.7	

Eastbourne [222]

72,347†	72.8	Waterson, N.C.*	Con	22,183	42.1	-10.9
		Berry, C.J.	LD	20,189	38.3	-2.9
10.5		Lines, D.J.	Lab	6,576	12.5	+7.8
		Lowe, T.J.	Ref	2,724	5.2	
		Williamson, M-T. Ms.	Lib	741	1.4*	
		Dawkins, J.	UKI	254	0.5*	
1992: Con				1,994	3.8	

Eastleigh [223]

72,405†	76.6	Chidgey, D.W.G.*	LD	19,453	35.1	+5.4
		Reid, S.H.	Con	18,699	33.7	-17.2
26.5		Lloyd, A.	Lab	14,883	26.8	+7.4
		Eldridge, V.J.	Ref	2,013	3.6*	
		Robinson, P.W.	UKI	446	0.8*	
1992: Con				754	1.4	

Eastwood [224]

66,769	78.3	Murphy, J.	Lab	20,766	39.7	+15.6
		Cullen, P.B.	Con	17,530	33.5	-13.1
2.1		Yates, D.A.	SNP	6,826	13.1	+0.5
		Mason, C.M.	LD	6,110	11.7	-4.7
		Miller, D.I.	Ref	497	1.0*	
		Tayan, M.	PL	393	0.8*	
		McPherson, D.	UKI	130	0.2*	
1992: Con				3,236	6.2	

Eccles [225]

69,645†	65.6	Stewart, I.	Lab	30,468	66.7	+9.1
		Barker, G.L.G.	Con	8,552	18.7	-12.4
34.6		Boyd, R.D.	LD	4,905	10.7	+1.1
		de Roeck, J.	Ref	1,765	3.9*	
1992: Lab				21,916	48.0	

Eddisbury [226]

65,394†	75.6	Goodlad, A.R.*	Con	21,027	42.5	-10.2
		Hanson, M.R. Ms.	Lab	19,842	40.1	+9.1
47.4		Reaper, D.	LD	6,540	13.2	-1.6
		Napier, N.D. Ms.	Ref	2,041	4.1*	
1992: Con				1,185	2.4	

Edinburgh Central [227]

63,695†	67.1	Darling, A.M.*	Lab	20,125	47.1	+8.6
		Scott-Hayward, M.D.A.	Con	9,055	21.2	-8.2
38.4		Hyslop, F.J. Ms.	SNP	6,750	15.8	+0.6
		Utting, K.J. Ms.	LD	5,605	13.1	-1.7
		Hendry, L.M. Ms.	Grn	607	1.4*	
		Skinner, A.G.	Ref	495	1.2*	
		Benson, M.E.	Ind	98	0.2*	
1992: Lab				11,070	25.9	

Edinburgh East & Musselburgh [228]

59,648†	70.6	Strang, G.S.*	Lab	22,564	53.6	+8.9
		White, D.O.	SNP	8,034	19.1	+1.1
47.8		Ward, K.F.	Con	6,483	15.4	-8.6
		MacKellar, C.I.	LD	4,511	10.7	-0.8
		Sibbet, J.A.	Ref	526	1.2*	
1992: Lab				14,530	34.5	

Edinburgh North & Leith [229]

61,617†	66.5	Chisholm, M.G.R.*	Lab	19,209	46.9	+12.0
		Dana, A.C. Ms.	SNP	8,231	20.1	-0.2
43.0		Stewart, E.N.	Con	7,312	17.9	-7.0
		Campbell, H.C. Ms.	LD	5,335	13.0	+1.3
		Graham, A.G.	Ref	441	1.1*	
		Brown, G.	SSA	320	0.8*	
		Douglas-Reid, P.B.	NLP	97	0.2*	
1992: Lab				10,978	26.8	

Edinburgh Pentlands [230]

59,635†	76.7	Clark, L.M. Ms.	Lab	19,675	43.0	+11.8
		Rifkind, M.L.*	Con	14,813	32.4	-7.8
7.6		Gibb, S.	SNP	5,952	13.0	-2.7
		Dawe, J.A. Ms.	LD	4,575	10.0	-2.7
		McDonald, M.	Ref	422	0.9*	
		Harper, R.C.M.	Grn	224	0.5*	
		McConnachie, A.D.	UKI	81	0.2*	
1992: Con				4,862	10.6	

Edinburgh South [231]

62,467†	71.8	Griffiths, N.*	Lab	20,993	46.8	+5.3
		Smith, E.J. Ms.	Con	9,541	21.3	-10.9
2.7		Pringle, M.S.R.	LD	7,911	17.6	+4.5
		Hargreaves, J.	SNP	5,791	12.9	+0.0
		McLean, I.R.	Ref	504	1.1*	
		Dunn, B.R.	NLP	98	0.2*	
1992: Lab				11,452	25.5	

Edinburgh West [232]

61,133†	77.9	Gorrie, D.C.E.	LD	20,578	43.2	+13.3
		Douglas-Hamilton, J.A.*	Con	13,325	28.0	-10.2
52.2		Hinds, L.A. Ms.	Lab	8,948	18.8	+1.4
		Sutherland, G.D.	SNP	4,210	8.8	-3.7
		Elphick, S.C.	Ref	277	0.6*	
		Coombes, P.N.	Lib	263	0.6*	
		Jack, A.C.O.	Ind	30	0.1*	
1992: Con				7,253	15.2	

Edmonton [233]

63,793	70.3	Love, A.M.	Lab	27,029	60.3	+15.2
		Twinn, I.D.*	Con	13,557	30.2	-16.0
None		Wiseman, A.D.	LD	2,847	6.3	-1.9
		Wright, J.	Ref	708	1.6*	
		Cowd, B.	BNP	437	1.0*	
		Weald, P.S. Ms.	UKI	260	0.6*	
1992: Con				13,472	30.0	

Ellesmere Port & Neston [234]

67,573	77.8	Miller, A.P.*	Lab	31,310	59.6	+11.7
		Turnbull, L. Ms.	Con	15,275	29.1	-13.0
6.9		Pemberton, J.L. Ms.	LD	4,673	8.9	-0.0
		Rodden, C.S.	Ref	1,305	2.5*	
1992: Lab				16,035	30.5	

Elmet [235]

70,423†	76.8	Burgon, C.	Lab	28,348	52.4	+10.5
		Batiste, S.L.*	Con	19,569	36.2	-11.3
None		Jennings, B.D.T.	LD	4,691	8.7	-1.9
		Zawadski, C.A.	Ref	1,487	2.7*	
1992: Con				8,779	16.2	

Eltham [236]

57,358†	75.7	Efford, C.S.	Lab	23,710	54.6	+14.5
		Blackwood, C.D.	Con	13,528	31.2	-12.8
25.6		Taylor, A.J. Ms.	LD	3,701	8.5	-7.0
		Clark, M.D.	Ref	1,414	3.3*	
		Middleton, H.	Lib	584	1.3*	
		Hitches, W.A.	BNP	491	1.1*	
1992: Con				10,182	23.4	

Enfield North [237]

67,748	70.4	Ryan, J.M. Ms.	Lab	24,148	50.7	+15.7
		Field, M.C.	Con	17,326	36.3	-16.6
None		Hopkins, M.S.	LD	4,264	8.9	-2.1
		Ellingham, R.	Ref	857	1.8*	
		Griffin, J. Ms.	BNP	590	1.2*	
		O'Ware, J.S. Ms.	UKI	484	1.0*	
1992: Con				6,822	14.3	

Enfield Southgate [238]

65,887	70.6	Twigg, S.	Lab	20,570	44.2	+18.0
		Portillo, M.D.X.*	Con	19,137	41.1	-16.8
0.1		Browne, J.R.	LD	4,966	10.7	-3.8
		Luard, N.L.	Ref	1,342	2.9*	
		Storkey, A.J.	CD	289	0.6*	
		Malakouna, A.	Ind	229	0.5*	
1992: Con				1,433	3.1	

Epping Forest [239]

72,690	72.9	Laing, E.F. Ms.	Con	24,117	45.5	-14.3
		Murray, S.W.	Lab	18,865	35.6	+13.0
7.6		Robinson, S.J.	LD	7,074	13.3	-3.4
		Berry, J.F.R.	Ref	2,208	4.2*	
		Henderson, P.	BNP	743	1.4*	
1992: Con				5,252	9.9	

Epsom & Ewell [240]

73,222†	74.0	Hamilton, A.G.*	Con	24,717	45.6	-15.4
		Woodford, P.J.	Lab	13,192	24.3	+9.3
24.8		Vincent, J.W.	LD	12,380	22.8	-0.4
		MacDonald, C.P.	Ref	2,355	4.3*	
		Green, H.S.	UKI	544	1.0*	
		Charlton, H.	Grn	527	1.0*	
		Weeks, K.F. Ms.	PL	466	0.9*	
1992: Con				11,525	21.3	

Erewash [241]

77,402†	78.0	Blackman, E.M. Ms.	Lab	31,196	51.7	+13.5
		Knight, A.A. Ms.*	Con	22,061	36.6	-10.6
0.2		Garnett, M.C.	LD	5,181	8.6	-5.0
		Stagg, S.A.	Ref	1,404	2.3*	
		Simmons, M.A.	SL	496	0.8*	
1992: Con				9,135	15.1	

Erith & Thamesmead [242]

63,417	65.6	Austin-Walker, J.E.*	Lab	25,812	62.1	+19.1
		Zahawi, N.	Con	8,388	20.2	-11.4
94.1		Grigg, A.H.C.	LD	5,001	12.0	-13.4
		Flunder, J.E.	Ref	1,394	3.4*	
		Dooley, V.J.	BNP	718	1.7*	
		Jackson, M.L.	UKI	274	0.7*	
1992: Lab				17,424	41.9	

Esher & Walton [243]

72,236	74.3	Taylor, I.C.*	Con	26,747	49.8	-10.9
		Reay, J.A. Ms.	Lab	12,219	22.8	+5.4
64.7		Miles, G.M.	LD	10,937	20.4	-1.6
		Cruickshank, A.A.C.	Ref	2,904	5.4	
		Collignon, B.M.	UKI	558	1.0*	
		Kay, S. Ms.	Rainbow	302	0.6*	
1992: Con				14,528	27.1	

Essex North [244]

68,008†	75.3	Jenkin, B.C.*	Con	22,480	43.9	-13.8
		Young, T.J.	Lab	17,004	33.2	+14.1
80.3		Phillips, A.J.	LD	10,028	19.6	-2.6
		Lord, R.G.	UKI	1,202	2.3*	
		Ransome, S.J. Ms.	Grn	495	1.0*	
1992: Con				5,476	10.7	

Exeter [245]

79,418	77.9	Bradshaw, B.P.J.	Lab	29,398	47.5	+11.3
		Rogers, A.R.	Con	17,693	28.6	-12.5
0.6		Brewer, D.	LD	11,148	18.0	-1.4
		Morrish, D.J.	Lib	2,062	3.3*	
		Edwards, P.A.	Grn	643	1.0*	
		Haynes, C.P. Ms.	UKI	638	1.0*	
		Meakin, J.K.	Ind	282	0.5*	
1992: Con				11,705	18.9	

Falkirk East [246]

56,792†	73.2	Connarty, M.*	Lab	23,344	56.1	+12.0
		Brown, K.J.	SNP	9,959	23.9	-4.4
29.2		Nicol, M.	Con	5,813	14.0	-6.2
		Spillane, R.J.	LD	2,153	5.2	-2.1
		Mowbray, S.C.	Ref	325	0.8*	
1992: Lab				13,385	32.2	

Falkirk West [247]

52,850†	72.6	Canavan, D.*	Lab	22,772	59.3	+7.9
		Alexander, D.	SNP	8,989	23.4	-0.1
14.7		Buchanan, C.A. Ms.	Con	4,639	12.1	-6.8
		Houston, D.	LD	1,970	5.1	-1.0
1992: Lab				13,783	35.9	

Falmouth & Camborne [248]

71,383†	75.1	Atherton, C.K. Ms.	Lab	18,151	33.8	+4.7
		Coe, S.N.*	Con	15,463	28.8	-8.1
None		Jones, T.L. Ms.	LD	13,512	25.2	-6.0
		de Savary, P.J.	Ref	3,534	6.6	
		Geach, J.H.	Ind Lab	1,691	3.2*	
		Holmes, P.T.	Lib	527	1.0*	
		Smith, R.L.	UKI	355	0.7*	
		Lewarne, R. Ms.	MK	238	0.4*	
		Glitter, G.	MRLP	161	0.3*	
1992: Con				2,688	5.0	

Fareham [249]

68,787†	75.9	Lloyd, P.R.C.*	Con	24,436	46.8	-13.8
		Pryor, M.A.	Lab	14,078	27.0	+12.1
19.0		Hill, G. Ms.	LD	10,234	19.6	-3.6
		Markham, W.D.	Ref	2,914	5.6	
		O'Brien, W.	Ind	515	1.0*	
1992: Con				10,358	19.9	

Faversham & Kent Mid [250]

67,130	73.9	Rowe, A.J.B.*	Con	22,016	44.4	-14.8
		Stewart, A.	Lab	17,843	36.0	+13.0
124.5		Parmenter, B.E.	LD	6,138	12.4	-4.7
		Birley, R.M.	Ref	2,073	4.2*	
		Davidson, N.A.	MRLP	511	1.0*	
		Cunningham, M.J.	UKI	431	0.9*	
		Currer, D.J.	Grn	380	0.8*	
		Morgan, C. Ms.	Ind	115	0.2*	
		Pollard, N.P.J.	NLP	99	0.2*	
1992: Con				4,173	8.4	

Feltham & Heston [251]

71,868†	64.9	Keen, A.*	Lab	27,836	59.7	+14.2
		Ground, R.P.	Con	12,563	26.9	-15.9
11.8		Penning, C.D.	LD	4,264	9.1	-2.4
		Stubbs, R.A.	Ref	1,099	2.4*	
		Church, R.	BNP	682	1.5*	
		Fawcett, D.J.	NLP	177	0.4*	
1992: Lab				15,273	32.8	

Fermanagh & South Tyrone [252]

64,740	74.6	Maginnis, K.*	UU	24,862	51.5	-0.9
		McHugh, G.	SF	11,174	23.1	+4.0
12.7		Gallagher, T.J.	SDLP	11,060	22.9	-0.0
		Farry, S.A.	APNI	977	2.0*	+0.3
		Gillan, S.T.	NLP	217	0.4*	
1992: UU				13,688	28.3	

Fife Central [253]

58,394	69.8	McLeish, H.B.*	Lab	23,912	58.7	+7.9
		Marwick, T. Ms.	SNP	10,199	25.0	+0.1
2.3		Rees-Mogg, J.W.	Con	3,669	9.0	-8.4
		Laird, R.	LD	2,610	6.4	-0.5
		Scrymgeour-Wedderburn, J.F.	Ref	375	0.9*	
1992: Lab				13,713	33.6	

Fife North East [254]

58,794†	71.2	Campbell, M.*	LD	21,432	51.2	+4.8
		Bruce, A.R.	Con	11,076	26.5	-12.0
0.1		Welsh, C.	SNP	4,545	10.9	+2.3
		Milne, C.	Lab	4,301	10.3	+4.7
		Stewart, W.N.	Ref	485	1.2*	
1992: LD				10,356	24.8	

Finchley & Golders Green [255]

72,357	69.5	Vis, R.J.	Lab	23,180	46.1	+15.2
		Marshall, J.L.*	Con	19,991	39.7	-15.0
73.4		Davies, J.M.	LD	5,670	11.3	-1.5
		Shaw, G.D.	Ref	684	1.4*	
		Gunstock, A.	Grn	576	1.1*	
		Barraclough, D.N.G.	UKI	205	0.4*	
1992: Con				3,189	6.3	

Folkestone & Hythe [256]

71,561†	72.7	Howard, M.*	Con	20,313	39.0	-13.3
		Laws, D.A.	LD	13,981	26.9	-8.5
0.0		Doherty, P.	Lab	12,939	24.9	+12.8
		Aspinall, J.V.	Ref	4,188	8.0	
		Baker, J.A.	UKI	378	0.7*	
		Segal, E.	Soc	182	0.3*	
		Saint, R.W.	Ind	69	0.1*	
1992: Con				6,332	12.2	

Forest of Dean [257]

63,732	78.7	Organ, D.M. Ms.	Lab	24,203	48.2	+5.8
		Marland, P.*	Con	17,860	35.6	-5.5
22.1		Lynch, A.S.	LD	6,165	12.3	-3.8
		Hopkins, D.J.	Ref	1,624	3.2*	
		Morgan, G.R.	Ind	218	0.4*	
		Palmer, C.R.	Ind	80	0.2*	
		Porter, S.R.	Ind	34	0.1*	
1992: Lab				6,343	12.6	

Foyle [258]

67,905	70.4	Hume, J.*	SDLP	25,109	52.5	-1.5
		McLaughlin, M.	SF	11,445	23.9	+6.6
16.8		Hay, W.	DUP	10,290	21.5	-3.5
		Bell, H.M. Ms.	APNI	817	1.7*	-0.3
		Brennan, D.	NLP	154	0.3*	
1992: SDLP				13,664	28.6	

Fylde [259]

71,460	72.9	Jack, J.M.*	Con	25,443	48.9	-11.4
		Garrett, J.L.	Lab	16,480	31.7	+13.1
12.5		Greene, W.L.	LD	7,609	14.6	-6.1
		Britton, D.J.	Ref	2,372	4.6*	
		Kerwin, T.B.	NLP	163	0.3*	
1992: Con				8,963	17.2	

Gainsborough [260]

64,106†	74.6	Leigh, E.J.E.*	Con	20,593	43.1	-10.3
		Taylor, P.	Lab	13,767	28.8	+7.9
13.3		Taylor, N.	LD	13,436	28.1	+2.4
1992: Con				6,826	14.3	

Galloway & Upper Nithsdale [261]

52,751†	79.7	Morgan, A.N.	SNP	18,449	43.9	+7.5
		Lang, I.B.*	Con	12,825	30.5	-11.5
2.7		Clark, K. Ms.	Lab	6,861	16.3	+3.4
		McKerchar, J.E.	LD	2,700	6.4	-2.2
		Wood, R.S.	Ind	566	1.3*	
		Kennedy, A.G.	Ref	428	1.0*	
		Smith, J.W.	UKI	189	0.4*	
1992: Con				5,624	13.4	

Gateshead East & Washington West [262]

64,114†	67.2	Quin, J.G. Ms.*	Lab	31,047	72.1	+14.1
		Burns, J.M. Ms.	Con	6,097	14.2	-13.6
68.9		Ord, A.	LD	4,622	10.7	-3.6
		Daley, M.	Ref	1,315	3.1*	
1992: Lab				24,950	57.9	

Gedling [263]

68,878	75.7	Coaker, V.R.	Lab	24,390	46.8	+12.3
		Mitchell, A.J.B.*	Con	20,588	39.5	-13.7
None		Poynter, R.A.	LD	5,180	9.9	-2.2
		Connor, J.D.	Ref	2,006	3.8*	
1992: Con				3,802	7.3	

Gillingham [264]

70,389†	72.0	Clark, P.G.	Lab	20,187	39.8	+16.0
		Couchman, J.R.*	Con	18,207	35.9	-16.0
2.8		Sayer, R.J.	LD	9,649	19.0	-4.4
		Cann, G.S.	Ref	1,492	2.9*	
		Mackinlay, C.	UKI	590	1.2*	
		Robinson, D.A.	MRLP	305	0.6*	
		Jury, C.J.	BNP	195	0.4*	
		Duguay, G.	NLP	58	0.1*	
1992: Con				1,980	3.9	

Glasgow Anniesland [265]

53,112†	63.8	Dewar, D.*	Lab	20,951	61.8	+8.8
		Wilson, W.L.	SNP	5,797	17.1	+0.1
29.1		Brocklehurst, R.A.P.	Con	3,881	11.5	-4.2
		McGinty, C.P.	LD	2,453	7.2	-6.5
		Majid, A.	PL	374	1.1*	
		Bonnar, W.	SSA	229	0.7*	
		Milligan, A.H.	UKI	86	0.3*	
		McKay, G. Ms.	Ref	84	0.2*	
		Pringle, T.J.	NLP	24	0.1*	
1992: Lab				15,154	44.7	

Glasgow Baillieston [266]

51,185†	62.2	Wray, J.*	Lab	20,925	65.7	+2.5
		Thomson, P.J. Ms.	SNP	6,085	19.1	-3.5
93.8		Kelly, M.G.	Con	2,468	7.7	-2.1
		Rainger, S.J. Ms.	LD	1,217	3.8*	-0.5
		McVicar, J.	SSA	970	3.0*	
		McClafferty, J.	Ref	188	0.6*	
1992: Lab				14,840	46.6	

Glasgow Cathcart [267]

49,416†	67.6	Maxton, J.A.*	Lab	19,158	57.4	+8.0
		Whitehead, M. Ms.	SNP	6,193	18.5	-0.5
45.6		Muir, A.J.	Con	4,248	12.7	-8.8
		Dick, G.C.	LD	2,302	6.9	-0.3
		Indyk, Z.	PL	687	2.1*	
		Stevenson, R.	SSA	458	1.4*	
		Haldane, S.W.S.	Ref	344	1.0*	
1992: Lab				12,965	38.8	

Glasgow Govan [268]

49,978†	64.5	Sarwar, M.	Lab	14,216	44.1	+1.0
		Sturgeon, N. Ms.	SNP	11,302	35.1	+7.4
123.1		Thomas, W.J.	Con	2,839	8.8	-10.9
		Stewart, R.	LD	1,918	5.9	+0.4
		McCombes, A.	SSA	755	2.3*	
		Paton, P.J.	Ind Lab	325	1.0*	
		Badar, I.M.	Ind Lab	319	1.0*	
		Abbasi, Z.J.	Ind Con	221	0.7*	
		MacDonald, K.	Ref	201	0.6*	
		White, J.	BNP	149	0.5*	
1992: Lab				2,914	9.0	

Glasgow Kelvin [269]

58,198†	56.1	Galloway, G.*	Lab	16,643	51.0	+4.1
		White, S. Ms.	SNP	6,978	21.4	+2.1
35.2		Buchanan, E. Ms.	LD	4,629	14.2	-4.7
		McPhie, D.H.	Con	3,539	10.8	-2.3
		Green, A.	SSA	386	1.2*	
		Grigor, R.J.M.	Ref	282	0.9*	
		Vanni, V.	Soc	102	0.3*	
		Stidolph, G.W.	NLP	95	0.3*	
1992: Lab				9,665	29.6	

Glasgow Maryhill [270]

52,693†	56.4	Fyfe, M. Ms.*	Lab	19,301	64.9	+2.3
		Wailes, J.G.	SNP	5,037	16.9	-2.5
16.7		Attwooll, E.M. Ms.	LD	2,119	7.1	+0.5
		Baldwin, S.A.	Con	1,747	5.9	-3.8
		Blair, L.J. Ms.	NLP	651	2.2*	
		Baker, M. Ms.	SSA	409	1.4*	
		Hanif, J.K.	PL	344	1.2*	
		Paterson, R.	Ref	77	0.3*	
		Johnstone, S.	Ind	36	0.1*	
1992: Lab				14,264	48.0	

Glasgow Pollok [271]

49,328†	66.5	Davidson, I.G.*	Lab	19,653	59.9	+10.1
		Logan, D.	SNP	5,862	17.9	-7.1
99.7		Sheridan, T.	SSA	3,639	11.1	
		Hamilton, E.S.	Con	1,979	6.0	-2.1
		Jago, D.M.	LD	1,137	3.5*	-0.9
		Gott, M. Ms.	PL	380	1.2*	
		Haldane, D.G.	Ref	152	0.5*	
1992: Lab				13,791	42.0	

Glasgow Rutherglen [272]

50,673†	70.1	McAvoy, T.M.*	Lab	20,430	57.5	+4.1
		Gray, I.G.M.	SNP	5,423	15.3	-0.3
15.8		Brown, R.E.	LD	5,167	14.5	+2.9
		Campbell Bannerman, D.	Con	3,288	9.3	-9.9
		Easton, G.D.	Ind Lab	812	2.3*	
		Kane, R. Ms.	SSA	251	0.7*	
		Kerr, J. Ms.	Ref	150	0.4*	
1992: Lab				15,007	42.2	

Glasgow Shettleston [273]

48,104†	55.7	Marshall, D.*	Lab	19,616	73.2	+7.7
		Hanif, H.	SNP	3,748	14.0	-2.2
99.9		Simpson, C.	Con	1,484	5.5	-6.7
		Hiles, K.J. Ms.	LD	1,061	4.0*	-2.2
		McVicar, C. Ms.	SSA	482	1.8*	
		Currie, R.	BNP	191	0.7*	
		Montguire, T.	Ref	151	0.6*	
		Graham, J.M.M.	WRP	80	0.3*	
1992: Lab				15,868	59.2	

Glasgow Springburn [274]

53,576†	58.9	Martin, M.J.*	Lab	22,534	71.4	+6.4
		Brady, J.R.	SNP	5,208	16.5	-3.4
44.3		Holdsworth, M.B.	Con	1,893	6.0	-4.9
		Alexander, J.	LD	1,349	4.3*	-0.1
		Lawson, J.	SSA	407	1.3*	
		Keating, A.J.	Ref	186	0.6*	
1992: Lab				17,326	54.9	

Gloucester [275]

78,852†	73.4	Kingham, T.J. Ms.	Lab	28,943	50.0	+13.2
		French, D.C.*	Con	20,684	35.7	-9.8
6.1		Munisamy, P.	LD	6,069	10.5	-7.2
		Reid, A.J.	Ref	1,482	2.6*	
		Harris, A.L.	UKI	455	0.8*	
		Hamilton, M.T. Ms.	NLP	281	0.5*	
1992: Con				8,259	14.3	

Gordon [276]

58,762	71.9	Bruce, M.G.*	LD	17,999	42.6	+15.4
		Porter, J.A.	Con	11,002	26.0	-21.9
64.1		Lochhead, R.N.	SNP	8,435	20.0	+1.4
		Kirkhill, L.A. Ms.	Lab	4,350	10.3	+4.0
		Pidcock, F.	Ref	459	1.1*	
1992: Con				6,997	16.6	

Gosport [277]

68,830†	70.3	Viggers, P.J.*	Con	21,085	43.6	-14.5
		Gray, I.L.	Lab	14,827	30.7	+17.1
None		Hogg, S.M.	LD	9,479	19.6	-8.0
		Blowers, A.M.	Ref	2,538	5.2	
		Ettie, P.F.F.	Ind	426	0.9*	
1992: Con				6,258	12.9	

Gower [278]

57,707†	75.1	Caton, M.P.	Lab	23,313	53.8	+3.7
		Cairns, A.H.	Con	10,306	23.8	-11.3
None		Evans, H.W.	LD	5,624	13.0	+3.0
		Williams, D.E.	PC	2,226	5.1	+1.6
		Lewis, R.D.	Ref	1,745	4.0*	
		Popham, A.G.	Ind	122	0.3*	
1992: Lab				13,007	30.0	

Grantham & Stamford [279]

72,310†	73.3	Davies, J.Q.*	Con	22,672	42.8	-15.1
		Denning, P.J.	Lab	19,980	37.7	+11.6
91.1		Sellick, J.C.L.	LD	6,612	12.5	-3.6
		Swain, M.J. Ms.	Ref	2,721	5.1	
		Charlesworth, M.	UKI	556	1.0*	
		Clark, R.R. Ms.	PL	314	0.6*	
		Harper, I.N.	NLP	115	0.2*	
1992: Con				2,692	5.1	

Gravesham [280]

69,288	76.9	Pond, C.R.	Lab	26,460	49.7	+9.3
		Arnold, J.A.*	Con	20,681	38.8	-10.8
0.9		Canet, J.M. Ms.	LD	4,128	7.8	-1.1
		Curtis, P. Ms.	Ref	1,441	2.7*	
		Leyshon, A.	Ind	414	0.8*	
		Palmer, D.L.	NLP	129	0.2*	
1992: Con				5,779	10.9	

Great Grimsby [281]

65,216†	66.1	Mitchell, A.V.*	Lab	25,765	59.8	+8.8
		Godson, D.	Con	9,521	22.1	-14.1
None		de Freitas, A.	LD	7,810	18.1	+5.4
1992: Lab				16,244	37.7	

Great Yarmouth [282]

68,525	71.3	Wright, A.D.	Lab	26,084	53.4	+15.4
		Carttiss, M.R.H.*	Con	17,416	35.6	-12.3
None		Wood, D.F.J.	LD	5,381	11.0	-2.6
1992: Con				8,668	17.7	

Greenock & Inverclyde [283]

48,971	70.8	Godman, N.A.*	Lab	19,480	56.2	+8.4
		Goodall, B.J.	SNP	6,440	18.6	+1.3
54.3		Ackland, R.	LD	4,791	13.8	-0.1
		Swire, H.G.W.	Con	3,976	11.5	-9.6
1992: Lab				13,040	37.6	

Greenwich & Woolwich [284]

61,352†	65.9	Raynsford, W.R.N.*	Lab	25,630	63.4	+18.8
		Mitchell, A.M.	Con	7,502	18.6	+0.3
37.5		Luxton, C.M. Ms.	LD	5,049	12.5	-22.6
		Ellison, D.B.	Ref	1,670	4.1*	
		Mallone, R.S.	Ind	428	1.1*	
		Martin-Eagle, D.H.	Ind	124	0.3*	
1992: Lab				18,128	44.9	

Guildford [285]

76,301	74.6	St Aubyn, N.F.	Con	24,230	42.5	-12.8
		Sharp, M.L. Ms.	LD	19,439	34.1	+1.3
2.2		Burns, J.G.D.	Lab	9,945	17.5	+6.1
		Gore, J.M.	Ref	2,650	4.7*	
		McWhirter, R.A.	UKI	400	0.7*	
		Morris, J.H.	Ind	294	0.5*	
1992: Con				4,791	8.4	

Hackney North & Stoke Newington [286]

62,308	52.0	Abbott, D.J. Ms.*	Lab	21,110	65.2	+7.4
		Lavender, M.D.	Con	5,483	16.9	-10.0
None		Taylor, D.A.	LD	3,306	10.2	-1.3
		Chit Chong, Y.	Grn	1,395	4.3*	
		Maxwell, B.M.	Ref	544	1.7*	
		Tolson, D.K.	Ind	368	1.1*	
		Lovebucket, L. Ms.	Rainbow	176	0.5*	
1992: Lab				15,627	48.3	

Hackney South & Shoreditch [287]

62,000	54.5	Sedgemore, B.C.J.*	Lab	20,048	59.4	+6.0
		Pantling, M.J.	LD	5,058	15.0	+0.0
0.1		O'Leary, C.P.	Con	4,494	13.3	-15.7
		Betts, T.V.	Ind Lab	2,436	7.2	
		Franklin, R.K.	Ref	613	1.8*	
		Callow, G.T.	BNP	531	1.6*	
		Goldman, M.	Ind	298	0.9*	
		Goldberg, M.L. Ms.	NLP	145	0.4*	
		Rogers, W.P.	WRP	139	0.4*	
1992: Lab				14,990	44.4	

Halesowen & Rowley Regis [288]

66,538	73.3	Heal, S.L. Ms.	Lab	26,366	54.1	+9.6
		Kennedy, J.K.	Con	16,029	32.9	-11.9
87.7		Todd, E. Ms.	LD	4,169	8.5	-1.4
		White, A.P.R.	Ref	1,244	2.6*	
		Meeds, K.M. Ms.	Nat Dem	592	1.2*	
		Weller, T.	Grn	361	0.7*	
1992: Con				10,337	21.2	

Halifax [289]

71,701†	70.5	Mahon, A. Ms.*	Lab	27,465	54.3	+10.8
		Light, R.C.	Con	16,253	32.1	-10.5
None		Waller, E.J.	LD	6,059	12.0	-0.8
		Whitaker, C. Ms.	UKI	779	1.5*	
1992: Lab				11,212	22.2	

Haltemprice & Howden [290]

65,685	75.4	Davis, D.M.*	Con	21,809	44.0	-15.3
		Wallis, D.P. Ms.	LD	14,295	28.8	+3.7
68.2		McManus, G.	Lab	11,701	23.6	+8.3
		Pearson, T.J.	Ref	1,370	2.8*	
		Bloom, G.W.	UKI	301	0.6*	
		Stevens, B.G.	NLP	74	0.1*	
1992: Con				7,514	15.2	

Halton [291]

65,058	68.3	Twigg, J.D.	Lab	31,497	70.9	+11.3
		Balmer, P.	Con	7,847	17.7	-12.6
13.4		Jones, J.E. Ms.	LD	3,263	7.3	-1.5
		Atkins, R.F.	Ref	1,036	2.3*	
		Proffitt, D.S.	Lib	600	1.4*	
		Alley, J.	Ind	196	0.4*	
1992: Lab				23,650	53.2	

Hamilton North & Bellshill [292]

53,607†	70.9	Reid, J.*	Lab	24,322	64.0	+5.7
		Matheson, M.S.	SNP	7,255	19.1	-0.6
62.3		McIntosh, G.	Con	3,944	10.4	-4.8
		Legg, K.M.	LD	1,924	5.1	-1.7
		Conn, R.P.D.	Ref	554	1.5*	
1992: Lab				17,067	44.9	

Hamilton South [293]

46,562†	71.1	Robertson, G.*	Lab	21,709	65.6	+8.7
		Black, I.	SNP	5,831	17.6	-2.7
24.8		Kilgour, R.D.	Con	2,858	8.6	-7.4
		Pitts, R.	LD	1,693	5.1	-1.5
		Gunn, C.S.	PL	684	2.1*	
		Brown, S.W.	Ref	316	1.0*	
1992: Lab				15,878	48.0	

Hammersmith & Fulham [294]

78,637†	68.7	Coleman, I.	Lab	25,262	46.8	+8.1
		Carrington, M.H.M.*	Con	21,420	39.6	-12.0
38.7		Sugden, A.E. Ms.	LD	4,728	8.8	+0.5
		Bremner, E.M. Ms.	Ref	1,023	1.9*	
		Johnson-Smith, W.F.P.	Ind Lab	695	1.3*	
		Streeter, E.J.A. Ms.	Grn	562	1.0*	
		Roberts, G.	UKI	183	0.3*	
		Phillips, A.S.P.	NLP	79	0.1*	
		Elston, A.	Ind	74	0.1*	
1992: Con				3,842	7.1	

Hampshire East [295]

76,890†	75.6	Mates, M.J.*	Con	27,927	48.0	-12.6
		Booker, R.A.	LD	16,337	28.1	+0.6
109.9		Hoyle, R.	Lab	9,945	17.1	+7.7
		Hayter, J.W.	Ref	2,757	4.7*	
		Foster, I.C.	Grn	649	1.1*	
		Coles, S.R.	UKI	513	0.9*	
1992: Con				11,590	19.9	

Hampshire North East [296]

69,437†	73.6	Arbuthnot, J.N.*	Con	26,017	50.9	-13.1
		Mann, I.H.	LD	11,619	22.7	-2.4
42.5		Dare, P.R.	Lab	8,203	16.0	+6.9
		Rees, W.D.	Ref	2,420	4.7*	
		Jessavala, K.P.	Ind	2,400	4.7*	
		Berry, C.W.	UKI	452	0.9*	
1992: Con				14,398	28.2	

Hampshire North West [297]

73,663	74.2	Young, G.S.K. Sir*	Con	24,730	45.2	-12.8
		Fleming, C.D.	LD	13,179	24.1	-3.9
25.7		Mumford, M.J.	Lab	12,900	23.6	+11.0
		Callaghan, P.J. Ms.	Ref	1,533	2.8*	
		Rolt, T.M.	UKI	1,383	2.5*	
		Baxter, W.E.	Grn	486	0.9*	
		Anscomb, H.M. Ms.	Ind	231	0.4*	
		Dodd, B.	Ind	225	0.4*	
1992: Con				11,551	21.1	

Hampstead & Highgate [298]

64,889†	67.9	Jackson, G.M. Ms.*	Lab	25,275	57.4	+11.2
		Gibson, E.M. Ms.	Con	11,991	27.2	-13.5
7.3		Fox, B. Ms.	LD	5,481	12.4	+1.4
		Siddique, M. Ms.	Ref	667	1.5*	
		Leslie, J.	NLP	147	0.3*	
		Carroll, R.	Rainbow	141	0.3*	
		Prince, P. Ms.	UKI	123	0.3*	
		Harris, R.J.	Hum	105	0.2*	
		Rizz, C.	Ind	101	0.2*	
1992: Lab				13,284	30.2	

Harborough [299]

70,424†	75.3	Garnier, E.H.*	Con	22,170	41.8	-10.9
		Cox, M.A.	LD	15,646	29.5	-4.9
11.5		Holden, N.R.	Lab	13,332	25.2	+12.9
		Wright, N.E.	Ref	1,859	3.5*	
1992: Con				6,524	12.3	

Harlow [300]

64,314	74.3	Rammell, W.E.	Lab	25,861	54.1	+11.3
		Hayes, J.J.J.*	Con	15,347	32.1	-13.9
6.3		Spenceley, L.H. Ms.	LD	4,523	9.5	-1.8
		Wells, M.J.D.	Ref	1,422	3.0*	
		Batten, G.	UKI	340	0.7*	
		Bowles, J.	BNP	319	0.7*	
1992: Con				10,514	22.0	

Harrogate & Knaresborough [301]

65,394†	72.9	Willis, G.P.	LD	24,558	51.5	+18.2
		Lamont, N.S.H.*	Con	18,322	38.5	-13.3
15.6		Boyce, B.A. Ms.	Lab	4,151	8.7	-4.8
		Blackburn, J.M.	Ind Con	614	1.3*	
1992: Con				6,236	13.1	

Harrow East [302]

79,981	71.2	McNulty, A.J.	Lab	29,923	52.5	+18.7
		Dykes, H.J.*	Con	20,189	35.4	-17.5
2.4		Sharma, B.K.	LD	4,697	8.2	-2.6
		Casey, B.J.	Ref	1,537	2.7*	
		Scholefield, A.J.	UKI	464	0.8*	
		Planton, A.W.	NLP	171	0.3*	
1992: Con				9,734	17.1	

Harrow West [303]

72,146	72.8	Thomas, G.R.	Lab	21,811	41.5	+19.0
		Hughes, R.G.*	Con	20,571	39.2	-16.0
0.0		Nandhra, P.K. Ms.	LD	8,127	15.5	-4.7
		Crossman, H.W.	Ref	1,997	3.8*	
1992: Con				1,240	2.4	

Hartlepool [304]

67,712†	65.6	Mandelson, P.B.*	Lab	26,997	60.7	+8.9
		Horsley, M.A.	Con	9,489	21.3	-13.5
None		Clark, R.B.	LD	6,248	14.1	+0.8
		Henderson, M.A. Ms.	Ref	1,718	3.9*	
1992: Lab				17,508	39.4	

Harwich [305]

75,927†	70.5	Henderson, I.J.	Lab	20,740	38.8	+14.1
		Sproat, I.M.*	Con	19,524	36.5	-15.2
8.1		Elvin, A.M. Ms.	LD	7,037	13.1	-10.0
		Titford, J.W.	Ref	4,923	9.2	
		Knight, R.	Ind	1,290	2.4*	
1992: Con				1,216	2.3	

Hastings & Rye [306]

70,388†	69.7	Foster, M.J.	Lab	16,867	34.4	+18.6
		Lait, J.A.H. Ms.*	Con	14,307	29.2	-18.4
None		Palmer, M.E.	LD	13,717	28.0	-7.3
		McGovern, C.J.M.	Ref	2,511	5.1	
		Amstad, J.M.E. Ms.	Lib	1,046	2.1*	
		Andrews, W.N.	UKI	472	1.0*	
		Tiverton, D.H.	Ind	149	0.3*	
1992: Con				2,560	5.2	

Havant [307]

68,625	70.4	Willetts, D.L.*	Con	19,204	39.7	-13.1
		Armstrong, L.R. Ms.	Lab	15,475	32.0	+12.3
49.5		Kooner, M.D.	LD	10,806	22.4	-3.7
		Green, A.F.	Ref	2,395	5.0*	
		Atwal, M.	Ind	442	0.9*	
1992: Con				3,729	7.7	

Hayes & Harlington [308]

56,783	72.4	McDonnell, J.M.	Lab	25,458	62.0	+17.2
		Retter, A.J.	Con	11,167	27.2	-17.7
0.1		Little, A.J.	LD	3,049	7.4	-2.9
		Page, F.J.	Ref	778	1.9*	
		Hutchins, G.S.	NF	504	1.2*	
		Farrow, D.J.	Ind	135	0.3*	
1992: Con				14,291	34.8	

Hazel Grove [309]

63,863†	77.3	Stunell, A.	LD	26,883	54.5	+11.4
		Murphy, B.P.	Con	15,069	30.5	-14.3
None		Lewis, J.W.	Lab	5,882	11.9	+0.2
		Stanyer, J.B.	Ref	1,055	2.1*	
		Black, G.	UKI	268	0.5*	
		Firkin-Flood, D.	Hum	183	0.4*	
1992: Con				11,814	23.9	

Hemel Hempstead [310]

71,924†	76.6	McWalter, T.	Lab	25,175	45.7	+13.2
		Jones, R.*	Con	21,539	39.1	-10.8
19.0		Lindsley, P. Ms.	LD	6,789	12.3	-3.0
		Such, P.	Ref	1,327	2.4*	
		Harding, D. Ms.	NLP	262	0.5*	
1992: Con				3,636	6.6	

Hemsworth [311]

66,967	67.9	Trickett, J.H.*	Lab	32,088	70.6	+6.8
		Hazell, N.J.	Con	8,096	17.8	-8.0
21.2		Kirby, J.D. Ms.	LD	4,033	8.9	-1.5
		Irvine, D.M.	Ref	1,260	2.8*	
1992: Lab				23,992	52.8	

Hendon [312]

76,264	65.6	Dismore, A.H.	Lab	24,683	49.3	+15.8
		Gorst, J.M.*	Con	18,528	37.0	-16.6
40.9		Casey, W.J.	LD	5,427	10.8	-0.8
		Rabbow, S.	Ref	978	2.0*	
		Wright, B.P.	UKI	267	0.5*	
		Taylor, S. Ms.	WRP	153	0.3*	
1992: Con				6,155	12.3	

Henley [313]

66,424†	77.6	Heseltine, M.R.D.*	Con	23,908	46.4	-13.6
		Horton, T.R.	LD	12,741	24.7	+0.8
3.2		Enright, D.S.T.	Lab	11,700	22.7	+7.9
		Sainsbury, S.C.	Ref	2,299	4.5*	
		Miles, S. Ms.	Grn	514	1.0*	
		Barlow, N.V.P.	NLP	221	0.4*	
		Hibbert, T.R.	Ind	160	0.3*	
1992: Con				11,167	21.7	

Hereford [314]

69,864†	75.2	Keetch, P.S.	LD	25,198	47.9	+6.6
		Shepherd, C.R.*	Con	18,550	35.3	-11.7
1.3		Chappell, A.C.R.	Lab	6,596	12.6	+2.0
		Easton, C.G.	Ref	2,209	4.2*	
1992: Con				6,648	12.7	

Hertford & Stortford [315]

72,259†	75.5	Wells, B.*	Con	24,027	44.0	-12.5
		Speller, S.K.	Lab	17,142	31.4	+14.6
26.3		Wood, M.	LD	9,679	17.7	-7.7
		Page Croft, H.D.	Ref	2,105	3.9*	
		Smalley, B.G.	UKI	1,233	2.3*	
		Franey, M.J.	PL	259	0.5*	
		Molloy, D.E.	Ind	126	0.2*	
1992: Con				6,885	12.6	

Hertfordshire North East [316]

67,469	77.1	Heald, O.*	Con	21,712	41.8	-9.9
		Gibbons, I.A.	Lab	18,624	35.8	+14.5
62.8		Jarvis, S.K.	LD	9,493	18.3	-8.2
		Grose, J.J.	Ref	2,166	4.2*	
1992: Con				3,088	5.9	

Hertfordshire South West [317]

72,276†	76.7	Page, R.L.*	Con	25,462	46.0	-13.3
		Wilson, M.D.D.	Lab	15,441	27.9	+10.4
38.4		Shaw, A. Ms.	LD	12,381	22.3	-0.2
		Millward, T.M.	Ref	1,853	3.3*	
		Adamson, C.J.	NLP	274	0.5*	
1992: Con				10,021	18.1	

Hertsmere [318]

68,093	73.9	Clappison, W.J.*	Con	22,305	44.3	-13.5
		Kelly, E.M. Ms.	Lab	19,230	38.2	+16.4
8.5		Gray, A. Ms.	LD	6,466	12.8	-6.9
		Marlow, J.J.	Ref	1,703	3.4*	
		Saunders, R.A.	UKI	453	0.9*	
		Kahn, N.D.	NLP	191	0.4*	
1992: Con				3,075	6.1	

Hexham [319]

58,914†	77.5	Atkinson, P.L.*	Con	17,701	38.8	-13.7
		McMinn, I.A.	Lab	17,479	38.3	+14.1
None		Carr, P.	LD	7,959	17.4	-4.3
		Waddell, R.E.O.	Ref	1,362	3.0*	
		Lott, D.C.	UKI	1,170	2.6*	
1992: Con				222	0.5	

Heywood & Middleton [320]

73,898†	68.4	Dobbin, J.	Lab	29,179	57.7	+11.2
		Grigg, E.S.	Con	11,637	23.0	-8.6
29.6		Clayton, D.	LD	7,908	15.6	-4.3
		West, C.M. Ms.	Ref	1,076	2.1*	
		Burke, P.	Lib	750	1.5*	
1992: Lab				17,542	34.7	

High Peak [321]

72,448†	78.9	Levitt, T.	Lab	29,052	50.8	+12.9
		Hendry, C.*	Con	20,261	35.5	-10.5
0.0		Barber, S.P. Ms.	LD	6,420	11.2	-3.6
		Hanson-Orr, C.V.	Ref	1,420	2.5*	
1992: Con				8,791	15.4	

Hitchin & Harpenden [322]

67,219†	78.0	Lilley, P.B.*	Con	24,038	45.9	-15.6
		Sanderson, R. Ms.	Lab	17,367	33.1	+15.3
101.7		White, C.J.	LD	10,515	20.1	+0.3
		Cooke, D.R.H.	NLP	290	0.6*	
		Horton, J.D.O.	Soc	217	0.4*	
1992: Con				6,671	12.7	

Holborn & St Pancras [323]

63,037†	60.3	Dobson, F.G.*	Lab	24,707	65.0	+10.8
		Smith, J.L.	Con	6,804	17.9	-10.3
6.6		McGuinness, J. Ms.	LD	4,758	12.5	-1.4
		Carr, J.T.G. Ms.	Ref	790	2.1*	
		Bedding, T.P.J.	NLP	191	0.5*	
		Smith, S.	Ind	173	0.5*	
		Conway, B. Ms.	WRP	171	0.4*	
		Rosenthal, M.	Rainbow	157	0.4*	
		Rice-Evans, P.	Ind	140	0.4*	
		Quintavalle, B.F.	PL	114	0.3*	
1992: Lab				17,903	47.1	

Hornchurch [324]

60,392	72.8	Cryer, J.R.	Lab	22,066	50.2	+15.7
		Squire, R.C.*	Con	16,386	37.3	-16.2
None		Martins, R.	LD	3,446	7.8	-3.3
		Khilkoff-Boulding, R.E.B.	Ref	1,595	3.6*	
		Trueman, J. Ms.	Ind	259	0.6*	
		Sowerby, J.	PL	189	0.4*	
1992: Con				5,680	12.9	

Hornsey & Wood Green [325]

74,537†	69.1	Roche, B.M. Ms.*	Lab	31,792	61.7	+13.3
		Hart, H.D. Ms.	Con	11,293	21.9	-17.2
None		Featherstone, L.C. Ms.	LD	5,794	11.3	+1.3
		Jago, H. Ms.	Grn	1,214	2.4*	
		Miller, R. Ms.	Ref	808	1.6*	
		Sikorski, P.W.	SL	586	1.1*	
1992: Lab				20,499	39.8	

Horsham [326]

75,899†	75.3	Maude, F.A.A.	Con	29,015	50.8	-11.5
		Millson, M.E. Ms.	LD	14,153	24.8	+2.0
56.8		Walsh, M.D. Ms.	Lab	10,691	18.7	+6.8
		Grant, R.D.M.	Ref	2,281	4.0*	
		Miller, H.P.J.	UKI	819	1.4*	
		Corbould, M.C.	Ind	206	0.4*	
1992: Con				14,862	26.0	

Houghton & Washington East [327]

67,343†	62.1	Kemp, F.	Lab	31,946	76.4	+9.4
		Booth, P.M.	Con	5,391	12.9	-8.8
41.7		Miller, K.	LD	3,209	7.7	-3.6
		Joseph, C.J.	Ref	1,277	3.1*	
1992: Lab				26,555	63.5	

Hove [328]

69,178	69.6	Caplin, I.K.	Lab	21,458	44.6	+20.1
		Guy, J.R.C.	Con	17,499	36.4	-12.6
None		Pearce, T.	LD	4,645	9.7	-9.7
		Field, S.R.	Ref	1,931	4.0*	
		Furness, J.N.P.	Ind Con	1,735	3.6*	
		Mulligan, P.A.T.	Grn	644	1.3*	
		Vause, J.E.	UKI	209	0.4*	
1992: Con				3,959	8.2	

Huddersfield [329]

65,837	67.7	Sheerman, B.J.*	Lab	25,171	56.5	+7.8
		Forrow, N.W.	Con	9,323	20.9	-13.0
None		Beever, G.J.	LD	7,642	17.2	+1.2
		McNulty, P.A.	Ref	1,480	3.3*	
		Phillips, J.L.	Grn	938	2.1*	
1992: Lab				15,848	35.6	

Hull East [330]

68,400	59.2	Prescott, J.L.*	Lab	28,870	71.3	+8.4
		West, A.J.	Con	5,552	13.7	-10.1
None		Wastling, J.H.	LD	3,965	9.8	-2.9
		Rogers, G.	Ref	1,788	4.4*	
		Nolan, M.R. Ms.	PL	190	0.5*	
		Whitley, D.F.	NLP	121	0.3*	
1992: Lab				23,318	57.6	

Hull North [331]

68,091	57.0	McNamara, J.K.*	Lab	25,542	65.8	+9.9
		Lee, D.S.	Con	5,837	15.0	-8.6
None		Nolan, D.P.	LD	5,667	14.6	-5.4
		Scott, N.A.	Ref	1,533	4.0*	
		Brotheridge, T.L.	NLP	215	0.6*	
1992: Lab				19,705	50.8	

Hull West & Hessle [332]

65,349	58.7	Johnson, A.A.	Lab	22,520	58.7	+7.1
		Tress, R.D.	LD	6,995	18.2	+0.8
19.4		Moore, C.J.	Con	6,933	18.1	-12.2
		Bate, R.F.	Ref	1,596	4.2*	
		Franklin, B.J.	NLP	310	0.8*	
1992: Lab				15,525	40.5	

Huntingdon [333]

76,094†	74.9	Major, J.*	Con	31,501	55.3	-4.7
		Reece, J.	Lab	13,361	23.5	+9.0
85.0		Owen, M.J.	LD	8,390	14.7	-6.6
		Bellamy, D.J.	Ref	3,114	5.5	
		Coyne, C.R.	UKI	331	0.6*	
		Hufford, V. Ms.	CD	177	0.3*	
		Robertson, D.J.	Ind	89	0.2*	
1992: Con				18,140	31.8	

Hyndburn [334]

66,931	72.1	Pope, G.J.*	Lab	26,831	55.6	+8.7
		Britcliffe, P.	Con	15,383	31.9	-11.3
12.5		Jones, L.	LD	4,141	8.6	-1.0
		Congdon, P.S.M.	Ref	1,627	3.4*	
		Brown, J.M.	Ind	290	0.6*	
1992: Lab				11,448	23.7	

Ilford North [335]

67,151	72.7	Perham, L. Ms.	Lab	23,135	47.4	+17.5
		Bendall, V.W.H.*	Con	19,911	40.8	-17.1
75.5		Dean, A.	LD	5,049	10.3	-1.9
		Wilson, P.	BNP	755	1.5*	
1992: Con				3,224	6.6	

Ilford South [336]

71,202	70.2	Gapes, M.J.*	Lab	29,273	58.5	+16.4
		Thorne, N.G.	Con	15,073	30.1	-16.8
39.3		Khan, A. Ms.	LD	3,152	6.3	-4.1
		Hodges, D.	Ref	1,073	2.1*	
		Ramsey, B.G.	SL	868	1.7*	
		Owens, A.	BNP	580	1.2*	
1992: Con				14,200	28.4	

Inverness East, Nairn & Lochaber [337]

65,701†	72.7	Stewart, D.J.	Lab	16,187	33.9	+10.7
		Ewing, F.	SNP	13,848	29.0	+3.9
12.1		Gallagher, S.	LD	8,364	17.5	-9.2
		Scanlon, M.E. Ms.	Con	8,355	17.5	-6.0
		Wall, W.A.B. Ms.	Ref	436	0.9*	
		Falconer, M.T.	Grn	354	0.7*	
		Hart, D.	Ind	224	0.5*	
1992: LD				2,339	4.9	

Ipswich [338]

66,947†	72.2	Cann, J.C.*	Lab	25,484	52.7	+8.8
		Castle, S.C.	Con	15,048	31.1	-12.2
0.4		Roberts, N.	LD	5,881	12.2	+0.8
		Agnew, T.T.M.	Ref	1,637	3.4*	
		Vinyard, W.J.	UKI	208	0.4*	
		Kaplan, E.S.	NLP	107	0.2*	
1992: Lab				10,436	21.6	

Isle of Wight [339]

101,680†	72.0	Brand, P.	LD	31,274	42.7	-2.9
		Turner, A.J.	Con	24,868	34.0	-13.9
None		Gardiner, D.I. Ms.	Lab	9,646	13.2	+7.2
		Bristow, T.D.I.J.	Ref	4,734	6.5	
		Turner, M.K.	UKI	1,072	1.5*	
		Rees, H.	Ind	848	1.2*	
		Scivier, P.K.	Grn	544	0.7*	
		Daly, C.A.	NLP	87	0.1*	
		Eveleigh, J.L.G.	Rainbow	86	0.1*	
1992: Con				6,406	8.8	

Islington North [340]

57,385†	62.5	Corbyn, J.B.*	Lab	24,834	69.3	+11.8
		Kempton, J.	LD	4,879	13.6	-1.5
None		Fawthrop, S.H.	Con	4,631	12.9	-10.8
		Ashby, C.	Grn	1,516	4.2*	
1992: Lab				19,955	55.6	

Islington South & Finsbury [341]

55,468†	63.7	Smith, C.*	Lab	22,079	62.5	+11.3
		Ludford, S.A. Ms.	LD	7,516	21.3	-1.9
1.6		Berens, D.A.	Con	4,587	13.0	-11.7
		Bryett, J.A. Ms.	Ref	741	2.1*	
		Laws, A.J.	Ind	171	0.5*	
		Creese, M.R.	NLP	121	0.3*	
		Basarik, E.	Ind	101	0.3*	
1992: Lab				14,563	41.2	

Islwyn [342]

50,540†	72.0	Touhig, J.D.*	Lab	26,995	74.2	-0.2
		Worker, C.J.	LD	3,064	8.4	+2.8
None		Walters, R.	Con	2,864	7.9	-7.0
		Jones, D.	PC	2,272	6.2	+2.4
		Monaghan, S.M. Ms.	Ref	1,209	3.3*	
1992: Lab				23,931	65.7	

Jarrow [343]

63,963	68.7	Hepburn, S.	Lab	28,497	64.9	+2.4
		Allatt, M.C.	Con	6,564	14.9	-8.5
21.9		Stone, T.N.	LD	4,865	11.1	-3.0
		LeBlond, A.J.	Ind Lab	2,538	5.8	
		Mailer, P.W.	Ref	1,034	2.4*	
		Bissett, J.	Soc	444	1.0*	
1992: Lab				21,933	49.9	

Keighley [344]

67,231†	76.6	Cryer, C.A. Ms.	Lab	26,039	50.6	+9.7
		Waller, G.P.A.*	Con	18,907	36.7	-10.7
None		Doyle, M.P.	LD	5,064	9.8	-0.7
		Carpenter, L.C.	Ref	1,470	2.9*	
1992: Con				7,132	13.9	

Kensington & Chelsea [345]

67,786†	54.7	Clark, A.K.M.	Con	19,887	53.6	-14.6
		Atkinson, J.R.	Lab	10,368	28.0	+11.3
50.2		Woodthorpe Browne, R.	LD	5,668	15.3	+2.1
		Ellis-Jones, A.K.F. Ms.	UKI	540	1.5*	
		Bear, E.	Ind	218	0.6*	
		Oliver, G.P.	Ind	176	0.5*	
		Hamza, S.J. Ms.	NLP	122	0.3*	
		Sullivan, P.	Rainbow	65	0.2*	
		Parliament, P.	Ind	44	0.1*	
1992: Con				9,519	25.7	

Kettering [346]

75,456	75.5	Sawford, P.A.	Lab	24,650	43.3	+11.4
		Freeman, R.N.*	Con	24,461	42.9	-9.8
5.3		Aron, R.J.	LD	6,098	10.7	-4.7
		Smith, A.E.	Ref	1,551	2.7*	
		le Carpentier, R. Ms.	NLP	197	0.3*	
1992: Con						
				189	0.3	

Kilmarnock & Loudoun [347]

61,466	77.1	Browne, D.	Lab	23,621	49.8	+5.0
		Neil, A.	SNP	16,365	34.5	+3.8
None		Taylor, D.S.	Con	5,125	10.8	-8.2
		Stewart, J.D.	LD	1,891	4.0*	-1.5
		Sneddon, W.G.	Ref	284	0.6*	
		Gilmour, W.M.R.	NLP	123	0.3*	
1992: Lab				7,256	15.3	

Kingston & Surbiton [348]

73,836	75.4	Davey, E.J.	LD	20,411	36.7	+10.7
		Tracey, R.P.*	Con	20,355	36.6	-16.5
65.0		Griffin, S.B. Ms.	Lab	12,811	23.0	+3.4
		Tchiprout, G.S. Ms.	Ref	1,470	2.6*	
		Burns, P.A. Ms.	UKI	418	0.8*	
		Leighton, M.C.	NLP	100	0.2*	
		Port, C.	Rainbow	100	0.2*	
1992: Con				56	0.1	

Kingswood [349]

77,221	77.6	Berry, R.L.*	Lab	32,181	53.7	+13.1
		Howard, J.L.	Con	17,928	29.9	-15.9
51.0		Pinkerton, J.B. Ms.	LD	7,672	12.8	-0.8
		Reather, A.H. Ms.	Ref	1,463	2.4*	
		Hart, P.G.	BNP	290	0.5*	
		Harding, A.E.	NLP	238	0.4*	
		Nicolson, A.D.	Ind	115	0.2*	
1992: Con				14,253	23.8	

Kirkcaldy [350]

52,266	66.9	Moonie, L.G.*	Lab	18,730	53.6	+8.0
		Hosie, S.	SNP	8,020	22.9	+0.3
2.6		Black, C. Ms.	Con	4,779	13.7	-8.4
		Mainland, J.M.	LD	3,031	8.7	-1.0
		Baxter, V.	Ref	413	1.2*	
1992: Lab				10,710	30.6	

Knowsley North & Sefton East [351]

70,918†	70.1	Howarth, G.E.*	Lab	34,747	69.9	+15.5
		Doran, C.C.J.	Con	8,600	17.3	-9.5
87.7		Bamber, D.	LD	5,499	11.1	-4.5
		Jones, C.R.	SL	857	1.7*	
1992: Lab				26,147	52.6	

Knowsley South [352]

70,532†	67.5	O'Hara, E.*	Lab	36,695	77.1	+7.6
		Robertson, G.R.	Con	5,987	12.6	-7.9
14.9		Mainey, C.A.	LD	3,954	8.3	-0.7
		Wright, A.	Ref	954	2.0*	
1992: Lab				30,708	64.5	

Lagan Valley [353]

71,341	62.1	Donaldson, J.M.	UU	24,560	55.4	-11.5
		Close, S.A.	APNI	7,635	17.2	+5.4
27.1		Poots, E.C.	DUP	6,005	13.6	+13.6
		Kelly, D. Ms.	SDLP	3,436	7.8	-1.3
		Sexton, S.E.	Con	1,212	2.7*	-6.3
		Ramsey, S. Ms.	SF	1,110	2.5*	+0.4
		McCarthy, F. Ms.	WP	203	0.5*	
		Finlay, H.	NLP	149	0.3*	
1992: UU				16,925	38.2	

Lancashire West [354]

73,320	74.6	Pickthall, C.*	Lab	33,022	60.3	+10.9
		Varley, C.J.	Con	15,903	29.1	-13.3
20.6		Wood, A.R.	LD	3,938	7.2	+0.2
		Carter, M.	Ref	1,025	1.9*	
		Collins, J.D.	NLP	449	0.8*	
		Hill, D.	Ind	392	0.7*	
1992: Lab				17,119	31.3	

Lancaster & Wyre [355]

78,684†	74.8	Dawson, T.H.	Lab	25,173	42.8	+9.7
		Mans, K.D.R.*	Con	23,878	40.6	-11.6
76.3		Humberstone, J.C.	LD	6,802	11.6	-2.4
		Ivell, J.V. Ms.	Ref	1,516	2.6*	
		Barry, J.	Grn	795	1.4*	
		Whittaker, J.	UKI	698	1.2*	
1992: Con				1,295	2.2	

Leeds Central [356]

68,309†	54.2	Fatchett, D.J.*	Lab	25,766	69.6	+5.9
		Wild, W.E.	Con	5,077	13.7	-8.6
18.7		Freeman, D.R.	LD	4,164	11.3	-2.7
		Myers, P.	Ref	1,042	2.8*	
		Rix, M.D.	SL	656	1.8*	
		Hill, C.	Soc	304	0.8*	
1992: Lab				20,689	55.9	

Leeds East [357]

57,023†	62.8	Mudie, G.E.*	Lab	24,151	67.5	+9.8
		Emsley, J.	Con	6,685	18.7	-9.6
None		Kirk, M.A. Ms.	LD	3,689	10.3	-3.7
		Parish, L.M.D.	Ref	1,267	3.5*	
1992: Lab				17,466	48.8	

Leeds North East [358]

63,399†	71.8	Hamilton, F.	Lab	22,368	49.2	+12.3
		Kirkhope, T.J.R.*	Con	15,409	33.9	-11.5
None		Winlow, W.	LD	6,318	13.9	-2.8
		Rose, I.S.	Ref	946	2.1*	
		Egan, J. Ms.	SL	468	1.0*	
1992: Con				6,959	15.3	

Leeds North West [359]

70,833†	69.7	Best, H.	Lab	19,694	39.9	+12.6
		Hampson, K.*	Con	15,850	32.1	-10.9
None		Pearce, B.A. Ms.	LD	11,689	23.7	-4.2
		Emmett, S.N.	Ref	1,325	2.7*	
		Lamb, R.	SL	335	0.7*	
		Toone, R.F.	PL	251	0.5*	
		Duffy, D.S.	Ind	232	0.5*	
1992: Con				3,844	7.8	

Leeds West [360]

64,194†	62.7	Battle, J.D.*	Lab	26,819	66.7	+11.6
		Whelan, J.A.	Con	7,048	17.5	-8.6
None		Amor, N.M.	LD	3,622	9.0	+0.1
		Finley, W.	Ref	1,210	3.0*	
		Blackburn, D.	Grn	896	2.2*	
		Nowosielski, N.A.B.	Lib	625	1.6*	
1992: Lab				19,771	49.2	

Leicester East [361]

64,253†	69.1	Vaz, K.*	Lab	29,083	65.5	+9.2
		Milton, S.H.	Con	10,661	24.0	-9.7
None		Matabudul, J.	LD	3,105	7.0	-1.1
		Iwaniw, W.P.	Ref	1,015	2.3*	
		Singh Sidhu, S.	SL	436	1.0*	
		Slack, N.O.	Ind	102	0.2*	
1992: Lab				18,422	41.5	

Leicester South [362]

72,583†	66.3	Marshall, J.*	Lab	27,914	58.0	+5.7
		Heaton-Harris, C.	Con	11,421	23.7	-10.9
None		Coles, B.	LD	6,654	13.8	+2.1
		Hancock, J.N.D.	Ref	1,184	2.5*	
		Dooher, J.	SL	634	1.3*	
		Sills, K.J.	Nat Dem	307	0.6*	
1992: Lab				16,493	34.3	

Leicester West [363]

64,878†	63.1	Hewitt, P.H. Ms.	Lab	22,580	55.2	+8.4
		Thomas, R.H.	Con	9,716	23.7	-14.8
None		Jones, M.D.	LD	5,795	14.2	+0.9
		Shooter, W.K.	Ref	970	2.4*	
		Forse, G.J.	Grn	586	1.4*	
		Roberts, D.P.	SL	452	1.1*	
		Nicholls, J. Ms.	Soc	327	0.8*	
		Belshaw, A.P.	BNP	302	0.7*	
		Potter, C.B.	Nat Dem	186	0.5*	
1992: Lab				12,864	31.4	

Leicestershire North West [364]

65,069†	80.0	Taylor, D.L.	Lab	29,332	56.4	+12.5
		Goodwill, R.	Con	16,113	31.0	-14.5
13.6		Heptinstall, S.	LD	4,492	8.6	-1.7
		Abney-Hastings, M.M.H.	Ref	2,088	4.0*	
1992: Con				13,219	25.4	

Leigh [365]

69,908†	65.7	Cunliffe, L.F.*	Lab	31,652	68.9	+9.6
		Young, E.	Con	7,156	15.6	-11.7
30.9		Hough, P.A.	LD	5,163	11.2	-1.2
		Constable, R.	Ref	1,949	4.2*	
1992: Lab				24,496	53.3	

Leominster [366]

65,993†	76.6	Temple-Morris, P.*	Con	22,888	45.3	-11.1
		James, T.M.	LD	14,053	27.8	-0.0
19.8		Westwood, R.J.	Lab	8,831	17.5	+5.2
		Parkin, A.J.	Ref	2,815	5.6	
		Norman, F.M. Ms.	Grn	1,086	2.1*	
		Chamings, R.J.	UKI	588	1.2*	
		Haycock, J.B.	BNP	292	0.6*	
1992: Con				8,835	17.5	

Lewes [367]

64,340†	76.4	Baker, N.J.	LD	21,250	43.2	+4.1
		Rathbone, J.R.*	Con	19,950	40.6	-10.8
32.3		Patton, M.A.	Lab	5,232	10.6	+2.4
		Butler, L.D. Ms.	Ref	2,481	5.0	
		Harvey, J.S.	UKI	256	0.5*	
1992: Con				1,300	2.6	

Lewisham Deptford [368]

58,141†	57.9	Ruddock, J.M. Ms.*	Lab	23,827	70.8	+10.2
		Kimm, I.A. Ms.	Con	4,949	14.7	-12.9
1.5		Appiah, K.	LD	3,004	8.9	-2.8
		Mulrenan, J.A.	SL	996	3.0*	
		Shepherd, S. Ms.	Ref	868	2.6*	
1992: Lab				18,878	56.1	

Lewisham East [369]

56,333†	66.4	Prentice, B. Ms.*	Lab	21,821	58.3	+13.0
		Hollobone, P.T.	Con	9,694	25.9	-16.9
0.3		Buxton, D.C.	LD	4,178	11.2	-0.2
		Drury, S.	Ref	910	2.4*	
		Croucher, R.C.	NF	431	1.2*	
		White, P.	Lib	277	0.7*	
		Rizz, C.	Rainbow	97	0.3*	
1992: Lab				12,127	32.4	

Lewisham West [370]

58,659†	64.0	Dowd, J.P.*	Lab	23,273	62.0	+15.0
		Whelan, C.R. Ms.	Con	8,956	23.8	-19.0
None		McGrath, K.M.B. Ms.	LD	3,672	9.8	-0.1
		Leese, A.R.G.	Ref	1,098	2.9*	
		Long, N.R.	SL	398	1.1*	
		Oram, E.A. Ms.	Lib	167	0.4*	
1992: Lab				14,317	38.1	

Leyton & Wanstead [371]

62,176†	63.2	Cohen, H.M.*	Lab	23,922	60.8	+15.0
		Vaudry, R.T.	Con	8,736	22.2	-8.7
40.8		Anglin, C.A.	LD	5,920	15.1	-5.4
		Duffy, S.F.	PL	488	1.2*	
		Mian, A.K.	Ind	256	0.7*	
1992: Lab				15,186	38.6	

Lichfield [372]

62,753	77.4	Fabricant, M.L.D.*	Con	20,853	42.9	-14.1
		Woodward, S.E. Ms.	Lab	20,615	42.4	+5.8
103.3		Bennion, R.P.	LD	5,473	11.3	+5.5
		Seward, G.	Ref	1,652	3.4*	
1992: Con				238	0.5	

Lincoln [373]

65,565	71.0	Merron, G.J. Ms.	Lab	25,563	54.9	+8.9
		Brown, A.G.	Con	14,433	31.0	-13.2
17.0		Gabriel, L.M. Ms.	LD	5,048	10.8	+2.0
		Ivory, J.	Ref	1,329	2.9*	
		Myers, A.D.S.	NLP	175	0.4*	
1992: Lab				11,130	23.9	

Linlithgow [374]

53,706†	73.8	Dalyell, T.*	Lab	21,469	54.1	+4.9
		MacAskill, K.	SNP	10,631	26.8	-3.3
14.5		Kerr, T.	Con	4,964	12.5	-1.2
		Duncan, A.W.	LD	2,331	5.9	-1.1
		Plomer, K.R.	Ref	259	0.7*	
1992: Lab				10,838	27.3	

Liverpool Garston [375]

66,873†	65.0	Eagle, M. Ms.	Lab	26,667	61.3	+10.2
		Clucas, H.F. Ms.	LD	8,250	19.0	-2.7
21.0		Gordon-Johnson, N.I.	Con	6,819	15.7	-9.3
		Dunne, F.	Ref	833	1.9*	
		Copeland, G.I.	Lib	666	1.5*	
		Parsons, J.V.	NLP	127	0.3*	
		Nolan, S.	Ind	120	0.3*	
1992: Lab				18,417	42.4	

Liverpool Riverside [376]

73,954†	51.6	Ellman, L.J. Ms.	Lab	26,858	70.4	+2.0
		Fraenkel, B.L. Ms.	LD	5,059	13.3	-5.2
44.5		Sparrow, D.	Con	3,635	9.5	-1.3
		Wilson, C. Ms.	Soc	776	2.0*	
		Green, D.W.	Lib	594	1.6*	
		Skelly, G.	Ref	586	1.5*	
		Neilson, H.M. Ms.	PL	277	0.7*	
		Braid, D.O.	Ind	179	0.5*	
		Gay, G.N.W.	NLP	171	0.4*	
1992: Lab				21,799	57.2	

Liverpool Walton [377]

67,606†	59.5	Kilfoyle, P.*	Lab	31,516	78.4	+6.0
		Roberts, R.J.	LD	4,478	11.1	-0.9
None		Kotecha, M.K.	Con	2,551	6.3	-6.2
		Grundy, C.	Ref	620	1.5*	
		Mahmood, L.E. Ms.	Soc	444	1.1*	
		Williams, H.L. Ms.	Lib	352	0.9*	
		Mearns, V.P. Ms.	PL	246	0.6*	
1992: Lab				27,038	67.2	

Liverpool Wavertree [378]

73,251†	62.7	Kennedy, J.E. Ms.*	Lab	29,592	64.4	+23.1
		Kemp, R.C.	LD	9,891	21.5	-13.2
63.2		Malthouse, C.L.	Con	4,944	10.8	-1.7
		Worthington, P.A.	Ref	576	1.3*	
		McCullough, K.	Lib	391	0.9*	
		Kingsley, R.A. Ms.	PL	346	0.8*	
		Corkhill, C. Ms.	WRP	178	0.4*	
1992: Lab				19,701	42.9	

Liverpool West Derby [379]

68,775†	61.3	Wareing, R.N.*	Lab	30,002	71.2	+6.6
		Radford, S.R.	Lib	4,037	9.6	
21.1		Hines, A. Ms.	LD	3,805	9.0	-6.3
		Morgan, N.C.	Con	3,656	8.7	-5.9
		Forrest, P.R.	Ref	657	1.6*	
1992: Lab				25,965	61.6	

Livingston [380]

60,296†	71.0	Cook, R.*	Lab	23,510	54.9	+9.0
		Johnston, P.J.B.A.	SNP	11,763	27.5	+1.5
12.6		Craigie Halkett, H.D.	Con	4,028	9.4	-8.7
		Hawthorn, E.G.	LD	2,876	6.7	-2.4
		Campbell, H.M. Ms.	Ref	444	1.0*	
		Culbert, M.	Soc	213	0.5*	
1992: Lab				11,747	27.4	

Llanelli [381]

58,293	70.7	Davies, D.J.D.*	Lab	23,851	57.9	+3.4
		Phillips, D.M.	PC	7,812	19.0	+3.2
8.5		Hayes, R.A.	Con	5,003	12.1	-4.9
		Burree, N.C.	LD	3,788	9.2	-3.6
		Willock, J.	SL	757	1.8*	
1992: Lab				16,039	38.9	

Londonderry East [382]

58,938	64.6	Ross, W.*	UU	13,558	35.6	-29.3
		Campbell, G.L.	DUP	9,764	25.6	+25.6
27.1		Doherty, A.	SDLP	8,273	21.7	+1.8
		O'Kane, M.B.	SF	3,463	9.1	+5.6
		Boyle, Y.I.M. Ms.	APNI	2,427	6.4	-1.0
		Holmes, J.D.R.	Con	436	1.1*	-3.3
		Gallen, C. Ms.	NLP	100	0.3*	
		Anderson, I.H.M.	Nat Dem	81	0.2*	
1992: UU				3,794	10.0	

Loughborough [383]

68,973	75.9	Reed, A.J.	Lab	25,448	48.6	+8.8
		Andrew, K.	Con	19,736	37.7	-9.1
34.8		Brass, D. Ms.	LD	6,190	11.8	+0.6
		Gupta, R.P.	Ref	991	1.9*	
1992: Con				5,712	10.9	

Louth & Horncastle [384]

68,824†	72.6	Tapsell, P.H.B.*	Con	21,699	43.4	-9.3
		Hough, J.D.	Lab	14,799	29.6	+16.0
41.6		Martin, F.M. Ms.	LD	12,207	24.4	-7.2
		Robinson, R.E. Ms.	Grn	1,248	2.5*	
1992: Con				6,900	13.8	

Ludlow [385]

61,267†	75.5	Gill, C.J.F.*	Con	19,633	42.4	-9.2
		Huffer, T.I.	LD	13,724	29.7	+4.1
15.2		O'Kane, N. Ms.	Lab	11,745	25.4	+4.0
		Andrewes, T.H.	Grn	798	1.7*	
		Freeman-Keel, E.	UKI	385	0.8*	
1992: Con				5,909	12.8	

Luton North [386]

64,618†	73.2	Hopkins, K.P.	Lab	25,860	54.6	+17.4
		Senior, D.N.	Con	16,234	34.3	-16.9
35.5		Newbound, K. Ms.	LD	4,299	9.1	-1.1
		Brown, C.D.	UKI	689	1.5*	
		Custance, A.	NLP	250	0.5*	
1992: Con				9,626	20.3	

Luton South [387]

68,395†	70.4	Moran, M. Ms.	Lab	26,428	54.8	+11.6
		Bright, G.F.J.*	Con	15,109	31.4	-12.9
10.1		Fitchett, K.	LD	4,610	9.6	-1.6
		Jacobs, C.	Ref	1,205	2.5*	
		Lawman, C.S.	UKI	390	0.8*	
		Scheimann, M.	Grn	356	0.7*	
		Perrin, C.L. Ms.	NLP	86	0.2*	
1992: Con				11,319	23.5	

Macclesfield [388]

72,049†	75.2	Winterton, N.R.*	Con	26,888	49.6	-6.4
		Jackson, J.A. Ms.	Lab	18,234	33.6	+10.8
8.1		Flynn, F.M.	LD	9,075	16.7	-4.0
1992: Con				8,654	16.0	

Maidenhead [389]

67,302†	75.6	May, T.M. Ms.	Con	25,344	49.8	-11.8
		Ketteringham, A.T.	LD	13,363	26.3	-3.6
61.6		Robson, D.M. Ms.	Lab	9,205	18.1	+9.5
		Taverner, C.T.	Ref	1,638	3.2*	
		Munkley, D.J.	Lib	896	1.8*	
		Spiers, N.A.	UKI	277	0.5*	
		Ardley, K.J.	Ind	166	0.3*	
1992: Con				11,981	23.5	

Maidstone & The Weald [390]

72,735	73.7	Widdecombe, A.N. Ms.*	Con	23,657	44.1	-11.9
		Morgan, J.	Lab	14,054	26.2	+13.8
62.9		Nelson, J.E. Ms.	LD	11,986	22.4	-7.9
		Hopkins, S.L. Ms.	Ref	1,998	3.7*	
		Cleator, M. Ms.	SL	979	1.8*	
		Kemp, P.A. Ms.	Grn	480	0.9*	
		Owen, R. Ms.	UKI	339	0.6*	
		Oldbury, J.D.	NLP	115	0.2*	
1992: Con				9,603	17.9	

Makerfield [391]

67,358†	66.8	McCartney, I.*	Lab	33,119	73.6	+10.2
		Winstanley, M.W.	Con	6,942	15.4	-9.0
26.4		Hubbard, B.L.	LD	3,743	8.3	-0.9
		Seed, A.D.	Ref	1,210	2.7*	
1992: Lab				26,177	58.2	

Maldon & Chelmsford East [392]

64,680	77.9	Whittingdale, J.F.L.*	Con	24,524	48.7	-15.2
		Freeman, K.A.	Lab	14,485	28.7	+16.0
80.9		Pooley, G.H.J.	LD	9,758	19.4	-2.7
		Overy-Owen, L.T.	UKI	935	1.9*	
		Burgess, E.J. Ms.	Grn	685	1.4*	
1992: Con				10,039	19.9	

Manchester Blackley [393]

62,474†	57.2	Stringer, G.E.	Lab	25,042	70.0	+7.9
		Barclay, S.P.	Con	5,454	15.3	-10.8
17.6		Wheale, S.D.	LD	3,937	11.0	-0.0
		Stanyer, P.A.	Ref	1,323	3.7*	
1992: Lab				19,588	54.8	

Manchester Central [394]

64,823†	51.7	Lloyd, A.J.*	Lab	23,803	71.0	+1.8
		Firth, A.P. Ms.	LD	4,121	12.3	+1.8
49.4		McIlwaine, S.P.	Con	3,964	11.8	-7.6
		Rafferty, F.D.	SL	810	2.4*	
		Maxwell, J.W.	Ref	742	2.2*	
		Rigby, T.D.J.	Ind	97	0.3*	
1992: Lab				19,682	58.7	

Manchester Gorton [395]

65,352†	55.6	Kaufman, G.B.*	Lab	23,704	65.3	+2.9
		Pearcey, J. Ms.	LD	6,362	17.5	+3.5
0.1		Senior, J.G.B.	Con	4,249	11.7	-7.8
		Hartley, K.J.	Ref	812	2.2*	
		Fitz-Gibbon, S.S.	Grn	683	1.9*	
		Wongsam, T.E.	SL	501	1.4*	
1992: Lab				17,342	47.8	

Manchester Withington [396]

66,894†	65.8	Bradley, K.J.C.*	Lab	27,103	61.6	+8.9
		Smith, J.M.	Con	8,522	19.4	-11.9
0.2		Zalzala, Y. Ms.	LD	6,000	13.6	-0.6
		Sheppard, M.B.B.	Ref	1,079	2.5*	
		Caldwell, S.P.	PL	614	1.4*	
		White, J. Ms.	Soc	376	0.9*	
		Kingston, S.	Rainbow	181	0.4*	
		Gaskell, M.E.J.	NLP	152	0.3*	
1992: Lab				18,581	42.2	

Mansfield [397]

67,093	70.7	Meale, J.A.*	Lab	30,556	64.4	+10.1
		Frost, T.J.A.	Con	10,038	21.2	-11.9
None		Smith, P.A.	LD	5,244	11.1	-1.5
		Bogusz, W.Z.J.	Ref	1,588	3.3*	
1992: Lab				20,518	43.3	

Medway [398]

61,878	72.3	Marshall-Andrews, R.G.	Lab	21,858	48.9	+14.3
		Fenner, P.E. Ms.*	Con	16,504	36.9	-15.5
None		Roberts, R.D.C.	LD	4,555	10.2	+0.6
		Main, J.	Ref	1,420	3.2*	
		Radlett, S.P. Ms.	UKI	405	0.9*	
1992: Con				5,354	12.0	

Meirionnydd Nant Conwy [399]

32,345†	76.0	Llwyd, E.*	PC	12,465	50.7	+6.8
		Rees, H.E.	Lab	5,660	23.0	+4.2
None		Quin, J.M.	Con	3,922	16.0	-10.5
		Feeley, R.L. Ms.	LD	1,719	7.0	-1.9
		Hodge, P.H.	Ref	809	3.3*	
1992: PC				6,805	27.7	

Meriden [400]

76,348	71.7	Spelman, C.A. Ms.	Con	22,997	42.0	-13.1
		Seymour-Smith, B.R.	Lab	22,415	41.0	+10.1
None		Dupont, A.R.	LD	7,098	13.0	-1.0
		Gilbert, P.G.	Ref	2,208	4.0*	
1992: Con				582	1.1	

Merthyr Tydfil & Rhymney [401]

56,507†	69.3	Rowlands, E.*	Lab	30,012	76.7	+5.1
		Anstey, D.J.	LD	2,926	7.5	-3.8
None		Morgan, J.B.	Con	2,508	6.4	-4.7
		Cox, A.G.	PC	2,344	6.0	-0.1
		Cowdell, A.B.	Ind Lab	691	1.8*	
		Hutchings, R.W.	Ref	660	1.7*	
1992: Lab				27,086	69.2	

Middlesbrough [402]

70,931†	65.0	Bell, S.*	Lab	32,925	71.4	+10.3
		Benham, L.J.	Con	7,907	17.2	-12.8
24.9		Charlesworth, A.D. Ms.	LD	3,934	8.5	-0.4
		Edwards, R.	Ref	1,331	2.9*	
1992: Lab				25,018	54.3	

Middlesbrough South & Cleveland East [403]

70,481†	76.0	Kumar, A.	Lab	29,319	54.7	+11.4
		Bates, M.W.*	Con	18,712	34.9	-10.9
12.9		Garrett, L.J.	LD	4,004	7.5	-3.5
		Batchelor, R.D.L.	Ref	1,552	2.9*	
1992: Con				10,607	19.8	

Midlothian [404]

47,600	74.1	Clarke, E.L.*	Lab	18,861	53.5	+5.3
		Millar, L.	SNP	8,991	25.5	+2.3
21.8		Harper, A.C. Ms.	Con	3,842	10.9	-6.7
		Pinnock, R.F.	LD	3,235	9.2	-0.8
		Docking, K.L.	Ref	320	0.9*	
1992: Lab				9,870	28.0	

Milton Keynes North East [405]

70,395†	72.8	White, B.A.R.	Lab	20,201	39.4	+15.7
		Butler, P.*	Con	19,961	39.0	-12.6
0.0		Mabbutt, G.A.G.	LD	8,907	17.4	-5.6
		Phillips, M.S.	Ref	1,492	2.9*	
		Francis, A.H.	Grn	576	1.1*	
		Simson, M.J.	NLP	99	0.2*	
1992: Con				240	0.5	

Milton Keynes South West [406]

71,070†	71.4	Starkey, P.M. Ms.	Lab	27,298	53.8	+16.3
		Legg, B.C.*	Con	17,006	33.5	-13.1
None		Jones, P.M.	LD	6,065	11.9	-2.6
		Kelly, H.W.	NLP	389	0.8*	
1992: Con				10,292	20.3	

Mitcham & Morden [407]

65,402	73.3	McDonagh, S.A. Ms.	Lab	27,984	58.4	+15.3
		Rumbold, A.C.R. Ms.*	Con	14,243	29.7	-16.8
None		Harris, N.P.	LD	3,632	7.6	-1.6
		Isaacs, P.J.	Ref	810	1.7*	
		Miller, L. Ms.	BNP	521	1.1*	
		Walsh, T.J.	Grn	415	0.9*	
		Vaikunstha Vasan, K.	Ind	144	0.3*	
		Barrett, J.R.	UKI	117	0.2*	
		Dixon, N.T.V.	Ind	80	0.2*	
1992: Con				13,741	28.7	

Mole Valley [408]

69,529	78.4	Beresford, P.A.*	Con	26,178	48.0	-13.3
		Cooksey, S.J.	LD	15,957	29.3	+0.6
35.5		Payne, C.G.	Lab	8,057	14.8	+5.4
		Taber, N.J.	Ref	2,424	4.4*	
		Burley, R.	Ind Con	1,276	2.3*	
		Cameron, I.P.N.	UKI	435	0.8*	
		Thomas, J.M. Ms.	NLP	197	0.4*	
1992: Con				10,221	18.7	

Monmouth [409]

60,873	80.5	Edwards, H.W.E.	Lab	23,404	47.7	+6.8
		Evans, R.K.*	Con	19,226	39.2	-8.0
None		Williams, M.F.	LD	4,689	9.6	-1.4
		Warry, T.N.	Ref	1,190	2.4*	
		Cotton, A.F.C.	PC	516	1.1*	+1.1
1992: Con				4,178	8.5	

Montgomeryshire [410]

42,753†	74.7	Opik, L.	LD	14,647	45.9	-2.6
		Davies, E.G.	Con	8,344	26.1	-6.6
None		Davies, A.L. Ms.	Lab	6,109	19.1	+6.7
		Jones, H.M. Ms.	PC	1,608	5.0	+0.3
		Bufton, J.A.	Ref	879	2.8*	
		Walker, S.M. Ms.	Grn	338	1.1*	
1992: LD				6,303	19.7	

Moray [411]

58,302†	68.2	Ewing, M.A. Ms.*	SNP	16,529	41.6	-3.0
		Findlay, A.J.	Con	10,963	27.6	-10.0
9.7		Macdonald, L.	Lab	7,886	19.8	+7.9
		Storr, D.M. Ms.	LD	3,548	8.9	+3.0
		Mieklejohn, I.P.F.	Ref	840	2.1*	
1992: SNP				5,566	14.0	

Morecambe & Lunesdale [412]

68,114†	72.3	Smith, G. Ms.	Lab	24,061	48.9	+19.4
		Lennox-Boyd, M.A.*	Con	18,096	36.7	-12.5
20.2		Greenwell, J. Ms.	LD	5,614	11.4	-7.7
		Ogilvie, I.R.	Ref	1,313	2.7*	
		Walne, D.	NLP	165	0.3*	
1992: Con				5,965	12.1	

Morley & Rothwell [413]

68,434†	67.1	Gunnell, J.*	Lab	26,836	58.5	+9.0
		Barraclough, A.H.	Con	12,086	26.3	-10.6
44.3		Galdas, M.	LD	5,087	11.1	-1.9
		Mitchell-Innes, D.I.	Ref	1,359	3.0*	
		Wood, R.I.	BNP	381	0.8*	
		Sammon, P.M. Ms.	PL	148	0.3*	
1992: Lab				14,750	32.1	

Motherwell & Wishaw [414]

52,252†	70.1	Roy, F.	Lab	21,020	57.4	+0.9
		McGuigan, J.	SNP	8,229	22.5	+1.0
5.1		Dickson, S.	Con	4,024	11.0	-4.6
		Mackie, A.G.	LD	2,331	6.4	+0.3
		Herriot, C.	SL	797	2.2*	
		Russell, T.	Ref	218	0.6*	
1992: Lab				12,791	34.9	

Neath [415]

55,541	74.3	Hain, P.*	Lab	30,324	73.5	+5.5
		Evans, D.M.	Con	3,583	8.7	-6.6
None		Jones, D.T.	PC	3,344	8.1	-3.2
		Little, F.H.	LD	2,597	6.3	+0.9
		Morris, P.A.	Ref	975	2.4*	
		Marks, D.H.	LC	420	1.0*	
1992: Lab				26,741	64.8	

New Forest East [416]

65,736	74.6	Lewis, J.M.	Con	21,053	42.9	-10.1
		Dawson, G.	LD	15,838	32.3	-1.1
51.2		Goodfellow, A.G.W.	Lab	12,161	24.8	+12.1
1992: Con				5,215	10.6	

New Forest West [417]

66,599	74.7	Swayne, D.A.	Con	25,149	50.6	-10.2
		Hale, R.C.H.	LD	13,817	27.8	-2.8
15.8		Griffiths, D.R.	Lab	7,092	14.3	+6.1
		Elliott, M.A. Ms.	Ref	2,150	4.3*	
		Holmes, M.J.	UKI	1,542	3.1*	
1992: Con				11,332	22.8	

Newark [418]

69,886	74.4	Jones, F.E.A. Ms.	Lab	23,496	45.2	+9.4
		Alexander, R.T.*	Con	20,480	39.4	-11.0
None		Harris, P.R.B.	LD	5,960	11.5	-1.5
		Creedy, G.J.T.	Ref	2,035	3.9*	
1992: Con				3,016	5.8	

Newbury [419]

74,046†	76.3	Rendel, D.D.*	LD	29,887	52.9	+15.8
		Benyon, R.H.R.	Con	21,370	37.8	-18.1
12.2		Hannon, J.P.R.	Lab	3,107	5.5	-0.6
		Snook, E.	Ref	992	1.8*	
		Stark, R.A. Ms.	Grn	644	1.1*	
		Tubb, R.B.	UKI	302	0.5*	
		Howse, K.R. Ms.	SL	174	0.3*	
1992: Con				8,517	15.1	

Newcastle-under-Lyme [420]

66,686†	73.7	Golding, L. Ms.*	Lab	27,743	56.5	+8.5
		Hayes, M.D.	Con	10,537	21.4	-8.1
None		Studd, J.R.	LD	6,858	14.0	-8.0
		Suttle, K. Ms.	Ref	1,510	3.1*	
		Mountford, S.J.	Lib	1,399	2.8*	
		Bell, B. Ms.	SL	1,082	2.2*	
1992: Lab				17,206	35.0	

Newcastle upon Tyne Central [421]

69,926	65.9	Cousins, J.M.*	Lab	27,272	59.2	+7.5
		Newmark, B.N.	Con	10,792	23.4	-12.2
14.2		Berry, R. Ms.	LD	6,911	15.0	+2.3
		Coxon, C.A.	Ref	1,113	2.4*	
1992: Lab				16,480	35.8	

Newcastle upon Tyne East & Wallsend [422]

63,272†	65.7	Brown, N.H.*	Lab	29,607	71.2	+14.0
		Middleton, J.P.	Con	5,796	13.9	-8.6
44.6		Morgan, G.D.	LD	4,415	10.6	-8.0
		Cossins, P.	Ref	966	2.3*	
		Carpenter, B. Ms.	SL	642	1.5*	
		Levy, M.R.	Comm	163	0.4*	
1992: Lab				23,811	57.3	

Newcastle upon Tyne North [423]

65,385	69.2	Henderson, D.J.*	Lab	28,125	62.2	+12.8
		White, G.B.	Con	8,793	19.4	-12.4
None		Allen, P.J.	LD	6,578	14.5	-4.2
		Chipchase, D. Ms.	Ref	1,733	3.8*	
1992: Lab				19,332	42.7	

Newport East [424]

50,676†	73.5	Howarth, A.T.*	Lab	21,481	57.7	+2.7
		Evans, D.M.	Con	7,958	21.4	-10.0
None		Cameron, A.R.	LD	3,880	10.4	-1.5
		Scargill, A.	SL	1,951	5.2	
		Chaney-Davis, E.G.	Ref	1,267	3.4*	
		Holland, C.K.	PC	721	1.9*	+1.9
1992: Lab				13,523	36.3	

Newport West [425]

53,914†	74.6	Flynn, P.P.*	Lab	24,331	60.5	+7.4
		Clarke, P.D.	Con	9,794	24.4	-11.6
None		Wilson, S.W.	LD	3,907	9.7	+0.3
		Thompsett, A.C.	Ref	1,199	3.0*	
		Jackson, H.V.	PC	648	1.6*	+1.6
		Moelwyn Hughes, H.	UKI	323	0.8*	
1992: Lab				14,537	36.2	

Newry and Armagh [426]

70,807	75.2	Mallon, S.*	SDLP	22,904	43.0	-6.3
		Kennedy, T.D.	UU	18,015	33.8	-2.5
1.3		McNamee, P.D.	SF	11,218	21.1	+8.5
		Whitcroft, P.W.R.	APNI	1,015	1.9*	+0.0
		Evans, D.	NLP	123	0.2*	
1992: SDLP				4,889	9.2	

Norfolk Mid [427]

75,311†	76.3	Simpson, K.R.	Con	22,739	39.6	-15.0
		Zeichner, D.S.	Lab	21,403	37.3	+11.2
9.9		Frary, S.J. Ms.	LD	8,617	15.0	-4.0
		Holder, N.R.	Ref	3,229	5.6	
		Park, T.A.	Grn	1,254	2.2*	
		Parker, B.H.	NLP	215	0.4*	
1992: Con				1,336	2.3	

Norfolk North [428]

77,365	76.0	Prior, D.G.L.	Con	21,456	36.5	-11.7
		Lamb, N.P.	LD	20,163	34.3	+6.9
None		Cullingham, M.A.	Lab	14,736	25.1	+1.9
		Allen, J.V.	Ref	2,458	4.2*	
1992: Con				1,293	2.2	

Norfolk North West [429]

77,083†	74.7	Turner, G.	Lab	25,250	43.8	+10.2
		Bellingham, H.C.*	Con	23,911	41.5	-10.6
None		Knowles, E. Ms.	LD	5,513	9.6	-4.2
		Percival, R.S.	Ref	2,923	5.1	
1992: Con				1,339	2.3	

Norfolk South [430]

79,239†	78.4	MacGregor, J.R.R.*	Con	24,935	40.2	-12.2
		Hacker, B.M. Ms.	LD	17,557	28.3	+1.4
6.6		Ross, J. Ms.	Lab	16,188	26.1	+7.7
		Bateson, P.A. Ms.	Ref	2,533	4.1*	
		Ross-Wagenknecht, S. Ms.	Grn	484	0.8*	
		Boddy, A.J.B.	UKI	400	0.6*	
1992: Con				7,378	11.9	

Norfolk South West [431]

80,406†	73.1	Shephard, G.P. Ms.*	Con	24,694	42.0	-12.7
		Heffernan, A.	Lab	22,230	37.8	+10.8
1.1		Buckton, D.J.	LD	8,178	13.9	-4.3
		Hoare, R.J.B.	Ref	3,694	6.3	
1992: Con				2,464	4.2	

Normanton [432]

62,983	68.3	O'Brien, W.*	Lab	26,046	60.6	+9.4
		Bulmer, F.L. Ms.	Con	10,153	23.6	-12.0
41.3		Ridgway, J.A.D.	LD	5,347	12.4	-0.9
		Shuttleworth, K.M.	Ref	1,458	3.4*	
1992: Lab				15,893	37.0	

Northampton North [433]

73,757	70.1	Keeble, S.C. Ms.	Lab	27,247	52.7	+14.1
		Marlow, A.R.*	Con	17,247	33.4	-12.4
4.5		Dunbar, L. Ms.	LD	6,579	12.7	-2.5
		Torbica, D.	UKI	464	0.9*	
		Spivack, B.	NLP	161	0.3*	
1992: Con				10,000	19.3	

Northampton South [434]

79,672	71.7	Clark, A.R.	Lab	24,214	42.4	+12.2
		Morris, M.W.L.*	Con	23,470	41.1	-14.6
11.7		Worgan, A.W.	LD	6,316	11.1	-3.1
		Petrie, C.C.	Ref	1,405	2.5*	
		Clark, D.R.	UKI	1,159	2.0*	
		Woollcombe, G.D.	NLP	541	0.9*	
1992: Con				744	1.3	

Northavon [435]

79,011	79.1	Webb, S.J.	LD	26,500	42.4	+7.9
		Cope, J.A.*	Con	24,363	39.0	-12.8
10.8		Stone, R.E.	Lab	9,767	15.6	+3.5
		Parfitt, J.	Ref	1,900	3.0*	
1992: Con				2,137	3.4	

Norwich North [436]

72,706†	75.7	Gibson, I.	Lab	27,346	49.7	+9.4
		Kinghorn, R.R.F.	Con	17,876	32.5	-11.7
12.2		Young, P.R.M.	LD	6,951	12.6	-2.0
		Bailey-Smith, T.M.	Ref	1,777	3.2*	
		Marks, D.H.	LC	512	0.9*	
		Hood, J.A.	SL	495	0.9*	
		Mills, D.B.L. Ms.	NLP	100	0.2*	
1992: Con				9,470	17.2	

Norwich South [437]

70,009†	72.6	Clarke, C.R.	Lab	26,267	51.7	+5.7
		Khanbhai, B.Y.	Con	12,028	23.7	-14.5
8.4		Aalders-Dunthorne, A.P.	LD	9,457	18.6	+4.5
		Holdsworth, D.K.	Ref	1,464	2.9*	
		Marks, D.H.	LC	765	1.5*	
		Holmes, A.St. J.	Grn	736	1.4*	
		Parsons, B.A.	NLP	84	0.2*	
1992: Lab				14,239	28.0	

Nottingham East [438]

65,644	60.5	Heppell, J.*	Lab	24,755	62.3	+9.7
		Raca, A.J.	Con	9,336	23.5	-12.9
None		Mulloy, K.J.V.D.	LD	4,008	10.1	+2.3
		Brown, B.M.	Ref	1,645	4.1*	
1992: Lab				15,419	38.8	

Nottingham North [439]

65,735	63.0	Allen, G.W.*	Lab	27,203	65.7	+10.0
		Shaw, G.C. Ms.	Con	8,402	20.3	-14.8
None		Oliver, R.C. Ms.	LD	3,301	8.0	-0.6
		Neal, J.W.E.	Ref	1,858	4.5*	
		Belfield, A.J.	Soc	637	1.5*	
1992: Lab				18,801	45.4	

Nottingham South [440]

72,479	66.9	Simpson, A.J.*	Lab	26,825	55.3	+7.6
		Kirsch, B.R.	Con	13,461	27.7	-14.1
None		Long, G.D.	LD	6,265	12.9	+2.9
		Thompson, K.J.	Ref	1,523	3.1*	
		Edwards, S.J. Ms.	Nat Dem	446	0.9*	
1992: Lab				13,364	27.5	

Nuneaton [441]

71,960	74.4	Olner, W.J.*	Lab	30,080	56.2	+10.5
		Blunt, R.	Con	16,540	30.9	-12.1
None		Cockings, R.E.	LD	4,732	8.8	-2.4
		English, R.G.	Ref	1,533	2.9*	
		Bray, D.J.	Ind	390	0.7*	
		Everitt, P.D.	UKI	238	0.4*	
1992: Lab				13,540	25.3	

Ochil [442]

56,572†	77.4	O'Neill, M.J.*	Lab	19,707	45.0	+1.9
		Reid, G.	SNP	15,055	34.4	+8.3
43.5		Hogarth, A.J.M.	Con	6,383	14.6	-9.4
		Watters, A.M. Ms.	LD	2,262	5.2	-1.7
		White, D.H.F.	Ref	210	0.5*	
		McDonald, I.D.	Ind	104	0.2*	
		Sullivan, M.S.	NLP	65	0.1*	
1992: Lab				4,652	10.6	

Ogmore [443]

52,193†	72.9	Powell, R.*	Lab	28,163	74.0	+2.2
		Unwin, D.A.	Con	3,716	9.8	-5.4
None		Williams, V.K. Ms.	LD	3,510	9.2	+2.4
		Rogers, J.D.	PC	2,679	7.0	+0.7
1992: Lab				24,447	64.2	

Old Bexley & Sidcup [444]

68,079	75.5	Heath, E.R.G.*	Con	21,608	42.0	-14.2
		Justham, R.J.	Lab	18,039	35.1	+14.0
38.6		King, I.B.	LD	8,284	16.1	-4.8
		Reading, B.	Ref	2,457	4.8*	
		Bullen, C.R.	UKI	489	1.0*	
		Tyndall, V. Ms.	BNP	415	0.8*	
		Stephens, R.T.	NLP	99	0.2*	
1992: Con				3,569	6.9	

Oldham East & Saddleworth [445]

73,189†	73.9	Woolas, P.J.	Lab	22,546	41.7	+11.5
		Davies, C.*	LD	19,157	35.4	+1.0
59.3		Hudson, J.	Con	10,666	19.7	-15.7
		Findlay, D.J.	Ref	1,116	2.1*	
		Smith, J.M.	SL	470	0.9*	
		Dalling, I.D.	NLP	146	0.3*	
1992: Con				3,389	6.3	

Oldham West & Royton [446]

69,203†	66.1	Meacher, M.H.*	Lab	26,894	58.8	+9.7
		Lord, J.G.C.	Con	10,693	23.4	-14.7
88.8		Cohen, H.L.	LD	5,434	11.9	+0.4
		Choudhury, G.U.	SL	1,311	2.9*	
		Etherden, P.W.	Ref	1,157	2.5*	
		Dalling, S.J. Ms.	NLP	249	0.5*	
1992: Lab				16,201	35.4	

Orkney & Shetland [447]

32,325	63.9	Wallace, J.R.*	LD	10,743	52.0	+5.6
		Paton, J.J.	Lab	3,775	18.3	-1.6
None		Ross, W.J.	SNP	2,624	12.7	+1.5
		Anderson, H.V.C.	Con	2,527	12.2	-9.8
		Adamson, F.A.	Ref	820	4.0*	
		Wharton, C.C. Ms.	NLP	116	0.6*	
		Robertson, A.A.	Ind	60	0.3*	
1992: LD				6,968	33.7	

Orpington [448]

78,831	76.3	Horam, J.R.*	Con	24,417	40.6	-14.7
		Maines, C.S.	LD	21,465	35.7	+7.4
41.1		Polydorou, S.A. Ms.	Lab	10,753	17.9	+3.1
		Clark, D.J.Q.	Ref	2,316	3.8*	
		Carver, J.B.	UKI	526	0.9*	
		Almond, R.	Lib	494	0.8*	
		Wilton, N.J.	PL	191	0.3*	
1992: Con				2,952	4.9	

Oxford East [449]

69,952†	68.4	Smith, A.D.*	Lab	27,205	56.8	+6.6
		Djanogly, J.S.	Con	10,540	22.0	-11.5
12.5		Kershaw, G.	LD	7,038	14.7	+0.7
		Young, J.M.B.	Ref	1,391	2.9*	
		Simmons, C.	Grn	975	2.0*	
		Harper-Jones, W.D.	PL	318	0.7*	
		Gardner, P.P.	UKI	234	0.5*	
		Thompson, J.C.H.	NLP	108	0.2*	
		Mylvaganam, P.S.	Ind	68	0.1*	
1992: Lab				16,665	34.8	

Oxford West & Abingdon [450]

78,425	78.0	Harris, E.	LD	26,268	42.9	+7.1
		Harris, L.M.	Con	19,983	32.7	-13.6
24.1		Brown, S.W. Ms.	Lab	12,361	20.2	+4.1
		Eustace, G.R. Ms.	Ref	1,258	2.1*	
		Woodin, M.E.	Grn	691	1.1*	
		Buckton, R.G.	UKI	258	0.4*	
		Hodge, L.J. Ms.	PL	238	0.4*	
		Wilson, A.M. Ms.	NLP	91	0.1*	
		Rose, J.A.	Ind	48	0.1*	
1992: Con				6,285	10.3	

Paisley North [451]

49,725†	68.6	Adams, K. Ms.*	Lab	20,295	59.5	+7.6
		Mackay, I.	SNP	7,481	21.9	-1.6
32.3		Brookes, K.	Con	3,267	9.6	-6.1
		Jelfs, A.	LD	2,365	6.9	-0.8
		Graham, R.	PL	531	1.6*	
		Mathew, E.	Ref	196	0.6*	
1992: Lab				12,814	37.5	

Paisley South [452]

54,040†	69.1	McMaster, G.*	Lab	21,482	57.5	+6.7
		Martin, B.	SNP	8,732	23.4	-1.2
15.0		McCartin, E. Ms.	LD	3,500	9.4	+0.5
		Reid, R.W.R.	Con	3,237	8.7	-6.7
		Lardner, J.	Ref	254	0.7*	
		Clerkin, S.A.	SSA	146	0.4*	
1992: Lab				12,750	34.1	

Pendle [453]

63,090	74.6	Prentice, G.*	Lab	25,059	53.3	+9.0
		Midgley, J.A.	Con	14,235	30.3	-10.0
None		Greaves, A.R.	LD	5,460	11.6	-3.4
		Hockney, N.R.A.D.	Ref	2,281	4.8*	
1992: Lab				10,824	23.0	

Penrith & The Border [454]

66,496†	73.6	Maclean, D.J.*	Con	23,300	47.6	-11.1
		Walker, K.G.	LD	13,067	26.7	-2.3
25.4		Meling, M.M. Ms.	Lab	10,576	21.6	+10.6
		Pope, C.H.	Ref	2,018	4.1*	
1992: Con				10,233	20.9	

Perth [455]

60,313†	73.9	Cunningham, R. Ms.*	SNP	16,209	36.4	+2.0
		Godfrey, J.P.	Con	13,068	29.3	-11.1
20.5		Alexander, D.G.	Lab	11,036	24.8	+11.6
		Brodie, C.G.	LD	3,583	8.0	-3.9
		MacAuley, R.J.	Ref	366	0.8*	
		Henderson, M.M.	UKI	289	0.6*	
1992: Con				3,141	7.1	

Peterborough [456]

66,506†	72.8	Brinton, H.R. Ms.	Lab	24,365	50.3	+12.5
		Foster, J. Ms.	Con	17,042	35.2	-14.3
43.7		Howarth, D.R.	LD	5,170	10.7	+1.4
		Slater, P.	Ref	924	1.9*	
		Brettell, C.R.	NLP	334	0.7*	
		Linskey, J.S.	UKI	317	0.7*	
		Goldspink, S.K.S.	PL	275	0.6*	
1992: Con				7,323	15.1	

Plymouth Devonport [457]

74,483†	69.8	Jamieson, D.C.*	Lab	31,629	60.9	+13.8
		Johnson, A.M.	Con	12,562	24.2	-11.4
15.3		Copus, R.A.A.	LD	5,570	10.7	-2.5
		Norsworthy, C.P.	Ref	1,486	2.9*	
		Farrand, C.A. Ms.	UKI	478	0.9*	
		Ebbs, S.	Nat Dem	238	0.5*	
1992: Lab				19,067	36.7	

Plymouth Sutton [458]

70,666†	67.4	Gilroy, L. Ms.	Lab	23,881	50.1	+10.4
		Crisp, A.G.	Con	14,441	30.3	-11.5
33.8		Melia, S.J.	LD	6,613	13.9	-2.6
		Hanbury, T.J.	Ref	1,654	3.5*	
		Bullock, R.P.	UKI	499	1.0*	
		Kelway, K.J.	Ind	396	0.8*	
		Lyons, F.A.	NLP	168	0.4*	
1992: Con				9,440	19.8	

Pontefract & Castleford [459]

62,397	66.3	Cooper, Y. Ms.	Lab	31,339	75.7	+5.8
		Flook, A.J.	Con	5,614	13.6	-7.4
None		Paxton, G.W.	LD	3,042	7.3	-1.8
		Wood, R.	Ref	1,401	3.4*	
1992: Lab				25,725	62.1	

Pontypridd [460]

64,185†	71.4	Howells, K.S.*	Lab	29,290	63.9	+3.1
		Howells, N.	LD	6,161	13.4	+4.9
None		Cowen, J.M.	Con	5,910	12.9	-7.4
		Llywelyn, G.O.	PC	2,977	6.5	-2.6
		Wood, A.J.	Ref	874	1.9*	
		Skelly, P.	SL	380	0.8*	
		Griffiths, R.D.	Comm	178	0.4*	
		Moore, A.G.	NLP	85	0.2*	
1992: Lab				23,129	50.4	

Poole [461]

65,928	71.0	Syms, R.A.R.	Con	19,726	42.1	-13.0
		Tetlow, A.G.	LD	14,428	30.8	+1.5
41.5		White, H.R.	Lab	10,100	21.6	+9.9
		Riddington, J.W.	Ref	1,932	4.1*	
		Tyler, P.C.	UKI	487	1.0*	
		Rosta, J.M. Ms.	NLP	137	0.3*	
1992: Con				5,298	11.3	

Poplar & Canning Town [462]

68,068†	57.7	Fitzpatrick, J.	Lab	24,807	63.2	+11.9
		Steinberg, B.	Con	5,892	15.0	-10.7
66.0		Ludlow, J. Ms.	LD	4,072	10.4	-9.2
		Tyndall, J.H.	BNP	2,849	7.3	
		Hare, I.K.	Ref	1,091	2.8*	
		Joseph, J. Ms.	SL	557	1.4*	
1992: Lab				18,915	48.2	

Portsmouth North [463]

64,539†	70.1	Rapson, S.N.J.	Lab	21,339	47.1	+13.9
		Griffiths, P.H.S.*	Con	17,016	37.6	-13.1
18.9		Sollitt, S.R.	LD	4,788	10.6	-4.5
		Evelegh, S.B.C.	Ref	1,757	3.9*	
		Coe, P.J.	UKI	298	0.7*	
		Bex, C.R.	Ind	72	0.2*	
1992: Con				4,323	9.5	

Portsmouth South [464]

81,014†	63.8	Hancock, M.T.	LD	20,421	39.5	-2.5
		Martin, D.J.P.*	Con	16,094	31.1	-11.4
None		Burnett, A.D.	Lab	13,086	25.3	+10.7
		Trim, C.G.	Ref	1,629	3.2*	
		Thompson, J.C.	Lib	184	0.4*	
		Evans, J.I. Ms.	UKI	141	0.3*	
		Treend, W.A.	NLP	140	0.3*	
1992: Con				4,327	8.4	

Preseli Pembrokeshire [465]

54,150†	78.3	Lawrence, J.R. Ms.	Lab	20,477	48.3	+10.2
		Buckland, R.J.	Con	11,741	27.7	-11.8
62.7		Clarke, J.J.	LD	5,527	13.0	+0.7
		Lloyd Jones, A.	PC	2,683	6.3	-2.3
		Berry, W.D.	Ref	1,574	3.7*	
		Cato, M.S. Ms.	Grn	401	0.9*	
1992: Con				8,736	20.6	

Preston [466]

73,097	65.8	Wise, A. Ms.*	Lab	29,220	60.8	+7.7
		Gray, P.S.	Con	10,540	21.9	-10.4
30.5		Chadwick, W.D.	LD	7,045	14.7	+0.8
		Porter, J.C.	Ref	924	1.9*	
		Ashforth, J.	NLP	345	0.7*	
1992: Lab				18,680	38.9	

Pudsey [467]

71,009†	74.3	Truswell, P.A.	Lab	25,370	48.1	+19.0
		Bone, P.W.	Con	19,163	36.3	-7.3
None		Brown, J.M.	LD	7,375	14.0	-12.4
		Crabtree, D.W.	Ref	823	1.6*	
1992: Con				6,207	11.8	

Putney [468]

60,015	73.3	Colman, A.	Lab	20,084	45.7	+9.0
		Mellor, D.J.*	Con	17,108	38.9	-13.3
None		Pyne, R.D.	LD	4,739	10.8	+1.2
		Goldsmith, J.M.	Ref	1,518	3.5*	
		Jamieson, W.B.	UKI	233	0.5*	
		Beige, L.	Ind	101	0.2*	
		Yardley, M.A.	Ind	90	0.2*	
		Small, J.D.	NLP	66	0.2*	
		Poole, A. Ms.	Ind	49	0.1*	
		Vanbraam, D.L.D.	Ind	7	0.0*	
1992: Con				2,976	6.8	

Rayleigh [469]

69,040	74.3	Clark, M.*	Con	25,516	49.7	-11.4
		Ellis, R.	Lab	14,832	28.9	+14.1
18.5		Cumberland, S.F.	LD	10,137	19.8	-2.2
		Farmer, A.	Lib	829	1.6*	
1992: Con				10,684	20.8	

Reading East [470]

71,586†	70.2	Griffiths, J.P. Ms.	Lab	21,461	42.7	+13.8
		Watts, J.A.*	Con	17,666	35.2	-13.9
66.8		Samuel, R.M.	LD	9,307	18.5	-1.9
		Harmer, P.D.	Ref	1,042	2.1*	
		Buckley, J.C.	NLP	254	0.5*	
		Thornton, A.L. Ms.	UKI	252	0.5*	
		Packer, B.M. Ms.	BNP	238	0.5*	
1992: Con				3,795	7.6	

Reading West [471]

69,073†	70.1	Salter, M.J.	Lab	21,841	45.1	+16.5
		Bennett, N.J.	Con	18,844	38.9	-13.4
18.9		Tomlin, D.D. Ms.	LD	6,153	12.7	-5.1
		Brown, S.G.	Ref	976	2.0*	
		Dell, I.B.	BNP	320	0.7*	
		Black, D.M.	UKI	255	0.5*	
1992: Con				2,997	6.2	

Redcar [472]

68,965†	71.0	Mowlam, M. Ms.*	Lab	32,975	67.3	+13.8
		Isaacs, A.G.	Con	11,308	23.1	-10.9
16.4		Benbow, J. Ms.	LD	4,679	9.6	-2.9
1992: Lab				21,667	44.3	

Redditch [473]

60,924	73.4	Smith, J.J. Ms.	Lab	22,280	49.8	+9.4
		McIntyre, A.E.J. Ms.	Con	16,155	36.1	-11.0
35.7		Hall, M.W.	LD	4,935	11.0	-0.7
		Cox, R.N.	Ref	1,151	2.6*	
		Davis, P.	NLP	227	0.5*	
1992: Con				6,125	13.7	

Regent's Park & Kensington North [474]

69,261	68.4	Buck, K.P. Ms.	Lab	28,367	59.9	+11.6
		McGuinness, P.A.	Con	13,710	29.0	-12.1
54.8		Gasson, E. Ms.	LD	4,041	8.5	+0.6
		Dangoor, S.R. Ms.	Ref	867	1.8*	
		Hinde, J.R.	NLP	192	0.4*	
		Sadowitz, D. Ms.	Rainbow	167	0.4*	
1992: Lab				14,657	31.0	

Reigate [475]

64,759	74.4	Blunt, C.J.R.	Con	21,123	43.8	-13.7
		Howard, A.P.	Lab	13,382	27.8	+10.3
29.2		Samuel, P.J.	LD	9,615	20.0	-4.1
		Gardiner, G.A. Sir*	Ref	3,352	7.0	
		Higgs, R.M.A.	Ind	412	0.9*	
		Smith, S.P.	UKI	290	0.6*	
1992: Con				7,741	16.1	

Renfrewshire West [476]

52,348†	76.0	Graham, T.*	Lab	18,525	46.6	+3.7
		Campbell, C.	SNP	10,546	26.5	+5.9
62.7		Cormack, C.J.S.	Con	7,387	18.6	-9.2
		Macpherson, B.J.S.	LD	3,045	7.7	-0.8
		Lindsay, S.T.	Ref	283	0.7*	
1992: Lab				7,979	20.1	

Rhondda [477]

57,105†	71.5	Rogers, A.R.*	Lab	30,381	74.5	-0.1
		Wood, L. Ms.	PC	5,450	13.4	+1.5
None		Berman, R.S.	LD	2,307	5.7	+0.4
		Whiting, S.J.	Con	1,551	3.8*	-4.0
		Gardener, S.M.	Ref	658	1.6*	
		Jakeway, K.	Grn	460	1.1*	
1992: Lab				24,931	61.1	

Ribble South [478]

71,670†	77.1	Borrow, D.S.	Lab	25,856	46.8	+12.0
		Atkins, R.J.*	Con	20,772	37.6	-12.2
36.3		Farron, T.J.	LD	5,879	10.6	-4.1
		Adams, G.M.	Ref	1,475	2.7*	
		Ashton, N.R.	Lib	1,127	2.0*	
		Leadbetter, J. Ms.	NLP	122	0.2*	
1992: Con				5,084	9.2	

Ribble Valley [479]

72,920	78.5	Evans, N.M.*	Con	26,702	46.7	-5.9
		Carr, M.	LD	20,062	35.1	-3.2
11.5		Johnstone, M.R.	Lab	9,013	15.8	+7.0
		Parkinson, J.A.	Ref	1,297	2.3*	
		Holmes, N.M. Ms.	NLP	147	0.3*	
1992: Con				6,640	11.6	

Richmond (Yorks) [480]

65,058†	73.4	Hague, W.J.*	Con	23,326	48.9	-11.6
		Merritt, S.L.	Lab	13,275	27.8	+16.3
22.5		Harvey, J. Ms.	LD	8,773	18.4	-8.8
		Bentley, A.M.	Ref	2,367	5.0*	
1992: Con				10,051	21.1	

Richmond Park [481]

71,951	79.0	Tonge, J.L. Ms.	LD	25,393	44.7	+7.0
		Hanley, J.J.*	Con	22,442	39.5	-12.4
57.4		Jenkins, S.P. Ms.	Lab	7,172	12.6	+3.8
		Pugh, E.F.	Ref	1,467	2.6*	
		Beaupre, D.J.	MRLP	204	0.4*	
		D'Arcy, B.H.M.	NLP	102	0.2*	
		Davies, P.	Rainbow	73	0.1*	
1992: Con				2,951	5.2	

Rochdale [482]

68,723†	70.0	Fitzsimons, L. Ms.	Lab	23,758	49.4	+11.7
		Lynne, E.L. Ms.*	LD	19,213	40.0	+2.0
46.8		Turnberg, M.J.	Con	4,237	8.8	-14.4
		Bergin, G.L.	BNP	653	1.4*	
		Salim, M.	Ind	221	0.5*	
1992: LD				4,545	9.5	

Rochford & Southend East [483]

73,075	63.7	Taylor, E.M.*	Con	22,683	48.7	-10.3
		Smith, N.J.M.	Lab	18,458	39.7	+12.2
19.2		Smith, P.A. Ms.	LD	4,387	9.4	-2.4
		Lynch, B.	Lib	1,007	2.2*	
1992: Con				4,225	9.1	

Romford [484]

59,276	71.1	Gordon, E. Ms.	Lab	18,187	43.2	+14.8
		Neubert, M.J.*	Con	17,538	41.6	-16.5
11.6		Meyer, N.L.	LD	3,341	7.9	-4.5
		Ward, S.P.	Ref	1,431	3.4*	
		Hurlstone, T.E.	Lib	1,100	2.6*	
		Carey, M.J.	BNP	522	1.2*	
1992: Con				649	1.5	

Romsey [485]

67,866	76.4	Colvin, M.K.B.*	Con	23,834	46.0	-17.2
		Cooper, M.G.	LD	15,249	29.4	+6.3
104.8		Ford, J.V. Ms.	Lab	9,623	18.6	+5.7
		Sked, A.	UKI	1,824	3.5*	
		Wigley, M.J.L.	Ref	1,291	2.5*	
1992: Con				8,585	16.6	

Ross, Skye & Inverness West [486]

55,780†	71.6	Kennedy, C.*	LD	15,472	38.7	+0.0
		Munro, D.	Lab	11,453	28.7	+9.8
33.2		Paterson, M.E. Ms.	SNP	7,821	19.6	+0.8
		Macleod, M.B. Ms.	Con	4,368	10.9	-10.9
		Durance, A.L.	Ref	535	1.3*	
		Hopkins, A.	Grn	306	0.8*	
1992: LD				4,019	10.1	

Rossendale & Darwen [487]

70,154	73.0	Anderson, J. Ms.*	Lab	27,470	53.6	+10.1
		Buzzard, P.M. Ms.	Con	16,521	32.3	-11.2
9.6		Dunning, B.F.	LD	5,435	10.6	-1.2
		Newstead, R.R.	Ref	1,108	2.2*	
		Wearden, A.	BNP	674	1.3*	
1992: Lab				10,949	21.4	

Rother Valley [488]

68,693†	67.2	Barron, K.J.*	Lab	31,184	67.6	+7.1
		Stanbury, S.G.	Con	7,699	16.7	-10.2
None		Burgess, S.B.	LD	5,342	11.6	-1.1
		Cook, S.D.	Ref	1,932	4.2*	
1992: Lab				23,485	50.9	

Rotherham [489]

59,942†	62.8	MacShane, D.*	Lab	26,852	71.3	+7.4
		Gordon, S.J.M.	Con	5,383	14.3	-9.4
None		Wildgoose, D.B.	LD	3,919	10.4	-1.9
		Hollebone, R.T.	Ref	1,132	3.0*	
		Neal, F.A.	PL	364	1.0*	
1992: Lab				21,469	57.0	

Roxburgh & Berwickshire [490]

47,288	73.9	Kirkwood, A.J.*	LD	16,243	46.5	+0.0
		Younger, D.H.	Con	8,337	23.9	-10.3
7.0		Eadie, H.S. Ms.	Lab	5,226	15.0	+6.2
		Balfour, M.T.	SNP	3,959	11.3	+0.7
		Curtis, J.R.	Ref	922	2.6*	
		Neilson, P.T.	UKI	202	0.6*	
		Lucas, D.J.	NLP	42	0.1*	
1992: LD				7,906	22.6	

Rugby & Kenilworth [491]

79,406	77.1	King, A.	Lab	26,356	43.1	+11.1
		Pawsey, J.F.*	Con	25,861	42.3	-10.2
0.3		Roodhouse, J.M.	LD	8,737	14.3	-1.0
		Twite, M.R.	NLP	251	0.4*	
1992: Con				495	0.8	

Ruislip Northwood [492]

60,393†	74.2	Wilkinson, J.A.D.*	Con	22,526	50.2	-12.6
		Barker, P.D.	Lab	14,732	32.9	+13.0
9.3		Edwards, C.D.J.	LD	7,279	16.2	-0.4
		Griffin, C.E. Ms.	NLP	296	0.7*	
1992: Con				7,794	17.4	

Runnymede & Weybridge [493]

72,123†	71.5	Hammond, P.	Con	25,051	48.6	-12.8
		Peacock, I.C.	Lab	15,176	29.4	+13.5
68.8		Taylor, G.E.	LD	8,397	16.3	-4.8
		Rolt, P.	Ref	2,150	4.2*	
		Slater, S.J.	UKI	625	1.2*	
		Sleeman, J.W.	NLP	162	0.3*	
1992: Con				9,875	19.2	

Rushcliffe [494]

78,849	78.8	Clarke, K.H.*	Con	27,558	44.4	-10.0
		Pettit, J. Ms.	Lab	22,503	36.2	+13.0
None		Boote, S.	LD	8,851	14.3	-5.7
		Chadd, S.C. Ms.	Ref	2,682	4.3*	
		Moore, J.D.	UKI	403	0.6*	
		Maszwska, A. Ms.	NLP	115	0.2*	
1992: Con				5,055	8.1	

Rutland & Melton [495]

70,239†	74.9	Duncan, A.J.C.*	Con	24,107	45.8	-15.6
		Meads, J.D.	Lab	15,271	29.0	+13.3
38.5		Lee, K.	LD	10,112	19.2	-1.6
		King, J.R.C.	Ref	2,317	4.4*	
		Abbott, J.S.	UKI	823	1.6*	
1992: Con				8,836	16.8	

Ryedale [496]

65,215†	74.8	Greenway, J.R.*	Con	21,351	43.8	-11.6
		Orrell, J.K.	LD	16,293	33.4	+3.4
38.4		Hiles, A.M. Ms.	Lab	8,762	18.0	+3.3
		Mackfall, J.E.	Ref	1,460	3.0*	
		Feaster, S.	UKI	917	1.9*	
1992: Con				5,058	10.4	

Saffron Walden [497]

74,184	76.9	Haselhurst, A.G.B.*	Con	25,871	45.3	-11.2
		Caton, M.H.	LD	15,298	26.8	-1.8
5.3		Fincken, M.J.	Lab	12,275	21.5	+7.2
		Glover, R.	Ref	2,308	4.0*	
		Evans, I.C.	UKI	658	1.2*	
		Tyler, R.T.	Ind	486	0.9*	
		Edwards, C.	NLP	154	0.3*	
1992: Con				10,573	18.5	

St Albans [498]

65,560†	77.5	Pollard, K.P.	Lab	21,338	42.0	+17.0
		Rutley, D.H.	Con	16,879	33.2	-12.4
61.8		Rowlands, A.F.	LD	10,692	21.0	-6.9
		Warrilow, J.R.	Ref	1,619	3.2*	
		Craigen, S. Ms.	Rainbow	166	0.3*	
		Docker, I.A.	NLP	111	0.2*	
1992: Con				4,459	8.8	

St Helens North [499]

71,416†	68.9	Watts, D.L.	Lab	31,953	64.9	+7.0
		Walker, P.J.C.	Con	8,536	17.3	-11.1
None		Beirne, J.	LD	6,270	12.7	-0.4
		Johnson, D.	Ref	1,276	2.6*	
		Waugh, R.	SL	833	1.7*	
		Rudin, R.D.	UKI	363	0.7*	
1992: Lab				23,417	47.6	

St Helens South [500]

66,554†	66.5	Bermingham, G.E.*	Lab	30,367	68.6	+7.6
		Russell, M.E.J.M. Ms.	Con	6,628	15.0	-9.5
0.6		Spencer, B.T.	LD	5,919	13.4	-0.5
		Holdaway, W.F.A.P.	Ref	1,165	2.6*	
		Jump, H.S. Ms.	NLP	179	0.4*	
1992: Lab				23,739	53.6	

St Ives [501]

71,680†	75.2	George, A.H.	LD	23,966	44.5	+4.4
		Rogers, W.J.G.	Con	16,796	31.2	-11.8
None		Fegan, C.	Lab	8,184	15.2	-0.8
		Faulkner, M.P.	Ref	3,714	6.9	
		Garnier, P.E. Ms.	UKI	567	1.1*	
		Stephens, F.G.	Lib	425	0.8*	
		Lippiatt, K.J.	Ind	178	0.3*	
		Hitchins, W.J.	Ind	71	0.1*	
1992: Con				7,170	13.3	

Salford [502]

58,851†	56.3	Blears, H.A. Ms.	Lab	22,848	69.0	+9.9
		Bishop, E.	Con	5,779	17.4	-9.0
15.4		Owen, N.J.	LD	3,407	10.3	-2.3
		Cumpsty, R.W.	Ref	926	2.8*	
		Herman, S. Ms.	NLP	162	0.5*	
1992: Lab				17,069	51.5	

Salisbury [503]

79,099	73.6	Key, S.R.*	Con	25,012	42.9	-9.1
		Emmerson-Peirce, Y.L. Ms.	LD	18,736	32.2	-5.0
None		Rogers, R.T.	Lab	10,242	17.6	+8.5
		Farage, N.P.	UKI	3,332	5.7	
		Soutar, H.D.	Grn	623	1.1*	
		Holmes, W.D.K.	Ind	184	0.3*	
		Haysom, S.A. Ms.	NLP	110	0.2*	
1992: Con				6,276	10.8	

Scarborough & Whitby [504]

75,862†	71.6	Quinn, L.W.	Lab	24,791	45.6	+15.8
		Sykes, J.D.*	Con	19,667	36.2	-13.6
None		Allinson, M.V.	LD	7,672	14.1	-4.8
		Murray, S. Ms.	Ref	2,191	4.0*	
1992: Con				5,124	9.4	

Scunthorpe [505]

60,393†	68.8	Morley, E.A.*	Lab	25,107	60.4	+6.1
		Fisher, M.B.	Con	10,934	26.3	-9.6
26.6		Smith, G.	LD	3,497	8.4	+0.7
		Smith, P.E.B.	Ref	1,637	3.9*	
		Hopper, B.S.	SL	399	1.0*	
1992: Lab				14,173	34.1	

Sedgefield [506]

65,181	72.3	Blair, A.C.L.*	Lab	33,526	71.2	+8.9
		Pitman, E.M.A. Ms.	Con	8,383	17.8	-10.3
56.7		Beadle, R.W.A.L.	LD	3,050	6.5	-3.2
		Hall, M. Ms.	Ref	1,683	3.6*	
		Gibson, B.	SL	474	1.0*	
1992: Lab				25,143	53.4	

Selby [507]

75,373†	74.7	Grogan, J.T.	Lab	25,838	45.9	+10.2
		Hind, K.H.	Con	22,002	39.1	-12.1
6.2		Batty, T.	LD	6,778	12.0	-1.0
		Walker, D.J.	Ref	1,162	2.1*	
		Spence, P.	UKI	536	1.0*	
1992: Con				3,836	6.8	

Sevenoaks [508]

66,531	75.4	Fallon, M.C.	Con	22,776	45.4	-12.2
		Hayes, J.P.	Lab	12,315	24.6	+8.4
22.1		Walshe, R.F.C.	LD	12,086	24.1	-0.5
		Large, N.R.A.	Ref	2,138	4.3*	
		Lawrence, M.E. Ms.	Grn	443	0.9*	
		Ellis, M.C.	Ind	244	0.5*	
		Hankey, A.M.A.	NLP	147	0.3*	
1992: Con				10,461	20.9	

Sheffield Attercliffe [509]

68,548†	64.7	Betts, C.J.C.*	Lab	28,937	65.3	+7.8
		Doyle, B.P.	Con	7,119	16.1	-10.3
None		Smith, A.G. Ms.	LD	6,973	15.7	+1.1
		Brown, J.C.	Ref	1,289	2.9*	
1992: Lab				21,818	49.2	

Sheffield Brightside [510]

58,930†	57.5	Blunkett, D.*	Lab	24,901	73.5	+3.1
		Butler, F.R.	LD	4,947	14.6	+2.1
None		Buckwell, C.B.	Con	2,850	8.4	-8.4
		Farnsworth, B.M.	Ref	624	1.8*	
		Davidson, P.F.	SL	482	1.4*	
		Scott, R.	NLP	61	0.2*	
1992: Lab				19,954	58.9	

Sheffield Central [511]

68,667†	53.0	Caborn, R.G.*	Lab	23,179	63.6	+4.0
		Qadar, A.	LD	6,273	17.2	-1.7
24.8		Hess, M.H.	Con	4,341	11.9	-6.8
		D'Agorne, A.M.	Grn	954	2.6*	
		Brownlow, A.M.	Ref	863	2.4*	
		Douglas, K.S.	Soc	466	1.3*	
		Aitken, M. Ms.	PL	280	0.8*	
		Driver, M.R.	WRP	63	0.2*	
1992: Lab				16,906	46.4	

Sheffield Hallam [512]

62,834†	72.4	Allan, R.B.	LD	23,345	51.3	+20.6
		Patnick, C.I.*	Con	15,074	33.1	-16.5
19.0		Conquest, S.G.	Lab	6,147	13.5	-4.9
		Davidson, I.S.	Ref	788	1.7*	
		Booler, P.	Ind	125	0.3*	
1992: Con				8,271	18.2	

Sheffield Heeley [513]

66,599†	65.0	Michie, B.*	Lab	26,274	60.7	+5.1
		Davison, R.N.	LD	9,196	21.3	+2.9
None		Harthman, J.P.	Con	6,767	15.6	-10.3
		Mawson, D.R.	Ref	1,029	2.4*	
1992: Lab				17,078	39.5	

Sheffield Hillsborough [514]

74,642†	71.0	Jackson, H.M. Ms.*	Lab	30,150	56.9	+10.7
		Dunworth, A.	LD	13,699	25.8	-8.5
None		Nuttall, D.J.	Con	7,707	14.5	-5.0
		Rusling, J.G.	Ref	1,468	2.8*	
1992: Lab				16,451	31.0	

Sherwood [515]

74,873	75.5	Tipping, S.P.*	Lab	33,071	58.5	+11.0
		Spencer, R.F.	Con	16,259	28.8	-14.1
None		Moult, B.N.	LD	4,889	8.6	-1.0
		Slack, L.F.	Ref	1,882	3.3*	
		Ballard, P.	BNP	432	0.8*	
1992: Lab				16,812	29.7	

Shipley [516]

69,281†	76.3	Leslie, C.M.	Lab	22,962	43.4	+15.0
		Fox, J.M.*	Con	19,966	37.8	-12.6
None		Cole, J.M.C.	LD	7,984	15.1	-4.9
		Ellams, S.D.	Ref	1,960	3.7*	
1992: Con				2,996	5.7	

Shrewsbury & Atcham [517]

73,563	75.2	Marsden, P.W.B.	Lab	20,484	37.0	+11.0
		Conway, D.L.*	Con	18,814	34.0	-11.8
None		Woolland, A.M. Ms.	LD	13,838	25.0	-2.0
		Barker, D.J.J.	Ref	1,346	2.4*	
		Rowlands, D.W.L.	UKI	477	0.9*	
		Dignan, A.S.W.	Ind	257	0.5*	
		Williams, A.D.	Ind	128	0.2*	
1992: Con				1,670	3.0	

Shropshire North [518]

70,970†	72.6	Paterson, O.W.	Con	20,730	40.2	-10.6
		Lucas, I.C.	Lab	18,535	36.0	+9.8
16.9		Stevens, H.J.	LD	10,489	20.4	-2.6
		Allen, D.G.	Ref	1,764	3.4*	
1992: Con				2,195	4.3	

Sittingbourne & Sheppey [519]

63,880	72.3	Wyatt, D.M.	Lab	18,723	40.6	+16.6
		Moate, R.D.*	Con	16,794	36.4	-12.4
26.5		Truelove, R.	LD	8,447	18.3	-8.5
		Moull, A.P.	Ref	1,082	2.3*	
		Driver, C.A.P.	MRLP	644	1.4*	
		Risi, N.	UKI	472	1.0*	
1992: Con				1,929	4.2	

Skipton & Ripon [520]

72,784	74.7	Curry, D.M.*	Con	25,294	46.5	-11.3
		Mould, T.A.	LD	13,674	25.2	-2.1
7.5		Marchant, R.J.S.	Lab	12,171	22.4	+7.6
		Holdsworth, N. Ms.	Ref	3,212	5.9	
1992: Con				11,620	21.4	

Sleaford & North Hykeham [521]

71,637†	74.2	Hogg, D.M.*	Con	23,358	43.9	-14.5
		Harriss, S.R.	Lab	18,235	34.3	+12.4
52.4		Marriott, J.R.	LD	8,063	15.2	-1.5
		Clery, P.A.	Ref	2,942	5.5	
		Overton, R.M.	Ind	578	1.1*	
1992: Con				5,123	9.6	

Slough [522]

70,283†	67.9	MacTaggart, F.M. Ms.	Lab	27,029	56.6	+12.5
		Buscombe, P.J. Ms.	Con	13,958	29.2	-14.8
7.4		Bushill, C.S.	LD	3,509	7.4	+0.2
		Bradshaw, A.J. Ms.	Lib	1,835	3.8*	
		Sharkey, T.J.	Ref	1,124	2.4*	
		Whitmore, P.P.	Ind	277	0.6*	
1992: Lab				13,071	27.4	

Solihull [523]

78,943	74.6	Taylor, J.M.*	Con	26,299	44.6	-16.2
		Southcombe, M.J.	LD	14,902	25.3	+4.3
0.3		Harris, R.N. Ms.	Lab	14,334	24.3	+7.6
		Nattrass, M.H.	Ref	2,748	4.7*	
		Caffery, J.	PL	623	1.1*	
1992: Con				11,397	19.3	

Somerton & Frome [524]

74,240	77.3	Heath, D.W.St.J.	LD	22,684	39.5	-0.8
		Robinson, M.N.F.*	Con	22,554	39.3	-8.1
1.1		Ashford, R.	Lab	9,385	16.3	+5.9
		Rodwell, R.E.H.	Ref	2,449	4.3*	
		Gadd, R.P.	UKI	331	0.6*	
1992: Con				130	0.2	

South Holland & The Deepings [525]

69,674	71.9	Hayes, J.H.	Con	24,691	49.3	-7.8
		Lewis, J.O.	Lab	16,700	33.3	+9.2
83.7		Millen, P.W.	LD	7,836	15.6	-3.3
		Erwood, G.R.E.	Ind Con	902	1.8*	
1992: Con				7,991	15.9	

South Shields [526]

62,324	62.5	Clark, D.G.*	Lab	27,834	71.4	+10.3
		Hoban, M.G.	Con	5,681	14.6	-12.1
9.6		Ord, D.	LD	3,429	8.8	-3.5
		Loraine, A.	Ref	1,660	4.3*	
		Wilburn, I.R.	Ind	374	1.0*	
1992: Lab				22,153	56.8	

Southampton Itchen [527]

76,910	70.0	Denham, J.Y.*	Lab	29,498	54.8	+10.8
		Fleet, P.D.	Con	15,269	28.4	-13.8
28.1		Harrison, D.	LD	6,289	11.7	-2.2
		Clegg, J.R.	Ref	1,660	3.1*	
		Rose, K.R.	SL	628	1.2*	
		Hoar, C.R.	UKI	172	0.3*	
		Marsh, G.L.	Soc	113	0.2*	
		Barry, R.J. Ms.	NLP	110	0.2*	
		McDermott, F.D.	PL	99	0.2*	
1992: Lab				14,229	26.4	

Southampton Test [528]

73,087	71.8	Whitehead, A.P.V.	Lab	28,396	54.1	+8.7
		Hill, S.J.A.*	Con	14,712	28.1	-12.4
28.6		Dowden, A.G.	LD	7,171	13.7	+0.6
		Day, P.A.	Ref	1,397	2.7*	
		Marks, D.H.	LC	388	0.7*	
		McCabe, A.M.	UKI	219	0.4*	
		Taylor, P.J.R.	Ind	81	0.2*	
		Sinel, J.	NLP	77	0.1*	
1992: Lab				13,684	26.1	

Southend West [529]

66,539	69.9	Amess, D.A.A.*	Con	18,029	38.8	-15.9
		Stimson, N. Ms.	LD	15,414	33.1	+2.3
None		Harley, A.J.	Lab	10,600	22.8	+10.5
		Webster, C.A.	Ref	1,734	3.7*	
		Lee, R.B.	UKI	636	1.4*	
		Warburton, P.N.	NLP	101	0.2*	
1992: Con				2,615	5.6	

Southport [530]

70,194†	72.1	Fearn, R.C.	LD	24,346	48.1	+6.6
		Banks, M.R.W.*	Con	18,186	35.9	-11.1
None		Norman, S.J. Ms.	Lab	6,129	12.1	+1.9
		Buckle, F.W.	Ref	1,368	2.7*	
		Ashton, S. Ms.	Lib	386	0.8*	
		Lines, E.A. Ms.	NLP	93	0.2*	
		Middleton, M.J.	Nat Dem	92	0.2*	
1992: Con				6,160	12.2	

Southwark North & Bermondsey [531]

67,546	60.4	Hughes, S.H.W.*	LD	19,831	48.6	-2.8
		Fraser, J.	Lab	16,444	40.3	+5.8
15.7		Shapps, G.	Con	2,835	6.9	-5.0
		Davidson, M.	BNP	713	1.7*	
		Newton, B.	Ref	543	1.3*	
		Grant, I.	Comm	175	0.4*	
		Munday, J.	Lib	157	0.4*	
		Yngvisson, I. Ms.	Nat Dem	95	0.2*	
1992: LD				3,387	8.3	

Spelthorne [532]

70,562†	73.6	Wilshire, D.*	Con	23,306	44.9	-13.7
		Dibble, K.	Lab	19,833	38.2	+15.3
None		Glynn, E.F.	LD	6,821	13.1	-3.4
		Coleman, B.W.	Ref	1,495	2.9*	
		Fowler, J.D.	UKI	462	0.9*	
1992: Con				3,473	6.7	

Stafford [533]

66,789	77.5	Kidney, D.N.	Lab	24,606	47.5	+12.6
		Cameron, D.W.D.	Con	20,292	39.2	-8.9
50.6		Hornby, P.A. Ms.	LD	5,480	10.6	-5.9
		Culley, S.R.	Ref	1,146	2.2*	
		May, A.A.N.	MRLP	248	0.5*	
1992: Con				4,314	8.3	

Staffordshire Moorlands [534]

65,742	77.8	Atkins, C. Ms.	Lab	26,686	52.2	+11.3
		Ashworth, A.J.	Con	16,637	32.5	-6.1
59.5		Jebb, C.R. Ms.	LD	6,191	12.1	-5.3
		Stanworth, D.F.	Ref	1,603	3.1*	
1992: Lab				10,049	19.7	

Staffordshire South [535]

68,896†	74.2	Cormack, P.T.C. Sir*	Con	25,568	50.0	-9.1
		Le Maistre, J.C. Ms.	Lab	17,747	34.7	+8.9
17.2		Calder, J.M.	LD	5,797	11.3	-3.7
		Carnell, P.G.	Ref	2,002	3.9*	
1992: Con				7,821	15.3	

Stalybridge & Hyde [536]

65,589†	65.7	Pendry, T.*	Lab	25,363	58.9	+7.3
		de Bois, G.N.	Con	10,557	24.5	-11.4
24.8		Cross, M.	LD	5,169	12.0	+3.0
		Clapham, R.J.D.	Ref	1,992	4.6*	
1992: Lab				14,806	34.4	

Stevenage [537]

67,086†	76.6	Follett, D.B. Ms.	Lab	28,440	55.3	+16.8
		Wood, T.J.R.*	Con	16,858	32.8	-11.1
5.7		Wilcock, A.I.C.	LD	4,588	8.9	-8.2
		Coburn, J.M.	Ref	1,194	2.3*	
		Bundy, D.W.	PL	196	0.4*	
		Calcraft, A.B.M.	NLP	110	0.2*	
1992: Con				11,582	22.5	

Stirling [538]

52,491†	81.8	McGuire, A. Ms.	Lab	20,382	47.4	+8.8
		Forsyth, M.B.*	Con	13,971	32.5	-6.7
11.8		Dow, E.G.	SNP	5,752	13.4	-1.1
		Tough, A.G.	LD	2,675	6.2	-0.5
		McMurdo, W.	UKI	154	0.4*	
		Olsen, E.L.M. Ms.	Ind	24	0.1*	
1992: Con				6,411	14.9	

Stockport [539]

65,437†	71.3	Coffey, A. Ms.*	Lab	29,338	62.9	+14.8
		Fitzsimmons, S.	Con	10,426	22.3	-15.5
13.8		Roberts, S.E. Ms.	LD	4,951	10.6	-2.2
		Morley-Scott, W.C.	Ref	1,280	2.7*	
		Southern, G.	SL	255	0.5*	
		Newitt, C.	MRLP	213	0.5*	
		Dronfield, C.J.	Ind	206	0.4*	
1992: Lab				18,912	40.5	

Stockton North [540]

64,472	69.0	Cook, F.*	Lab	29,726	66.8	+12.8
		Johnston, B.C.	Con	8,369	18.8	-14.1
5.0		Fletcher, S. Ms.	LD	4,816	10.8	-1.1
		McConnell, K.M.	Ref	1,563	3.5*	
1992: Lab				21,357	48.0	

Stockton South [541]

68,585	76.0	Taylor, D.J. Ms.	Lab	28,790	55.2	+19.7
		Devlin, T.R.*	Con	17,205	33.0	-12.0
23.9		Monck, P.J.	LD	4,721	9.1	-10.4
		Horner, J.E.	Ref	1,400	2.7*	
1992: Con				11,585	22.2	

Stoke-on-Trent Central [542]

64,396†	62.5	Fisher, M.*	Lab	26,662	66.2	+8.2
		Jones, D.N.	Con	6,738	16.7	-11.2
None		Fordham, E.T.	LD	4,809	11.9	-1.7
		Stanyer, P.L.	Ref	1,071	2.7*	
		Coleman, M.	BNP	606	1.5*	
		Oborski, F.M. Ms.	Lib	359	0.9*	
1992: Lab				19,924	49.5	

Stoke-on-Trent North [543]

59,165†	65.4	Walley, J.L. Ms.*	Lab	25,190	65.1	+10.4
		Day, C.	Con	7,798	20.2	-13.5
32.1		Jebb, H.W.G.	LD	4,141	10.7	+0.2
		Tobin, J. Ms.	Ref	1,537	4.0*	
1992: Lab				17,392	45.0	

Stoke-on-Trent South [544]

70,171†	65.9	Stevenson, G.W.*	Lab	28,645	62.0	+12.2
		Scott, S.M. Ms.	Con	10,342	22.4	-14.4
None		Barnett, P.J.	LD	4,710	10.2	-2.8
		Adams, R.W.	Ref	1,103	2.4*	
		Micklem, A.C. Ms.	Lib	580	1.3*	
		Batkin, S.R.	BNP	568	1.2*	
		Lawrence, B.C.	Nat Dem	288	0.6*	
1992: Lab				18,303	39.6	

Stone [545]

67,756	78.3	Cash, W.N.P.*	Con	24,859	46.8	-9.2
		Wakefield, V.T.J.	Lab	21,041	39.6	+10.8
127.3		Stamp, B.J.	LD	6,392	12.0	-1.5
		Winfield, A.C. Ms.	Lib	545	1.0*	
		Grice, D. Ms.	NLP	237	0.4*	
1992: Con				3,818	7.2	

Stourbridge [546]

64,984	76.5	Shipley, D.A. Ms.	Lab	23,452	47.2	+8.9
		Hawksley, P.W.*	Con	17,807	35.8	-13.0
83.3		Bramall, C.A.	LD	7,123	14.3	+2.5
		Quick, P.L.	Ref	1,319	2.7*	
1992: Con				5,645	11.4	

Strangford [547]

70,073	59.4	Taylor, J.D.*	UU	18,431	44.3	-4.8
		Robinson, I. Ms.	DUP	12,579	30.2	+10.4
65.0		McCarthy, K.	APNI	5,467	13.1	-3.0
		O'Reilly, P.J.	SDLP	2,775	6.7	+6.7
		Chalk, G.J.	Con	1,743	4.2*	-10.1
		O'Fachtna, G.S.	SF	503	1.2*	+1.2
		Mullins, S. Ms.	NLP	121	0.3*	
1992: UU				5,852	14.1	

Stratford-on-Avon [548]

81,542	76.2	Maples, J.C.	Con	29,967	48.3	-10.5
		Juned, S.A. Ms.	LD	15,861	25.5	-0.1
6.7		Stacey, S.C.	Lab	12,754	20.5	+7.1
		Hilton, A.K.	Ref	2,064	3.3*	
		Spilsbury, J.E.M.	UKI	556	0.9*	
		Brewster, J.L.	NLP	307	0.5*	
		Marcus, S.G.	Ind Con	306	0.5*	
		Miller, S.A. Ms.	PL	284	0.5*	
1992: Con				14,106	22.7	

Strathkelvin & Bearsden [549]

63,056†	78.8	Galbraith, S.L.*	Lab	26,278	52.9	+6.8
		Sharpe, D.J.	Con	9,986	20.1	-12.5
13.5		McCormick, G.	SNP	8,111	16.3	+3.4
		Morrison, J.	LD	4,843	9.7	+1.5
		Wilson, D.B.	Ref	339	0.7*	
		Fisher, C.J.L. Ms.	NLP	155	0.3*	
1992: Lab				16,292	32.8	

Streatham [550]

74,583†	60.2	Hill, T.K.*	Lab	28,181	62.8	+13.4
		Noad, E.G.	Con	9,758	21.7	-16.7
27.2		O'Brien, R.	LD	6,082	13.6	+3.6
		Wall, J.J.	Ref	864	1.9*	
1992: Lab				18,423	41.0	

Stretford & Urmston [551]

69,913†	69.7	Hughes, B.J. Ms.	Lab	28,480	58.5	+9.5
		Gregory, J.R.	Con	14,840	30.5	-10.3
98.1		Bridges, J.R.	LD	3,978	8.2	-1.1
		Dore, C. Ms.	Ref	1,397	2.9*	
1992: Lab				13,640	28.0	

Stroud [552]

77,856†	78.8	Drew, D.E.	Lab	26,170	42.7	+13.3
		Knapman, R.M.*	Con	23,260	37.9	-8.3
19.2		Hodgkinson, P.R.	LD	9,502	15.5	-6.1
		Marjoram, J.D.	Grn	2,415	3.9*	
1992: Con				2,910	4.7	

Suffolk Central & Ipswich North [553]

70,388†	75.0	Lord, M.N.*	Con	22,493	42.6	-13.2
		Jones, C.E. Ms.	Lab	18,955	35.9	+15.2
67.7		Goldspink, M.H. Ms.	LD	10,886	20.6	-1.3
		Bennell, S.A. Ms.	Ind	489	0.9*	
1992: Con				3,538	6.7	

Suffolk Coastal [554]

74,219†	75.8	Gummer, J.S.*	Con	21,696	38.6	-13.9
		Campbell, M.	Lab	18,442	32.8	+9.5
38.4		Jones, A. Ms.	LD	12,036	21.4	-1.3
		Caulfield, S.B.	Ref	3,416	6.1	
		Slade, A.C.	Grn	514	0.9*	
		Kaplan, F.B. Ms.	NLP	152	0.3*	
1992: Con				3,254	5.8	

Suffolk South [555]

67,335	77.2	Yeo, T.S.K.*	Con	19,402	37.3	-14.0
		Bishop, P.A.	Lab	15,227	29.3	+7.5
23.9		Pollard, A.K. Ms.	LD	14,395	27.7	+1.5
		de Chair, S.C.	Ref	2,740	5.3	
		Holland, A. Ms.	NLP	211	0.4*	
1992: Con				4,175	8.0	

Suffolk West [556]

68,638†	71.5	Spring, R.J.G.*	Con	20,081	40.9	-12.9
		Jefferys, M.J.	Lab	18,214	37.1	+13.1
67.7		Graves, A.P.	LD	6,892	14.0	-7.3
		Carver, J.J.T.	Ref	3,724	7.6	
		Shearer, A.J.M.	NLP	171	0.3*	
1992: Con				1,867	3.8	

Sunderland North [557]

64,711†	59.1	Etherington, W.*	Lab	26,067	68.2	+8.6
		Selous, A.E.A.	Con	6,370	16.7	-11.1
11.2		Pryke, G.M.	LD	3,973	10.4	-0.6
		Nicholson, M.T.	Ref	1,394	3.6*	
		Newby, K.J.	MRLP	409	1.1*	
1992: Lab				19,697	51.5	

Sunderland South [558]

67,937†	58.8	Mullin, C.J.*	Lab	27,174	68.1	+10.6
		Schofield, T.J.	Con	7,536	18.9	-10.4
25.9		Lennox, J.A.	LD	4,606	11.5	-0.3
		Wilkinson, M.A.M. Ms.	UKI	609	1.5*	
1992: Lab				19,638	49.2	

Surrey East [559]

73,224	74.6	Ainsworth, P.M.*	Con	27,389	50.1	-10.9
		Ford, B.J. Ms.	LD	12,296	22.5	-4.4
26.1		Ross, D.	Lab	11,573	21.2	+10.7
		Sydney, M.	Ref	2,656	4.9*	
		Stone, A.B.	UKI	569	1.0*	
		Bartrum, S.M. Ms.	NLP	173	0.3*	
1992: Con				15,093	27.6	

Surrey Heath [560]

73,813†	74.1	Hawkins, N.J.*	Con	28,231	51.6	-12.1
		Newman, D.I.	LD	11,944	21.8	-1.3
47.3		Jones, S.E. Ms.	Lab	11,511	21.0	+9.8
		Gale, J.E.	Ref	2,385	4.4*	
		Squire, R.P.F.	UKI	653	1.2*	
1992: Con				16,287	29.8	

Surrey South West [561]

72,841	77.5	Bottomley, V.H.B. Ms.*	Con	25,165	44.6	-13.9
		Sherlock, N.R.	LD	22,471	39.8	+6.3
None		Leicester, M.C. Ms.	Lab	5,333	9.4	+3.0
		Clementson, J.A. Ms.	Ref	2,830	5.0	
		Kirby, P.	UKI	401	0.7*	
		Quintavalle, J.M. Ms.	PL	258	0.5*	
1992: Con				2,694	4.8	

Sussex Mid [562]

68,928	77.6	Soames, A.N.W.*	Con	23,231	43.5	-15.5
		Collins, M.E. Ms.	LD	16,377	30.6	+2.4
15.0		Hamilton, M.F.M.M.	Lab	9,969	18.6	+8.0
		Large, L.H.T.	Ref	3,146	5.9	
		Barnett, J.V.	UKI	606	1.1*	
		Tudway, E.R.	Ind	134	0.3*	
1992: Con				6,854	12.8	

Sutton & Cheam [563]

62,824	75.0	Burstow, P.K.	LD	19,919	42.3	+8.5
		Maitland, O.H. Ms.*	Con	17,822	37.8	-17.3
None		Allison, M.G.	Lab	7,280	15.5	+5.5
		Atkinson, P.G.	Ref	1,784	3.8*	
		McKie, S.P.	UKI	191	0.4*	
		Wright, D. Ms.	NLP	96	0.2*	
1992: Con				2,097	4.5	

Sutton Coldfield [564]

71,918	72.9	Fowler, P.N. Sir*	Con	27,373	52.2	-12.9
		York, A.C.	Lab	12,488	23.8	+8.9
None		Whorwood, J.E.	LD	10,139	19.3	+0.0
		Hope, J.D.S.	Ref	2,401	4.6*	
1992: Con				14,885	28.4	

Swansea East [565]

57,371	67.4	Anderson, D.*	Lab	29,151	75.4	+5.7
		Dibble, E.C. Ms.	Con	3,582	9.3	-7.9
None		Jones, E.V.	LD	3,440	8.9	-0.6
		Pooley, M. Ms.	PC	1,308	3.4*	-0.2
		Maggs, C.E. Ms.	Ref	904	2.3*	
		Job, R.	Soc	289	0.7*	
1992: Lab				25,569	66.1	

Swansea West [566]

59,849	67.6	Williams, A.J.*	Lab	22,748	56.2	+3.2
		Baker, A.C.S.	Con	8,289	20.5	-10.9
None		Newbury, J.	LD	5,872	14.5	+4.0
		Lloyd, D.R.	PC	2,675	6.6	+2.8
		Proctor, D.	SL	885	2.2*	
1992: Lab				14,459	35.7	

Swindon North [567]

65,535†	73.7	Wills, M.D.	Lab	24,029	49.8	+7.1
		Opperman, G.T.	Con	16,341	33.9	-7.1
100.2		Evemy, M.S.	LD	6,237	12.9	-1.7
		Goldsmith, G.C. Ms.	Ref	1,533	3.2*	
		Fisken, A.W.	NLP	130	0.3*	
1992: Lab				7,688	15.9	

Swindon South [568]

70,207†	72.9	Drown, J.K. Ms.	Lab	23,943	46.8	+16.0
		Coombs, S.C.*	Con	18,298	35.8	-13.2
46.7		Pajak, S.J.	LD	7,371	14.4	-4.3
		Mackintosh, D.R.	Ref	1,273	2.5*	
		Charman, R.C.	Ind	181	0.4*	
		Buscombe, K.M.	NLP	96	0.2*	
1992: Con				5,645	11.0	

Tamworth [569]

67,205†	74.2	Jenkins, B.D.*	Lab	25,808	51.8	+12.6
		Lightbown, M.A. Ms.	Con	18,312	36.7	-12.6
7.8		Pinkett, J. Ms.	LD	4,025	8.1	-1.9
		Livesey, D.J. Ms.	Ref	1,163	2.3*	
		Lamb, C.A.	UKI	369	0.7*	
		Twelvetrees, C. Ms.	Lib	177	0.4*	
1992: Con				7,496	15.0	

Tatton [570]

64,099†	76.1	Bell, M.	Ind	29,354	60.2	
		Hamilton, M.N.*	Con	18,277	37.5	-24.7
28.6		Hill, S.	Ind	295	0.6*	
		Kinsey, S.L.	Ind	187	0.4*	
		Penhaul, B.G.	Ind	128	0.3*	
		Muir, J.R.	Ind	126	0.3*	
		Kennedy, M.P.	NLP	123	0.3*	
		Bishop, D.L.	Ind	116	0.2*	
		Nicholas, R.	Ind	113	0.2*	
		Price, J.M.	Ind	73	0.1*	
1992: Con				11,077	22.7	

Taunton [571]

79,783†	76.5	Ballard, J.M. Ms.	LD	26,064	42.7	+1.9
		Nicholson, D.J.*	Con	23,621	38.7	-7.3
None		Lisgo, E.S. Ms.	Lab	8,248	13.5	+0.8
		Ahern, B.J.	Ref	2,760	4.5*	
		Andrews, L.C.	BNP	318	0.5*	
1992: Con				2,443	4.0	

Tayside North [572]

61,398†	74.3	Swinney, J.R.	SNP	20,447	44.8	+6.1
		Walker, B.*	Con	16,287	35.7	-10.6
21.5		McFatridge, I.A.	Lab	5,141	11.3	+4.3
		Regent, P.F.	LD	3,716	8.2	+0.3
1992: Con				4,160	9.1	

Teignbridge [573]

82,098†	76.7	Nicholls, P.C,M.*	Con	24,679	39.2	-11.0
		Younger-Ross, R.	LD	24,398	38.8	+3.6
24.2		Dann, S.E. Ms.	Lab	11,311	18.0	+5.0
		Stokes, S.A.	UKI	1,601	2.5*	
		Banwell, N.J.	Grn	817	1.3*	
		Golding, L. Ms.	Rainbow	139	0.2*	
1992: Con				281	0.4	

Telford [574]

56,558†	65.6	Grocott, B.J.*	Lab	21,456	57.8	+5.1
		Gentry, B.A.R.	Con	10,166	27.4	-5.9
37.1		Green, N.J.	LD	4,371	11.8	-0.6
		Morris, C.J.	Ref	1,119	3.0*	
1992: Lab				11,290	30.4	

Tewkesbury [575]

68,453	76.2	Robertson, L.A.	Con	23,859	45.8	-8.1
		Sewell, J.M.	LD	14,625	28.0	-7.1
92.5		Tustin, K.M.	Lab	13,665	26.2	+16.1
1992: Con				9,234	17.7	

Thanet North [576]

71,112†	68.8	Gale, R.J.*	Con	21,586	44.1	-13.1
		Johnston, I. Ms.	Lab	18,820	38.4	+15.0
None		Kendrick, P.	LD	5,576	11.4	-6.3
		Chambers, M.R.	Ref	2,535	5.2	
		Haines, J.E. Ms.	UKI	438	0.9*	
1992: Con				2,766	5.7	

Thanet South [577]

62,792†	71.6	Ladyman, S.J.	Lab	20,777	46.2	+18.0
		Aitken, J.W.P.*	Con	17,899	39.8	-12.0
0.1		Hewett-Silk, B.M. Ms.	LD	5,263	11.7	-6.6
		Crook, C.P.	UKI	631	1.4*	
		Wheatley, D.	Grn	418	0.9*	
1992: Con				2,878	6.4	

Thurrock [578]

71,763	65.8	MacKinlay, A.S.*	Lab	29,896	63.3	+17.5
		Rosindell, A.R.	Con	12,640	26.8	-16.9
None		White, J.	LD	3,843	8.1	-1.4
		Compobassi, P.	UKI	833	1.8*	
1992: Lab				17,256	36.6	

Tiverton & Honiton [579]

76,154	77.6	Browning, A.F. Ms.*	Con	24,438	41.3	-9.9
		Barnard, J.A.W.	LD	22,785	38.5	+6.8
30.6		King, J.	Lab	7,598	12.8	+1.9
		Lowings, S.J.	Ref	2,952	5.0*	
		Roach, J. Ms.	Lib	635	1.1*	
		McIvor, E.R. Ms.	Grn	485	0.8*	
		Charles, D.	Nat Dem	236	0.4*	
1992: Con				1,653	2.8	

Tonbridge & Malling [580]

64,988	75.8	Stanley, J.P.*	Con	23,640	48.0	-12.8
		Withstandley, B. Ms.	Lab	13,410	27.2	+10.2
45.8		Brown, K.J.	LD	9,467	19.2	-1.5
		Scrivenor, J.P.	Ref	2,005	4.1*	
		Bullen, B. Ms.	UKI	502	1.0*	
		Valente, G.J.	NLP	205	0.4*	
1992: Con				10,230	20.8	

Tooting [581]

66,536	69.3	Cox, T.M.*	Lab	27,516	59.7	+11.5
		Hutchings, J.B.B.	Con	12,505	27.1	-13.0
None		James, S.A.	LD	4,320	9.4	+2.0
		Husband, A.M. Ms.	Ref	829	1.8*	
		Rattray, J.M.	Grn	527	1.1*	
		Boddington, P.J.	Ind	161	0.3*	
		Koene, J.	Ind	94	0.2*	
		Bailey-Bond, D.J.	Rainbow	83	0.2*	
		Miller, P.J.	NLP	70	0.2*	
1992: Lab				15,011	32.6	

Torbay [582]

72,258†	73.8	Sanders, A.M.	LD	21,094	39.6	-0.2
		Allason, R.W.S.*	Con	21,082	39.5	-10.3
None		Morey, M.J.	Lab	7,923	14.9	+5.3
		Booth, G.H.	UKI	1,962	3.7*	
		Cowling, B.H.	Lib	1,161	2.2*	
		Wild, P.D.	Rainbow	100	0.2*	
1992: Con				12	0.0	

Torfaen [583]

60,343†	71.7	Murphy, P.P.*	Lab	29,863	69.1	+4.9
		Parish, N.Q.G.	Con	5,327	12.3	-8.0
None		Gray, J.E. Ms.	LD	5,249	12.1	-0.9
		Holler, D.J. Ms.	Ref	1,245	2.9*	
		Gough, R.W.	PC	1,042	2.4*	-0.1
		Coghill, R.W.	Grn	519	1.2*	
1992: Lab				24,536	56.7	

Totnes [584]

70,920	75.8	Steen, A.D.*	Con	19,637	36.5	-14.3
		Chave, R.F.	LD	18,760	34.9	-0.7
38.4		Ellery, V.S.	Lab	8,796	16.4	+4.3
		Cook, P.H. Ms.	Ref	2,552	4.7*	
		Venmore, C.	Ind Con	2,369	4.4*	
		Thomas, H.W.	UKI	999	1.9*	
		Pratt, A.R.	Grn	548	1.0*	
		Golding, J.S.M.	Rainbow	108	0.2*	
1992: Con				877	1.6	

Tottenham [585]

66,251†	56.9	Grant, B.A.M.*	Lab	26,121	69.3	+12.8
		Scantlebury, A.R.	Con	5,921	15.7	-14.1
None		Hughes, N.	LD	4,064	10.8	-0.6
		Budge, P.	Grn	1,059	2.8*	
		Tay, L.L.E. Ms.	PL	210	0.6*	
		Anglin, C.F.	WRP	181	0.5*	
		Kent, T. Ms.	Ind	148	0.4*	
1992: Lab				20,200	53.6	

Truro & St Austell [586]

76,634†	74.0	Taylor, M.O.J.*	LD	27,502	48.5	-2.0
		Badcock, N.	Con	15,001	26.4	-11.8
None		Dooley, M.	Lab	8,697	15.3	+5.5
		Hearn, C.P.	Ref	3,682	6.5	
		Haithwaite, A.T.	UKI	576	1.0*	
		Robinson, D. Ms.	Grn	482	0.8*	
		Hicks, D.A.	MK	450	0.8*	
		Yelland, L.M. Ms.	Ind	240	0.4*	
		Boland, P.A.	NLP	117	0.2*	
1992: LD				12,501	22.0	

Tunbridge Wells [587]

65,259†	74.1	Norman, A.J.	Con	21,853	45.2	-9.8
		Clayton, A.S.	LD	14,347	29.7	+0.2
14.0		Warner, P.G.	Lab	9,879	20.4	+5.7
		Macpherson, T.I.	Ref	1,858	3.8*	
		Smart, M.A.	UKI	264	0.5*	
		Levy, P.	NLP	153	0.3*	
1992: Con				7,506	15.5	

Tweeddale, Ettrick & Lauderdale [588]

51,114	76.3	Moore, M.K.	LD	12,178	31.2	-3.8
		Geddes, K.T.	Lab	10,689	27.4	+11.0
41.2		Jack, A.W.	Con	8,623	22.1	-8.6
		Goldie, I.R.	SNP	6,671	17.1	-0.1
		Mowbray, C.A.	Ref	406	1.0*	
		Hein, J.	Lib	387	1.0*	
		Paterson, D.J.	NLP	47	0.1*	
1992: LD				1,489	3.8	

Twickenham [589]

73,569	79.0	Cable, J.V.	LD	26,237	45.1	+5.8
		Jessel, T.F.H.*	Con	21,956	37.8	-11.8
14.0		Tutchell, E. Ms.	Lab	9,065	15.6	+5.2
		Harrison, M.J. Ms.	Ind Con	589	1.0*	
		Haggar, T.D.	Rainbow	155	0.3*	
		Hardy, A.J.W.	NLP	142	0.2*	
1992: Con				4,281	7.4	

Tyne Bridge [590]

61,058†	57.1	Clelland, D.G.*	Lab	26,767	76.8	+10.0
		Lee, A.H.	Con	3,861	11.1	-11.0
24.3		Wallace, M. Ms.	LD	2,785	8.0	-3.1
		Oswald, G.R.	Ref	919	2.6*	
		Brunskill, E. Ms.	Soc	518	1.5*	
1992: Lab				22,906	65.7	

Tynemouth [591]

66,341†	77.1	Campbell, A.	Lab	28,318	55.4	+13.1
		Callanan, M.J.	Con	17,045	33.3	-15.3
9.2		Duffield, A.J.R.	LD	4,509	8.8	+0.7
		Rook, C.	Ref	819	1.6*	
		Rogers, F.W.	UKI	462	0.9*	
1992: Con				11,273	22.0	

Tyneside North [592]

66,449†	67.9	Byers, S.J.*	Lab	32,810	72.7	+11.8
		McIntyre, M.	Con	6,167	13.7	-12.3
30.6		Mulvenna, T.	LD	4,762	10.6	-2.5
		Rollings, M.G.	Ref	1,382	3.1*	
1992: Lab				26,643	59.0	

Tyrone West [593]

58,428	79.2	Thompson, W.J.	UU	16,003	34.6	+34.6
		Byrne, J.	SDLP	14,842	32.1	+1.1
56.0		Doherty, P.	SF	14,280	30.9	+10.9
		Gormley, A. Ms.	APNI	829	1.8*	-2.9
		Owens, T.	WP	230	0.5*	
		Johnstone, R.A.	NLP	91	0.2*	
1992: DUP				1,161	2.5	

Ulster Mid [594]

59,086	85.8	McGuinness, M.	SF	20,294	40.1	+15.9
		McCrea, R.T.W.*	DUP	18,411	36.3	-4.7
105.6		Haughey, D.	SDLP	11,205	22.1	-8.5
		Bogues, E.	APNI	460	0.9*	-1.7
		Donnelly, M. Ms.	WP	238	0.5*	
		Murray, M. Ms.	NLP	61	0.1*	
1992: DUP				1,883	3.7	

Upminster [595]

56,793	72.8	Darvill, K.E.	Lab	19,085	46.2	+16.1
		Bonsor, N.C.*	Con	16,315	39.5	-14.7
9.9		Peskett, P.G. Ms.	LD	3,919	9.5	-6.3
		Murray, T.P.	Ref	2,000	4.8*	
1992: Con				2,770	6.7	

Upper Bann [596]

70,503	67.8	Trimble, D.*	UU	20,836	43.6	-15.4
		Rodgers, B. Ms.	SDLP	11,584	24.2	+0.8
0.0		O'Hagan, B.M.T. Ms.	SF	5,773	12.1	+6.0
		Carrick, W.M.	DUP	5,482	11.5	+11.5
		Ramsay, W.W.	APNI	3,017	6.3	+0.7
		French, T.	WP	554	1.2*	
		Price, B.D.	Con	433	0.9*	-2.5
		Lyons, J.	NLP	108	0.2*	
1992: UU				9,252	19.4	

Uxbridge [597]

57,414	72.4	Shersby, J.M. Sir*	Con	18,095	43.6	-12.8
		Williams, D.	Lab	17,371	41.8	+12.8
8.0		Malyan, A.D.	LD	4,528	10.9	-1.6
		Aird, G.R.	Ref	1,153	2.8*	
		Leonard, J.A. Ms.	Soc	398	1.0*	
1992: Con				724	1.7	

Vale of Clwyd [598]

52,426	74.6	Ruane, C.S.	Lab	20,617	52.7	+13.9
		Edwards, D.	Con	11,662	29.8	-13.9
91.1		Munford, D.N.	LD	3,425	8.8	-3.7
		Kensler, G.M. Ms.	PC	2,301	5.9	+1.1
		Vickers, S.R.	Ref	834	2.1*	
		Cooke, S.A.	UKI	293	0.7*	
1992: Con				8,955	22.9	

Vale of Glamorgan [599]

67,413†	80.0	Smith, J.W.P.	Lab	29,054	53.9	+9.6
		Sweeney, W.E.*	Con	18,522	34.4	-10.0
0.7		Campbell, S.M. Ms.	LD	4,945	9.2	-0.1
		Corp, M.J. Ms.	PC	1,393	2.6*	+0.5
1992: Con				10,532	19.5	

Vale of York [600]

70,128†	76.0	McIntosh, A.C.B. Ms.	Con	23,815	44.7	-15.9
		Carter, M.J.	Lab	14,094	26.5	+15.4
108.9		Hall, A.C.	LD	12,656	23.8	-4.1
		Fairclough, C.A.	Ref	2,503	4.7*	
		Pelton, T.	Ind	197	0.4*	
1992: Con				9,721	18.3	

Vauxhall [601]

70,424†	55.5	Hoey, C.L. Ms.*	Lab	24,920	63.8	+7.7
		Kerr, K.K.K.	LD	6,260	16.0	+1.6
12.6		Bacon, R.M.	Con	5,942	15.2	-11.4
		Driver, I.D.	SL	983	2.5*	
		Collins, W.S.B.	Grn	864	2.2*	
		Headicar, R.	Soc	97	0.2*	
1992: Lab				18,660	47.8	

Wakefield [602]

73,236	68.9	Hinchliffe, D.M.*	Lab	28,977	57.4	+9.1
		Peacock, J.D.	Con	14,373	28.5	-12.0
69.1		Dale, D.	LD	5,656	11.2	-0.1
		Shires, S.C.	Ref	1,480	2.9*	
1992: Lab				14,604	28.9	

Wallasey [603]

63,493	73.8	Eagle, A. Ms.*	Lab	30,264	64.6	+15.7
		Wilcock, M.P. Ms.	Con	11,190	23.9	-18.0
None		Reisdorf, P.T.C.	LD	3,899	8.3	+0.6
		Hayes, R.	Ref	1,490	3.2*	
1992: Lab				19,074	40.7	

Walsall North [604]

67,587†	64.1	Winnick, D.J.*	Lab	24,517	56.6	+9.9
		Bird, M.A.	Con	11,929	27.5	-11.8
None		O'Brien, T.J. Ms.	LD	4,050	9.4	-3.3
		Bennett, D.M.	Ref	1,430	3.3*	
		Pitt, M.G.	Ind	911	2.1*	
		Humphries, A.H.	NF	465	1.1*	
1992: Lab				12,588	29.1	

Walsall South [605]

64,221†	67.3	George, B.T.*	Lab	25,024	57.9	+9.7
		Leek, L.G.	Con	13,712	31.7	-10.2
None		Harris, H.R.	LD	2,698	6.2	-2.0
		Dent, T.F.	Ref	1,662	3.8*	
		Meads, L.P. Ms.	NLP	149	0.3*	
1992: Lab				11,312	26.2	

Walthamstow [606]

63,818†	62.8	Gerrard, N.F.*	Lab	25,287	63.1	+18.8
		Andrew, J.E. Ms.	Con	8,138	20.3	-16.9
33.3		Jackson, J.M. Ms.	LD	5,491	13.7	-2.1
		Hargreaves, J.G.	Ref	1,139	2.8*	
1992: Lab				17,149	42.8	

Wansbeck [607]

63,082†	71.6	Murphy, D.	Lab	29,569	65.5	+5.7
		Thompson, J.A.	LD	7,202	15.9	+0.7
None		Green, P.V.	Con	6,299	13.9	-9.6
		Gompertz, P.H.	Ref	1,146	2.5*	
		Best, N.F.	Grn	956	2.1*	
1992: Lab				22,367	49.5	

Wansdyke [608]

69,270	79.0	Norris, D.	Lab	24,117	44.1	+16.8
		Prisk, M.M.	Con	19,318	35.3	-11.9
58.6		Manning, J.S.	LD	9,205	16.8	-6.8
		Clinton, K.J.	Ref	1,327	2.4*	
		Hunt, T.S.	UKI	438	0.8*	
		House, P.J.	MRLP	225	0.4*	
		Lincoln, S.I. Ms.	NLP	92	0.2*	
1992: Con				4,799	8.8	

Wantage [609]

71,768	78.1	Jackson, R.V.*	Con	22,311	39.8	-14.3
		Wilson, C.M. Ms.	Lab	16,222	28.9	+9.6
None		Riley, J.G.A. Ms.	LD	14,862	26.5	+1.6
		Rising, S.F.	Ref	1,549	2.8*	
		Kennet, M.F. Ms.	Grn	640	1.1*	
		Tolstoy, N.	UKI	465	0.8*	
1992: Con				6,089	10.9	

Warley [610]

59,793	65.0	Spellar, J.F.*	Lab	24,813	63.8	+10.7
		Pincher, C.J.	Con	9,362	24.1	-10.2
18.6		Pursehouse, J.	LD	3,777	9.7	-1.7
		Gamre, K.B.	Ref	941	2.4*	
1992: Lab				15,451	39.7	

Warrington North [611]

72,815†	70.4	Jones, H.M. Ms.	Lab	31,827	62.1	+8.9
		Lacey, R. Ms.	Con	12,300	24.0	-10.9
9.5		Greenhalgh, I.	LD	5,308	10.4	-1.0
		Smith, A.T.	Ref	1,816	3.5*	
1992: Lab				19,527	38.1	

Warrington South [612]

72,461†	76.0	Southworth, H.M. Ms.	Lab	28,721	52.1	+11.4
		Grayling, C.S.	Con	17,914	32.5	-13.2
0.0		Walker, P.J.	LD	7,199	13.1	+0.1
		Kelly, G.D.	Ref	1,082	2.0*	
		Ross, S.G.	NLP	166	0.3*	
1992: Con				10,807	19.6	

Warwick & Leamington [613]

79,975	75.1	Plaskitt, J.A.	Lab	26,747	44.5	+13.3
		Smith, D.G.*	Con	23,349	38.9	-10.7
7.5		Hicks, N.S.	LD	7,133	11.9	-5.3
		Davis, V.L. Ms.	Ref	1,484	2.5*	
		Baptie, P.E.A.	Grn	764	1.3*	
		Warwick, G.J.G.	Ind	306	0.5*	
		Gibbs, M.C.	Ind	183	0.3*	
		McCarthy, R.	NLP	125	0.2*	
1992: Con				3,398	5.7	

Warwickshire North [614]

72,552	74.8	O'Brien, M.*	Lab	31,669	58.4	+12.3
		Hammond, S.W.	Con	16,902	31.2	-12.5
0.1		Powell, W.H.	LD	4,040	7.4	-2.8
		Mole, R.A.	Ref	917	1.7*	
		Cooke, C.T.	UKI	533	1.0*	
		Moorecroft, I.J.	Ind	178	0.3*	
1992: Lab				14,767	27.2	

Watford [615]

74,015†	74.6	Ward, C.M. Ms.	Lab	25,019	45.3	+11.3
		Gordon, R.I.N.	Con	19,227	34.8	-13.3
24.7		Canning, A.J.	LD	9,272	16.8	+0.0
		Roe, P.E.	Ref	1,484	2.7*	
		Davis, L.J.K.	NLP	234	0.4*	
1992: Con				5,792	10.5	

Waveney [616]

75,420†	74.6	Blizzard, R.J.	Lab	31,486	56.0	+16.2
		Porter, D.J.*	Con	19,393	34.5	-12.5
12.3		Thomas, C.F.	LD	5,054	9.0	-3.8
		Clark, N.H.	NLP	318	0.6*	
1992: Con				12,093	21.5	

Wealden [617]

80,206	73.7	Johnson Smith, G.*	Con	29,417	49.8	-12.0
		Skinner, M.D.	LD	15,213	25.7	-1.3
0.2		Levine, N.J.	Lab	10,185	17.2	+8.0
		Taplin, B.J.	Ref	3,527	6.0	
		English, M.J. Ms.	UKI	569	1.0*	
		Cragg, P.	NLP	188	0.3*	
1992: Con				14,204	24.0	

Weaver Vale [618]

66,125†	73.0	Hall, M.T.*	Lab	27,244	56.4	+7.7
		Byrne, J.P.	Con	13,796	28.6	-7.2
121.6		Griffiths, T.N.	LD	5,949	12.3	-2.2
		Cockfield, R.E.	Ref	1,312	2.7*	
1992: Lab				13,448	27.8	

Wellingborough [619]

75,221†	74.8	Stinchcombe, P.D.	Lab	24,854	44.2	+10.3
		Fry, P.D.*	Con	24,667	43.8	-9.6
None		Smith, P.D.G.	LD	5,279	9.4	-3.4
		Ellwood, A.R.	UKI	1,192	2.1*	
		Lorys, A. Ms.	NLP	297	0.5*	
1992: Con				187	0.3	

Wells [620]

72,426†	77.8	Heathcoat-Amory, D.P.*	Con	22,208	39.4	-10.2
		Gold, P.J.	LD	21,680	38.5	+0.4
None		Eavis, M.	Lab	10,204	18.1	+7.5
		Phelps, P.A. Ms.	Ref	2,196	3.9*	
		Royse, L. Ms.	NLP	92	0.2*	
1992: Con				528	0.9	

Welwyn Hatfield [621]

67,395†	78.6	Johnson, M.J. Ms.	Lab	24,936	47.1	+11.1
		Evans, D.J.*	Con	19,341	36.5	-11.0
6.5		Schwartz, R.S.	LD	7,161	13.5	-2.5
		Cox, V.E.	Ind	1,263	2.4*	
		Harold, H.T. Ms.	PL	267	0.5*	
1992: Con				5,595	10.6	

Wentworth [622]

63,951†	65.3	Healey, J.	Lab	30,225	72.3	+3.8
		Hamer, K.M.	Con	6,266	15.0	-6.8
None		Charters, J.J.	LD	3,867	9.3	-0.4
		Battley, A.	Ref	1,423	3.4*	
1992: Lab				23,959	57.3	

West Bromwich East [623]

63,432	65.4	Snape, P.C.*	Lab	23,710	57.2	+9.2
		Matsell, B.M.	Con	10,126	24.4	-13.5
16.0		Smith, M.G.	LD	6,179	14.9	+1.6
		Mulley, G.E.	Ref	1,472	3.5*	
1992: Lab				13,584	32.7	

West Bromwich West [624]

67,513	54.4	Boothroyd, B. Ms.*	Speaker	23,969	65.3	
		Silvester, R.E.W.	Ind Lab	8,546	23.3	
47.9		Edwards, S.	Nat Dem	4,181	11.4	
1992: Lab				15,423	42.0	

West Ham [625]

57,589†	58.5	Banks, A.L.*	Lab	24,531	72.9	+14.9
		MacGregor, M.C.	Con	5,037	15.0	-15.0
38.6		McDonough, S.L.C. Ms.	LD	2,479	7.4	-2.2
		Francis, K.F.A.	BNP	1,198	3.6*	
		Jug, T.	MRLP	300	0.9*	
		Rainbow, J.P.	Rainbow	116	0.3*	
1992: Lab				19,494	57.9	

Westbury [626]

74,457	76.2	Faber, D.J.C.*	Con	23,037	40.6	-11.6
		Miller, J.C.C.	LD	16,949	29.9	-4.1
15.5		Small, K.D.	Lab	11,969	21.1	+10.5
		Hawkins, G.F.J.	Lib	1,956	3.4*	
		Hawkings-Byass, N.G.E.	Ref	1,909	3.4*	
		Westbury, R.A.J.	UKI	771	1.4*	
		Haysom, C.A.	NLP	140	0.2*	
1992: Con				6,088	10.7	

Western Isles [627]

22,983†	70.1	MacDonald, C.A.*	Lab	8,955	55.6	+7.8
		Gillies, A.L. Ms.	SNP	5,379	33.4	-3.8
None		McGrigor, J.A.R.M.	Con	1,071	6.6	-1.8
		Mitchison, N.	LD	495	3.1*	-0.4
		Lionel, R.G.	Ref	206	1.3*	
1992: Lab				3,576	22.2	

Westmorland & Lonsdale [628]

68,563†	74.1	Collins, T.W.G.	Con	21,463	42.3	-14.6
		Collins, S.B.	LD	16,942	33.4	+5.9
6.3		Harding, J.L.	Lab	10,452	20.6	+5.5
		Smith, M.H.	Ref	1,924	3.8*	
1992: Con				4,521	8.9	

Weston-Super-Mare [629]

72,555	73.6	Cotter, B.J.	LD	21,407	40.1	+1.6
		Daly, M.E. Ms.	Con	20,133	37.7	-10.3
10.6		Kraft, D.	Lab	9,557	17.9	+6.5
		Sewell, T.R.M.	Ref	2,280	4.3*	
1992: Con				1,274	2.4	

Wigan [630]

64,689†	67.7	Stott, R.*	Lab	30,043	68.6	+7.9
		Loveday, M.A.	Con	7,400	16.9	-8.4
10.7		Beswick, T.R.	LD	4,390	10.0	-1.7
		Bradborn, A.H.	Ref	1,450	3.3*	
		Maile, C.J.	Grn	442	1.0*	
		Ayliffe, W.J.	NLP	94	0.2*	
1992: Lab				22,643	51.7	

Wiltshire North [631]

77,440†	74.9	Gray, J.W.	Con	25,390	43.8	-12.4
		Cordon, S.R.	LD	21,915	37.8	+6.3
16.5		Knowles, N.	Lab	8,261	14.2	+4.1
		Purves, M. Ms.	Ref	1,774	3.1*	
		Wood, A.S.	UKI	410	0.7*	
		Forsyth, J. Ms.	NLP	263	0.5*	
1992: Con				3,475	6.0	

Wimbledon [632]

64,113	75.4	Casale, R.M.	Lab	20,674	42.8	+19.5
		Goodson-Wickes, C.*	Con	17,684	36.6	-16.4
None		Willott, A.L. Ms.	LD	8,014	16.6	-4.7
		Abid, H.Z.	Ref	993	2.1*	
		Thacker, R.K.	Grn	474	1.0*	
		Davies, S.A.H. Ms.	PL	346	0.7*	
		Kirby, M.G.	Ind	112	0.2*	
		Stacey, G.L.	Rainbow	47	0.1*	
1992: Con				2,990	6.2	

Winchester [633]

79,272†	78.3	Oaten, M.	LD	26,100	42.1	+5.2
		Malone, G.*	Con	26,098	42.1	-9.6
44.3		Davies, P.	Lab	6,528	10.5	+3.0
		Strand, P.J.	Ref	1,598	2.6*	
		Huggett, R.J.	Ind	640	1.0*	
		Rumsey, D.L.	UKI	476	0.8*	
		Browne, J.E.D.D.	Ind	307	0.5*	
		Stockton, P.F.	MRLP	307	0.5*	
1992: Con				2	0.0	

Windsor [634]

69,132†	73.5	Trend, M.St. J.*	Con	24,476	48.2	-8.1
		Fox, C.F.	LD	14,559	28.7	-0.4
106.1		Williams, A.J. Ms.	Lab	9,287	18.3	+5.9
		McDermott, J.F.	Ref	1,676	3.3*	
		Bradshaw, P.E.	Lib	388	0.8*	
		Bigg, E. Ms.	UKI	302	0.6*	
		Parr, R.P.	Ind	93	0.2*	
1992: Con				9,917	19.5	

Wirral South [635]

59,321	81.1	Chapman, J.K.*	Lab	24,499	50.9	+16.4
		Byrom, L.T.	Con	17,495	36.4	-14.5
0.1		Gilchrist, P.N.	LD	5,018	10.4	-2.6
		Wilcox, D.	Ref	768	1.6*	
		Nielsen, J.W. Ms.	PL	264	0.5*	
		Mead, G.S.	NLP	51	0.1*	
1992: Con				7,004	14.6	

Wirral West [636]

60,732	77.2	Hesford, S.	Lab	21,035	44.9	+13.9
		Hunt, D.J.F.*	Con	18,297	39.0	-13.7
None		Thornton, J.L.	LD	5,945	12.7	-1.9
		Wharton, D.	Ref	1,613	3.4*	
1992: Con				2,738	5.8	

Witney [637]

73,520†	76.7	Woodward, S.A.	Con	24,282	43.1	-14.8
		Hollingsworth, A.J.	Lab	17,254	30.6	+12.5
18.2		Lawrence, A. Ms.	LD	11,202	19.9	-2.7
		Brown, G.M.C.	Ref	2,262	4.0*	
		Montgomery, M.S.J.	UKI	765	1.4*	
		Chaple-Perrie, S.N. Ms.	Grn	636	1.1*	
1992: Con				7,028	12.5	

Woking [638]

70,053†	72.7	Malins, H.J.	Con	19,553	38.4	-20.7
		Goldenberg, P.	LD	13,875	27.3	+0.2
14.9		Hanson, C.D. Ms.	Lab	10,695	21.0	+7.6
		Bell, H.M.I.	Ind Con	3,933	7.7	
		Skeate, C.T.W.	Ref	2,209	4.3*	
		Harvey, M.J.	UKI	512	1.0*	
		Sleeman, D.E. Ms.	NLP	137	0.3*	
1992: Con				5,678	11.2	

Wokingham [639]

66,781†	75.0	Redwood, J.A.*	Con	25,086	50.1	-11.7
		Longton, R.E.	LD	15,721	31.4	+5.7
67.6		Colling, P. Ms.	Lab	8,424	16.8	+5.5
		Owen, P.	MRLP	877	1.8*	
1992: Con				9,365	18.7	

Wolverhampton North East [640]

61,677	67.1	Purchase, K.*	Lab	24,534	59.3	+10.3
		Harvey, D.J.	Con	11,547	27.9	-13.5
1.7		Niblett, B.W.	LD	2,214	5.3	-2.0
		Hallmark, C.G.	Lib	1,560	3.8*	
		Muchall, A.C.	Ref	1,192	2.9*	
		Wingfield, M.	Nat Dem	356	0.9*	
1992: Lab				12,987	31.4	

Wolverhampton South East [641]

54,329	64.1	Turner, D.*	Lab	22,202	63.7	+7.0
		Hanbury, W.E.	Con	7,020	20.2	-11.6
None		Whitehouse, R.F.	LD	3,292	9.5	-0.0
		Stevenson-Platt, T.	Ref	980	2.8*	
		Worth, N.	SL	689	2.0*	
		Bullman, K.E.J.	Lib	647	1.9*	
1992: Lab				15,182	43.6	

Wolverhampton South West [642]

67,553	72.4	Jones, J.G. Ms.	Lab	24,657	50.4	+10.5
		Budgen, N.W.*	Con	19,539	39.9	-9.4
None		Green, M.R.	LD	4,012	8.2	-0.3
		Hyde, M.S.	Lib	713	1.5*	
1992: Con				5,118	10.5	

Woodspring [643]

70,069	78.4	Fox, L.*	Con	24,425	44.4	-8.9
		Kirsen, N.E. Ms.	LD	16,691	30.4	-1.3
33.9		Sander, D. Ms.	Lab	11,377	20.7	+8.3
		Hughes, R.C.	Ref	1,641	3.0*	
		Lawson, R.H.	Grn	667	1.2*	
		Glover, A.	Ind	101	0.2*	
		Mears, M.L.	NLP	52	0.1*	
1992: Con				7,734	14.1	

Worcester [644]

69,234†	74.6	Foster, M.J.	Lab	25,848	50.1	+10.2
		Bourne, N.H.	Con	18,423	35.7	-9.8
15.8		Chandler, P.	LD	6,462	12.5	-0.6
		Wood, P.A. Ms.	UKI	886	1.7*	
1992: Con				7,425	14.4	

Worcestershire Mid [645]

68,407	74.3	Luff, P.J.*	Con	24,092	47.4	-7.5
		Smith, D.C. Ms.	Lab	14,680	28.9	+11.3
107.8		Barwick, D.J.	LD	9,458	18.6	-7.5
		Watson, T.	Ref	1,780	3.5*	
		Ingles, D.C.	UKI	646	1.3*	
		Dyer, A.K.	NLP	163	0.3*	
1992: Con				9,412	18.5	

Worcestershire West [646]

64,712†	76.3	Spicer, W.M.H.*	Con	22,223	45.0	-9.7
		Hadley, M.P.J.	LD	18,377	37.2	+8.0
49.5		Stone, N.	Lab	7,738	15.7	+1.9
		Cameron, S.M. Ms.	Grn	1,006	2.0*	
1992: Con				3,846	7.8	

Workington [647]

65,766†	75.1	Campbell-Savours, D.N.*	Lab	31,717	64.2	+10.0
		Blunden, R.M.	Con	12,061	24.4	-12.0
15.7		Roberts, P.J.	LD	3,967	8.0	+0.6
		Donnan, G.W.	Ref	1,412	2.9*	
		Austin, C.	Ind	217	0.4*	
1992: Lab				19,656	39.8	

Worsley [648]

68,978†	67.8	Lewis, T.*	Lab	29,083	62.2	+8.4
		Garrido, D.R.L.	Con	11,342	24.2	-7.9
34.9		Bleakley, R.M.	LD	6,356	13.6	+0.9
1992: Lab				17,741	37.9	

Worthing East & Shoreham [649]

70,770	72.9	Loughton, T.P.	Con	20,864	40.5	-10.9
		King, M.	LD	15,766	30.6	-3.1
71.1		Williams, M.A.	Lab	12,335	23.9	+10.6
		McCulloch, J.	Ref	1,683	3.3*	
		Jarvis, R.L. Ms.	UKI	921	1.8*	
1992: Con				5,098	9.9	

Worthing West [650]

71,639†	71.8	Bottomley, P.J.*	Con	23,733	46.1	-15.6
		Hare, C.A.	LD	16,020	31.1	+3.6
57.0		Adams, J.P.	Lab	8,347	16.2	+7.6
		John, N.	Ref	2,313	4.5*	
		Cross, T.P.	UKI	1,029	2.0*	
1992: Con				7,713	15.0	

The Wrekin [651]

60,211†	75.2	Bradley, P.C.S.	Lab	21,243	46.9	+15.0
		Bruinvels, P.N.E.	Con	18,218	40.2	-7.5
89.6		Jenkins, I.C.	LD	5,807	12.8	-6.5
1992: Con				3,025	6.7	

Wrexham [652]

50,741†	71.8	Marek, J.*	Lab	20,450	56.1	+6.2
		Andrew, S.J.	Con	8,688	23.9	-8.6
32.1		Thomas, A.M.	LD	4,833	13.3	-1.7
		Cronk, J.E.	Ref	1,195	3.3*	
		Plant, J.K.	PC	1,170	3.2*	+0.6
		Low, N.J.	NLP	86	0.2*	
1992: Lab				11,762	32.3	

Wycombe [653]

73,589†	71.1	Whitney, R.W.*	Con	20,890	39.9	-13.3
		Bryant, C.J.	Lab	18,520	35.4	+14.0
3.9		Bensilum, P.K.	LD	9,678	18.5	-4.5
		Fulford, A.F.	Ref	2,394	4.6*	
		Laker, J.S.	Grn	716	1.4*	
		Heath, M.D.	NLP	121	0.2*	
1992: Con				2,370	4.5	

Wyre Forest [654]

73,083	75.3	Lock, D.A.	Lab	26,843	48.8	+17.5
		Coombs, A.M.V.*	Con	19,897	36.1	-11.3
2.7		Cropp, D.L.	LD	4,377	8.0	-13.3
		Till, W.	Ref	1,956	3.6*	
		Harvey, C.J.	Lib	1,670	3.0*	
		Millington, A.J.	UKI	312	0.6*	
1992: Con				6,946	12.6	

Wythenshawe & Sale East [655]

72,086†	63.2	Goggins, P.G.	Lab	26,448	58.1	+8.6
		Fleming, P.	Con	11,429	25.1	-9.8
47.8		Tucker, V.M. Ms.	LD	5,639	12.4	-2.1
		Stanyer, B.	Ref	1,060	2.3*	
		Flannery, J.D.	SL	957	2.1*	
1992: Lab				15,019	33.0	

Yeovil [656]

74,383	72.7	Ashdown, J.J.D.*	LD	26,349	48.7	-2.9
		Cambrook, N.D.J.	Con	14,946	27.7	-9.3
1.0		Conway, P.J.A.	Lab	8,053	14.9	+5.3
		Beveridge, J.C.	Ref	3,574	6.6	
		Taylor, D.R.	Grn	728	1.3*	
		Archer, J.R.	Ind	306	0.6*	
		Hudson, C.J.P.	Rainbow	97	0.2*	
1992: LD				11,403	21.1	

Ynys Mon [657]

53,294†	74.9	Jones, I.W.*	PC	15,756	39.5	+2.3
		Edwards, O.M.	Lab	13,275	33.2	+9.7
None		Owen, G.G.V.	Con	8,569	21.5	-13.1
		Burnham, D.W.L.	LD	1,537	3.8*	-0.5
		Gray Morris, R.H.	Ref	793	2.0*	
1992: PC				2,481	6.2	

York [658]

79,710†	73.2	Bayley, H.*	Lab	34,956	59.9	+10.8
		Mallett, S.J.	Con	14,433	24.7	-14.5
None		Waller, A.M.	LD	6,537	11.2	+0.6
		Sheppard, J.N.	Ref	1,083	1.9*	
		Hill, M.R.	Grn	880	1.5*	
		Wegener, E.G.	UKI	319	0.5*	
		Lightfoot, A.J.	Ind	137	0.2*	
1992: Lab				20,523	35.2	

Yorkshire East [659]

69,482	70.5	Townend, J.E.*	Con	20,904	42.7	-7.9
		Male, I.R.	Lab	17,567	35.9	+9.4
70.9		Leadley, D.R.	LD	9,070	18.5	-4.3
		Allerston, R.	Ind	1,049	2.1*	
		Cooper, M.P.	Nat Dem	381	0.8*	
1992: Con				3,337	6.8	

TABLES

Table 1: General Election 1997 : Summary Results

England	Votes	Votes %	%ch 92/97	Candidates	Elected
Con	8,780,881	33.7	-11.8	528	165
Lab	11,347,882	43.5	+9.6	527	328
Lib Dem	4,677,565	18.0	-1.2	527	34
Green	60,013	0.2	-0.3	85	-
NLP	25,958	0.1	-0.1	160	-
Referendum	746,624	2.9	-	445	-
UKInd	103,521	0.4	-	182	-
Others	316,268	1.2	+0.5	491	2*
Total Vote	26,058,712			2945	529
Electorate	36,516,012	71.4% turnout			

* These are Ms. B. Boothroyd (Speaker) and M. Bell (Independent)

Scotland	Votes	Votes %	%ch 92/97	Candidates	Elected
Con	493,059	17.5	-8.1	72	-
Lab	1,283,350	45.6	+6.6	72	56
Lib Dem	365,362	13.0	-0.1	72	10
SNP	621,550	22.1	+0.6	72	6
Green	1,721	0.1	-0.2	5	-
NLP	1,922	0.1	-0.0	14	-
Referendum	26,980	1.0	-	67	-
UKInd	1,585	0.1	-	9	-
Others	21,219	0.8	+0.3	48	-
Total Vote	2,816,748			431	72
Electorate	3,949,112	71.3% turnout			

Wales	Votes	Votes %	%ch 92/97	Candidates	Elected
Con	317,145	19.6	-9.0	40	-
Lab	886,935	54.7	+5.2	40	34
Lib Dem	200,020	12.3	-0.1	40	2
PC	161,030	9.9	+1.1	40	4
Green	1,718	0.1	-0.3	4	-
NLP	516	0.0	-0.0	5	-
Referendum	38,245	2.4	-	35	-
UKInd	616	0.0	-	2	-
Others	13,837	0.9	+0.7	17	-
Total Vote	1,620,062			223	40
Electorate	2,203,059	73.5% turnout			

N. Ireland	Votes	Votes %	%ch 92/97	Candidates	Elected
Con	9,858	1.2	-4.4	8	-
UU	258,349	32.7	-1.9	16	10
DUP	107,348	13.6	+0.5	9	2
UKU	12,817	1.6	-	1	1
Prog U	10,928	1.4	-	3	-
APNI	62,972	8.0	-0.8	17	-
SDLP	190,814	24.1	+0.6	18	3
SF	126,921	16.1	+6.1	17	2
NLP	2,208	0.3	+0.0	18	-
Others	8,547	1.1	-0.6	18	-
Total Vote	790,762			125	18
Electorate	1,177,969	67.1% turnout			

Great Britain	Votes	Votes %	%ch 92/97	Candidates	Elected
Con	9,591,085	31.5	-11.3	640	165
Lab	13,518,167	44.3	+9.1	639	418
Lib Dem	5,242,947	17.2	-1.1	639	46
SNP/PC	782,580	2.6	+0.2	112	10
Green	63,452	0.2	-0.3	94	-
NLP	28,396	0.1	-0.1	179	-
Referendum	811,849	2.7	-	547	-
UKInd	105,722	0.3	-	193	-
Others	351,324	1.2	+0.5	556	2
Total	30,495,522			3599	641
Electorate	42,668,183	71.5% turnout			

United Kingdom	Votes	Votes %	%ch 92/97	Candidates	Elected
Con	9,600,943	30.7	-11.2	648	165
Lab	13,518,167	43.2	+8.8	639	418
Lib Dem	5,242,947	16.8	-1.1	639	46
SNP/PC	782,580	2.5	+0.2	112	10
Green	63,991	0.2	-0.3	95	-
NLP	30,604	0.1	-0.1	197	-
Referendum	811,849	2.6	-	547	-
UKInd	105,722	0.3	-	193	-
Others	1,129,481	3.6	+0.8	654	20
Total Vote	31,286,284			3724	659
Electorate	43,846,152	71.4% turnout			

Table 2: Voting in the English Regions

East Anglia

	Con	Lab	Lib Dem	Other	Total
votes	460,612	456,417	213,474	60,735	1,191,238
votes% 1997	38.7	38.3	17.9	5.1	
votes% 1992	51.0	28.0	19.5	1.5	
change 92/97	-12.4	10.3	-1.6	3.6	
seats97	14	8	0	0	22
seats92	19	3	0	0	22

East Midlands

	Con	Lab	Lib Dem	Other	Total
votes	800,958	1,097,639	311,264	84,889	2,294,750
votes% 1997	34.9	47.8	13.6	3.7	
votes% 1992	46.6	37.4	15.3	0.7	
change 92/97	-11.7	10.4	-1.7	3.0	
seats97	14	30	0	0	44
seats92	29	15	0	0	44

Greater London

	Con	Lab	Lib Dem	Other	Total
votes	1,036,082	1,643,329	485,511	156,126	3,321,048
votes% 1997	31.2	49.5	14.6	4.7	
votes% 1992	45.3	37.1	15.9	1.7	
change 92/97	-14.1	12.4	-1.3	3.0	
seats97	11	57	6	0	74
seats92	41	32	1	0	74

Northern

	Con	Lab	Lib Dem	Other	Total
votes	360,973	991,745	215,900	60,322	1,628,940
votes% 1997	22.2	60.9	13.3	3.7	
votes% 1992	33.4	50.6	15.6	0.5	
change 92/97	-11.2	10.3	-2.3	3.2	
seats97	3	32	1	0	36
seats92	6	29	1	0	36

North West

	Con	Lab	Lib Dem	Other	Total
votes	905,877	1,812,401	477,547	147,330	3,343,155
votes% 1997	27.1	54.2	14.3	4.4	
votes% 1992	37.8	44.9	15.8	1.5	
change 92/97	-10.7	9.3	-1.5	2.9	
seats97	7	60	2	1	70
seats92	25	44	1	0	70

South East

	Con	Lab	Lib Dem	Other	Total
votes	2,521,508	1,945,998	1,303,360	326,671	6,097,537
votes% 1997	41.4	31.9	21.4	5.4	
votes% 1992	54.5	20.8	23.3	1.4	
change 92/97	-13.2	11.1	-2.0	4.0	
seats97	73	36	8	0	117
seats92	112	5	0	0	117

South West

	Con	Lab	Lib Dem	Other	Total
votes	1,020,635	734,361	869,486	153,564	2,778,046
votes% 1997	36.7	26.4	31.3	5.5	
votes% 1992	47.6	19.2	31.4	1.8	
change 92/97	-10.8	7.2	-0.1	3.7	
seats97	22	15	14	0	51
seats92	39	6	6	0	51

West Midlands

	Con	Lab	Lib Dem	Other	Total
votes	953,465	1,326,822	388,807	156,731	2,825,825
votes% 1997	33.7	47.0	13.8	5.5	
votes% 1992	44.8	38.8	15.0	1.5	
change 92/97	-11.0	8.2	-1.3	4.1	
seats97	14	43	1	1	59
seats92	31	28	0	0	59

Yorkshire & Humberside

	Con	Lab	Lib Dem	Other	Total
votes	720,771	1,339,170	412,216	106,016	2,578,173
votes% 1997	28.0	51.9	16.0	4.1	
votes% 1992	37.9	44.3	16.8	0.9	
change 92/97	-10.0	7.6	-0.8	3.2	
seats97	7	47	2	0	56
seats92	22	34	0	0	56

Table 3: Seats that Changed Hands

Labour gain from Conservative

	Con %ch 92/97	Lab %ch 92/97	Lib Dem %ch 92/97	Nats %ch 92/97
Aberdeen South	-11.0	11.4	1.0	-2.3
Amber Valley	-13.0	10.3	-1.4	-
Basildon	-14.3	15.1	-5.5	-
Batley & Spen	-8.3	6.4	-2.5	-
Battersea	-11.0	9.5	0.3	-
Bedford	-11.8	14.2	-4.1	-
Bexleyheath & Crayford	-15.8	14.2	-3.2	-
Birmingham Edgbaston	-10.7	9.3	-0.5	-
Birmingham Hall Green	-12.7	15.2	-6.0	-
Blackpool North & Fleetwood	-14.2	14.6	-3.4	-
Blackpool South	-9.7	13.6	-3.6	-
Bolton West	-12.2	10.4	-2.4	-
Braintree	-10.5	15.3	-9.2	-
Brent North	-17.3	20.4	-2.5	-
Brentford & Isleworth	-13.9	14.7	-1.9	-
Brigg & Goole	-13.3	14.5	-4.5	-
Brighton Kemptown	-13.9	14.0	-4.2	-
Brighton Pavilion	-17.6	14.4	-2.9	-
Bristol West	-12.3	11.9	-1.2	-
Broxtowe	-13.5	12.3	-1.8	-
Burton	-8.8	9.8	-2.1	-
Bury North	-12.1	10.2	-0.3	-
Bury South	-13.7	12.2	-0.6	-
Calder Valley	-10.4	8.7	-1.4	-
Cardiff North	-11.5	11.5	-2.7	0.6
Castle Point	-15.5	18.4	-9.9	-
Chatham & Aylesford	-13.8	16.4	-6.2	-
Chorley	-9.9	11.4	-3.5	-
City of Chester	-10.5	12.4	-4.1	-
Cleethorpes	-14.5	15.7	-3.3	-
Clwyd West	-16.0	6.2	-2.9	-
Colne Valley	-9.3	11.5	-4.4	-
Conwy	-9.5	9.3	-0.2	-0.5
Corby	-11.1	11.5	-2.7	-
Coventry South	-10.8	16.2	0.0	-
Crawley	-12.1	14.7	-6.3	-
Crosby	-13.9	22.4	-8.5	-
Croydon Central	-16.9	14.1	-2.1	-
Croydon North	-17.5	17.8	-3.2	-

Labour gain from Conservative contd.

	Con %ch 92/97	Lab %ch 92/97	Lib Dem %ch 92/97	Nats %ch 92/97
Dartford	-10.6	12.4	-2.8	-
Derby North	-14.2	12.3	-0.5	-
Derbyshire South	-15.9	10.5	0.7	-
Dover	-11.3	11.9	-2.9	-
Dumfries	-15.1	17.9	-0.6	-2.7
Ealing North	-14.2	17.9	-3.8	-
Eastwood	-13.1	15.6	-4.7	0.5
Edinburgh Pentlands	-7.8	11.8	-2.7	-2.7
Edmonton	-16.0	15.2	-1.9	-
Elmet	-11.3	10.5	-1.9	-
Eltham	-12.8	14.5	-7.0	-
Enfield North	-16.6	15.7	-2.1	-
Enfield Southgate	-16.8	18.0	-3.8	-
Erewash	-10.6	13.5	-5.0	-
Exeter	-12.5	11.3	-1.4	-
Falmouth & Camborne	-8.1	4.7	-6.0	-
Finchley & Golders Green	-15.0	15.2	-1.5	-
Gedling	-13.7	12.3	-2.2	-
Gillingham	-16.0	16.0	-4.4	-
Gloucester	-9.8	13.2	-7.2	-
Gravesham	-10.8	9.3	-1.1	-
Great Yarmouth	-12.3	15.4	-2.6	-
Halesowen & Rowley Regis	-11.9	9.6	-1.4	-
Hammersmith & Fulham	-12.0	8.1	0.5	-
Harlow	-13.9	11.3	-1.8	-
Harrow East	-17.5	18.7	-2.6	-
Harrow West	-16.0	19.0	-4.7	-
Harwich	-15.2	14.1	-10.0	-
Hastings & Rye	-18.4	18.6	-7.3	-
Hayes & Harlington	-17.7	17.2	-2.9	-
Hemel Hempstead	-10.8	13.2	-3.0	-
Hendon	-16.6	15.8	-0.8	-
High Peak	-10.5	12.9	-3.6	-
Hornchurch	-16.2	15.7	-3.3	-
Hove	-12.6	20.1	-9.7	-
Ilford North	-17.1	17.5	-1.9	-
Ilford South	-16.8	16.4	-4.1	-
Keighley	-10.7	9.7	-0.7	-
Kettering	-9.8	11.4	-4.7	-
Kingswood	-15.9	13.1	-0.8	-

Labour gain from Conservative contd.

	Con %ch 92/97	Lab %ch 92/97	Lib Dem %ch 92/97	Nats %ch 92/97
Lancaster & Wyre	-11.6	9.7	-2.4	-
Leeds North East	-11.5	12.3	-2.8	-
Leeds North West	-10.9	12.6	-4.2	-
Leicestershire North West	-14.5	12.5	-1.7	-
Loughborough	-9.1	8.8	0.6	-
Luton North	-16.9	17.4	-1.1	-
Luton South	-12.9	11.6	-1.6	-
Medway	-15.5	14.3	0.6	-
Middlesbrough S. & Cleveland E.	-10.9	11.4	-3.5	-
Milton Keynes North East	-12.6	15.7	-5.6	-
Milton Keynes South West	-13.1	16.3	-2.6	-
Mitcham & Morden	-16.8	15.3	-1.6	-
Monmouth	-8.0	6.8	-1.4	1.1
Morecambe & Lunesdale	-12.5	19.4	-7.7	-
Newark	-11.0	9.4	-1.5	-
Norfolk North West	-10.6	10.2	-4.2	-
Northampton North	-12.4	14.1	-2.5	-
Northampton South	-14.6	12.2	-3.1	-
Norwich North	-11.7	9.4	-2.0	-
Oldham East & Saddleworth	-15.7	11.5	1.0	-
Peterborough	-14.3	12.5	1.4	-
Plymouth Sutton	-11.5	10.4	-2.6	-
Portsmouth North	-13.1	13.9	-4.5	-
Preseli Pembrokeshire	-11.8	10.2	0.7	-2.3
Pudsey	-7.3	19.0	-12.4	-
Putney	-13.3	9.0	1.2	-
Reading East	-13.9	13.8	-1.9	-
Reading West	-13.4	16.5	-5.1	-
Redditch	-11.0	9.4	-0.7	-
Ribble South	-12.2	12.0	-4.1	-
Romford	-16.5	14.8	-4.5	-
Rugby & Kenilworth	-10.2	11.1	-1.0	-
Scarborough & Whitby	-13.6	15.8	-4.8	-
Selby	-12.1	10.2	-1.0	-
Shipley	-12.6	15.0	-4.9	-
Shrewsbury & Atcham	-11.8	11.0	-2.0	-
Sittingbourne & Sheppey	-12.4	16.6	-8.5	-
St Albans	-12.4	17.0	-6.9	-
Stafford	-8.9	12.6	-5.9	-
Stevenage	-11.1	16.8	-8.2	-
Stirling	-6.7	8.8	-0.5	-1.1

Labour gain from Conservative contd.

	Con %ch 92/97	Lab %ch 92/97	Lib Dem %ch 92/97	Nats %ch 92/97
Stockton South	-12.0	19.7	-10.4	-
Stourbridge	-13.0	8.9	2.5	-
Stroud	-8.3	13.3	-6.1	-
Swindon South	-13.2	16.0	-4.3	-
Tamworth	-12.6	12.6	-1.9	-
Thanet South	-12.0	18.0	-6.6	-
The Wrekin	-7.5	15.0	-6.5	-
Tynemouth	-15.3	13.1	0.7	-
Upminster	-14.7	16.1	-6.3	-
Vale of Clwyd	-13.9	13.9	-3.7	1.1
Vale of Glamorgan	-10.0	9.6	-0.1	0.5
Wansdyke	-11.9	16.8	-6.8	-
Warrington South	-13.2	11.4	0.1	-
Warwick & Leamington	-10.7	13.3	-5.3	-
Watford	-13.3	11.3	0.0	-
Waveney	-12.5	16.2	-3.8	-
Wellingborough	-9.6	10.3	-3.4	-
Welwyn Hatfield	-11.0	11.1	-2.5	-
Wimbledon	-16.4	19.5	-4.7	-
Wirral South	-14.5	16.4	-2.6	-
Wirral West	-13.7	13.9	-1.9	-
Wolverhampton South West	-9.4	10.5	-0.3	-
Worcester	-9.8	10.2	-0.6	-
Wyre Forest	-11.3	17.5	-13.3	-

Liberal Democrat gain from Conservative

	Con %ch 92/97	Lab %ch 92/97	Lib Dem %ch 92/97	Nats %ch 92/97
Aberdeenshire W & Kincardine	-10.2	2.3	6.4	0.6
Brecon & Radnorshire	-7.1	0.4	5.1	0.5
Carshalton & Wallington	-16.2	6.2	7.3	-
Colchester	-10.7	6.5	1.7	-
Cornwall South East	-15.1	3.6	9.0	-
Devon West & Torridge	-8.6	2.9	0.1	-
Eastleigh	-17.2	7.4	5.4	-
Edinburgh West	-10.2	1.4	13.3	-3.7
Gordon	-21.9	4.0	15.4	1.4
Harrogate & Knaresborough	-13.3	-4.8	18.2	-
Hazel Grove	-14.3	0.2	11.4	-
Hereford	-11.7	2.0	6.6	-
Isle of Wight	-13.9	7.2	-2.9	-
Kingston & Surbiton	-16.5	3.4	10.7	-
Lewes	-10.8	2.4	4.1	-
Newbury	-18.1	-0.6	15.8	-
Northavon	-12.8	3.5	7.9	-
Oxford West & Abingdon	-13.6	4.1	7.1	-
Portsmouth South	-11.4	10.7	-2.5	-
Richmond Park	-12.4	3.8	7.0	-
Sheffield Hallam	-16.5	-4.9	20.6	-
Somerton & Frome	-8.1	5.9	-0.8	-
Southport	-11.1	1.9	6.6	-
St Ives	-11.8	-0.8	4.4	-
Sutton & Cheam	-17.3	5.5	8.5	-
Taunton	-7.3	0.8	1.9	-
Torbay	-10.3	5.3	-0.2	-
Twickenham	-11.8	5.2	5.8	-
Weston-Super-Mare	-10.3	6.5	1.6	-
Winchester	-9.6	3.0	5.2	-

SNP gain from Conservative

	Con %ch 92/97	Lab %ch 92/97	Lib Dem %ch 92/97	Nats %ch 92/97
Galloway & Upper Nithsdale	-11.5	3.4	-2.2	7.5
Perth	-11.1	11.6	-3.9	2.0
Tayside North	-10.6	4.3	0.3	6.1

Independent gain from Conservative

	Con %ch 92/97	Lab %ch 92/97	Lib Dem %ch 92/97	Independent %ch 92/97
Tatton	-24.7	-19.0	-18.1	60.2

The Conservatives lost a total of 178 seats. Of these 144 were won by Labour, 30 by the Liberal Democrats, 3 by the SNP and 1 by an Independent.

Labour gain from Liberal Democrat

	Con %ch 92/97	Lab %ch 92/97	Lib Dem %ch 92/97	Nats %ch 92/97
Inverness East, Nairn & Lochaber	-6.0	10.7	-9.2	3.9
Rochdale	-14.4	11.7	2.0	-

UU gain from DUP

	UU %ch 92/97	DUP %ch 92/97	APNI %ch 92/97	SDLP %ch 92/97	SF %ch 92/97
Tyrone West	34.6	-38.8	-2.9	1.1	10.9

UKUP gain from UPUP

	UU %ch 92/97	DUP %ch 92/97	APNI %ch 92/97	SDLP %ch 92/97	SF %ch 92/97
Down North	31.1	-8.4	5.0	4.4	-

Sinn Fein gain from SDLP

	UU %ch 92/97	DUP %ch 92/97	APNI %ch 92/97	SDLP %ch 92/97	SF %ch 92/97
Belfast West	-8.2	-	-5.5	-	13.9

Sinn Fein gain from DUP

	UU %ch 92/97	DUP %ch 92/97	APNI %ch 92/97	SDLP %ch 92/97	SF %ch 92/97
Ulster Mid	-	-4.7	-1.7	-8.5	15.9

Table 4: Candidates Elected at By-elections during 1992/97 Parliament

Candidate	By-election constituency	By-election Date	Gen. Election constituency	Outcome
David Rendel	Newbury	6th May 1993	Newbury	Elected
Diana Maddock	Christchurch	28th July 1993	Christchurch	Defeated
Denis MacShane	Rotherham	5th May 1994	Rotherham	Elected
Margaret Hodge	Barking	9th June 1994	Barking	Elected
David Chidgey	Eastleigh	9th June 1994	Eastleigh	Elected
Judith Church	Dagenham	9th June 1994	Dagenham	Elected
Stephen Timms	Newham N.E.	9th June 1994	East Ham	Elected
Gerry Sutcliffe	Bradford S.	9th June 1994	Bradford S.	Elected
Helen Liddell	Monklands E.	30th June 1994	Airdrie & Shotts	Elected
Ian Pearson	Dudley W.	15th Dec 1994	Dudley S.	Elected
Don Touhig	Islwyn	16th Feb 1995	Islwyn	Elected
Roseanna Cunningham	Perth & Kinross	25th May 1995	Perth	Elected
Robert McCartney	Down North	15th June 1995	Down North	Elected
Chris Davies	Littleborough & Saddleworth	27th July 1995	Oldham E. & Saddleworth	Defeated
Jon Trickett	Hemsworth	1st Feb 1996	Hemsworth	Elected
Brian Jenkins	Staffordshire S.E.	11th April 1996	Tamworth	Elected
Jeff Ennis	Barnsley East	12th Dec 1996	Barnsley E. & Mexborough	Elected
Ben Chapman	Wirral South	27th Feb 1997	Wirral South	Elected

* Two 'old' constituencies - Don Valley and Meriden - were vacant at dissolution.

Table 5: Three-way marginal seats with winning party share 20% or less over third party

	1st	%maj	2nd	%maj	3rd
Tyrone West	UU	2.5	SDLP	3.7	SF
Colchester	LD	3.0	Con	3.8	Lab
Hastings & Rye	Lab	5.2	Con	6.4	LD
Bristol West	Lab	2.4	Con	7.2	LD
Eastleigh	LD	1.4	Con	8.2	Lab
Falmouth & Camborne	Lab	5.0	Con	8.6	LD
Aberdeen South	Lab	7.6	LD	8.9	Con
Tweeddale, Ettrick & Lauderdale	LD	3.8	Lab	9.1	Con
Suffolk South	Con	8.0	Lab	9.6	LD
Conwy	Lab	3.8	LD	10.8	Con
Norfolk North	Con	2.2	LD	11.4	Lab
Perth	Nats	7.1	Con	11.6	Lab
Shrewsbury & Atcham	Lab	3.0	Con	12.0	LD
Bridgwater	Con	3.3	LD	12.2	Lab

	1st	%maj	2nd	%maj	3rd
Caithness, Sutherland & Easter Ross	LD	7.7	Lab	12.6	SNP
Wantage	Con	10.9	Lab	13.3	LD
Kingston & Surbiton	LD	0.1	Con	13.7	Lab
Congleton	Con	11.5	LD	13.7	Lab
Londonderry East	UU	10.0	DUP	13.9	SDLP
Norfolk South	Con	11.9	LD	14.1	Lab
Folkestone & Hythe	Con	12.2	LD	14.2	Lab
Portsmouth South	LD	8.4	Con	14.2	Lab
Brecon & Radnorshire	LD	11.9	Con	14.2	Lab
Chelmsford West	Con	11.4	LD	14.2	Lab
Carshalton & Wallington	LD	4.7	Con	14.3	Lab
Down North	UKU	4.0	UU	14.4	APNI
Canterbury	Con	7.3	Lab	14.9	LD
Gainsborough	Con	14.3	Lab	15.0	LD
Dorset South	Con	0.2	Lab	15.9	LD
Southend West	Con	5.6	LD	16.0	Lab
Leeds North West	Lab	7.8	Con	16.2	LD
Inverness East, Nairn & Lochaber	Lab	4.9	SNP	16.4	LD
Worthing East & Shoreham	Con	9.9	LD	16.5	Lab
Harborough	Con	12.3	LD	16.7	Lab
Cambridgeshire South	Con	16.2	LD	16.9	Lab
Ludlow	Con	12.8	LD	17.0	Lab
Bournemouth West	Con	13.9	LD	17.1	Lab
Suffolk Coastal	Con	5.8	Lab	17.2	LD
Havant	Con	7.7	Lab	17.4	LD
Woking	Con	11.2	LD	17.4	Lab
Cambridgeshire South East	Con	16.5	Lab	17.9	LD
Ulster Mid	SF	3.7	DUP	17.9	SDLP
Ynys Mon	Nats	6.2	Lab	18.0	Con
New Forest East	Con	10.6	LD	18.1	Lab
Aldershot	Con	12.2	LD	18.6	Lab
Devizes	Con	16.3	LD	18.6	Lab
Colne Valley	Lab	8.6	Con	18.7	LD
Belfast East	DUP	17.3	UU	18.8	APNI
Louth & Horncastle	Con	13.8	Lab	19.0	LD
Ross, Skye & Inverness West	LD	10.1	Lab	19.1	SNP
Devon South West	Con	14.0	Lab	19.2	LD
Antrim East	UU	18.6	APNI	19.3	DUP
Westbury	Con	10.7	LD	19.5	Lab
Tewkesbury	Con	17.7	LD	19.5	Lab
Shropshire North	Con	4.3	Lab	19.9	LD

Table 6: Seats in rank order of %majority, vote majority and second party

Conservative seats

		%maj	vote	2nd
1	Dorset South	0.16	77	Lab
2	Bedfordshire South West	0.25	132	Lab
3	Teignbridge	0.45	281	LD
4	Hexham	0.49	222	Lab
5	Lichfield	0.49	238	Lab
6	Bury St Edmunds	0.66	368	Lab
7	Wells	0.94	528	LD
8	Meriden	1.06	582	Lab
9	Dorset Mid & Poole North	1.34	681	LD
10	Boston & Skegness	1.39	647	Lab
11	Totnes	1.63	877	LD
12	Uxbridge	1.74	724	Lab
13	Bosworth	1.97	1027	Lab
14	Chipping Barnet	2.09	1035	Lab
15	Norfolk North	2.20	1293	LD
16	Beverley & Holderness	2.30	1211	Lab
17	Norfolk Mid	2.33	1336	Lab
18	Eddisbury	2.40	1185	Lab
19	Billericay	2.45	1356	Lab
20	Tiverton & Honiton	2.80	1653	LD
21	Altrincham & Sale West	2.91	1505	Lab
22	Bridgwater	3.29	1796	LD
23	Dorset West	3.44	1840	LD
24	Eastbourne	3.79	1994	LD
25	Suffolk West	3.80	1867	Lab
26	Christchurch	3.85	2165	LD
27	Norfolk South West	4.19	2464	Lab
28	Basingstoke	4.20	2397	Lab
29	Shropshire North	4.26	2195	Lab
30	Wycombe	4.53	2370	Lab
31	Surrey South West	4.77	2694	LD
32	Orpington	4.91	2952	LD
33	Grantham & Stamford	5.08	2692	Lab
34	Dorset North	5.22	2746	LD
35	Aldridge - Brownhills	5.45	2526	Lab
36	Southend West	5.62	2615	LD
37	Thanet North	5.65	2766	Lab
38	Suffolk Coastal	5.78	3254	Lab
39	Hertfordshire North East	5.94	3088	Lab
40	Wiltshire North	5.99	3475	LD
41	Cheadle	6.08	3189	LD
42	Hertsmere	6.11	3075	Lab
43	Spelthorne	6.69	3473	Lab
44	Suffolk Central & Ipswich N.	6.70	3538	Lab
45	Yorkshire East	6.81	3337	Lab
46	Old Bexley & Sidcup	6.94	3569	Lab
47	Stone	7.19	3818	Lab
48	Canterbury	7.33	3964	Lab
49	Havant	7.72	3729	Lab
50	Worcestershire West	7.79	3846	LD
51	Suffolk South	8.03	4175	Lab
52	Banbury	8.10	4737	Lab
53	Rushcliffe	8.14	5055	Lab
54	Guildford	8.41	4791	LD
55	Faversham & Kent Mid	8.41	4173	Lab
56	Derbyshire West	8.59	4885	Lab
57	Westmorland & Lonsdale	8.90	4521	LD
58	Rochford & Southend E.	9.08	4225	Lab
59	Beckenham	9.11	4953	Lab
60	Cambridgeshire North E.	9.20	5101	Lab
61	Bromsgrove	9.27	4845	Lab
62	Sleaford & North Hykeham	9.63	5123	Lab
63	Ashford	9.68	5355	Lab
64	Worthing E. & Shoreham	9.89	5098	LD
65	Epping Forest	9.91	5252	Lab
66	Bournemouth East	10.00	4342	LD
67	Ryedale	10.37	5058	LD
68	Charnwood	10.50	5900	Lab
69	New Forest East	10.63	5215	LD
70	Essex North	10.69	5476	Lab
71	Westbury	10.73	6088	LD
72	Salisbury	10.78	6276	LD
73	Wantage	10.86	6089	Lab
74	Woking	11.15	5678	LD
75	Poole	11.32	5298	LD
76	Chelmsford West	11.42	6691	LD
77	Congleton	11.48	6130	LD
78	Ribble Valley	11.60	6640	LD
79	Bedfordshire N. E.	11.68	5883	Lab
80	Norfolk South	11.88	7378	LD
81	Daventry	11.95	7378	Lab
82	Blaby	12.08	6474	Lab
83	Cities of London & Westminster	12.16	4881	Lab
84	Folkestone & Hythe	12.17	6332	LD
85	Aldershot	12.23	6621	LD
86	Harborough	12.31	6524	LD
87	Witney	12.46	7028	Lab
88	Hertford & Stortford	12.62	6885	Lab
89	Hitchin & Harpenden	12.72	6671	Lab
90	Ludlow	12.77	5909	LD

91	Sussex Mid	12.82	6854	LD
92	Chingford & Woodford Green	12.86	5714	Lab
93	Gosport	12.94	6258	Lab
94	Bedfordshire Mid	13.50	7090	Lab
95	Louth & Horncastle	13.81	6900	Lab
96	Bournemouth West	13.90	5710	LD
97	Devon South West	14.01	7397	Lab
98	Woodspring	14.07	7734	LD
99	Broxbourne	14.16	6653	Lab
100	Devon East	14.26	7494	LD
101	Gainsborough	14.28	6826	Lab
102	Aylesbury	14.63	8419	LD
103	Worthing West	14.99	7713	LD
104	Haltemprice & Howden	15.16	7514	LD
105	Staffordshire South	15.30	7821	Lab
106	Tunbridge Wells	15.52	7506	LD
107	Bognor Regis & Littlehampton	15.76	7321	Lab
108	Cambridgeshire N. W.	15.88	7754	Lab
109	South Holland & The Deepings	15.94	7991	Lab
110	Macclesfield	15.97	8654	Lab
111	Reigate	16.07	7741	Lab
112	Cambridgeshire South	16.23	8712	LD
113	Devizes	16.29	9782	LD
114	Cambridgeshire S. E.	16.46	9349	Lab
115	Romsey	16.57	8585	LD
116	Rutland & Melton	16.79	8836	Lab
117	Fylde	17.21	8963	Lab
118	Ruislip Northwood	17.38	7794	Lab
119	Chichester	17.45	9734	LD
120	Leominster	17.48	8835	LD
121	Bracknell	17.58	10387	Lab
122	Tewkesbury	17.71	9234	LD
123	Maidstone & The Weald	17.91	9603	Lab
124	Hertfordshire S. W.	18.08	10021	Lab
125	Vale of York	18.25	9721	Lab
126	Worcestershire Mid	18.52	9412	Lab
127	Saffron Walden	18.53	10573	LD
128	Wokingham	18.69	9365	LD
129	Mole Valley	18.75	10221	LD
130	Brentwood & Ongar	19.10	9690	LD
131	Runnymede & Weybridge	19.15	9875	Lab
132	Solihull	19.35	11397	LD
133	Windsor	19.53	9917	LD
134	Fareham	19.85	10358	Lab
135	Maldon & Chelmsford E.	19.92	10039	Lab
136	Hampshire East	19.94	11590	LD
137	Tonbridge & Malling	20.78	10230	Lab
138	Rayleigh	20.82	10684	Lab
139	Sevenoaks	20.86	10461	Lab
140	Penrith & The Border	20.90	10233	LD
141	Richmond (Yorks)	21.05	10051	Lab
142	Bromley & Chislehurst	21.08	11118	Lab
143	Hampshire North W.	21.13	11551	LD
144	Epsom & Ewell	21.27	11525	Lab
145	Skipton & Ripon	21.38	11620	LD
146	Henley	21.67	11167	LD
147	Croydon South	22.01	11930	Lab
148	Bexhill & Battle	22.66	11100	LD
149	Stratford-on-Avon	22.72	14106	LD
150	New Forest West	22.78	11332	LD
151	Cotswold	23.41	11965	LD
152	Maidenhead	23.54	11981	LD
153	Wealden	24.03	14204	LD
154	Buckingham	25.07	12386	Lab
155	Kensington & Chelsea	25.67	9519	Lab
156	Horsham	26.00	14862	LD
157	Chesham & Amersham	26.55	13859	LD
158	Esher & Walton	27.07	14528	Lab
159	Arundel & South Downs	27.34	14035	LD
160	Surrey East	27.61	15093	LD
161	Beaconsfield	27.86	13987	LD
162	Hampshire North E.	28.17	14398	LD
163	Sutton Coldfield	28.41	14885	Lab
164	Surrey Heath	29.76	16287	LD
165	Huntingdon	31.85	18140	Lab

Labour seats

		%maj	vote	2nd
1	Kettering	0.33	189	Con
2	Wellingborough	0.33	187	Con
3	Milton Keynes North E.	0.47	240	Con
4	Rugby & Kenilworth	0.81	495	Con
5	Northampton South	1.30	744	Con
6	Romford	1.54	649	Con
7	Lancaster & Wyre	2.20	1295	Con
8	Harwich	2.27	1216	Con
9	Norfolk North West	2.32	1339	Con
10	Castle Point	2.35	1143	Con
11	Harrow West	2.36	1240	Con
12	Bristol West	2.38	1493	Con
13	Braintree	2.61	1451	Con
14	Shrewsbury & Atcham	3.02	1670	Con
15	Enfield Southgate	3.08	1433	Con
16	Conwy	3.84	1596	LD
17	Gillingham	3.91	1980	Con
18	Sittingbourne & Sheppey	4.18	1929	Con
19	Clwyd West	4.59	1848	Con
20	Stroud	4.74	2910	Con
21	Inverness East, Nairn & Lochaber	4.90	2339	SNP
22	Falmouth & Camborne	5.01	2688	Con

23	Hastings & Rye	5.22	2560	Con
24	Warwick & Leamington	5.65	3398	Con
25	Shipley	5.67	2996	Con
26	Chatham & Aylesford	5.68	2790	Con
27	Newark	5.80	3016	Con
28	Wirral West	5.84	2738	Con
29	Wimbledon	6.18	2990	Con
30	Eastwood	6.19	3236	Con
31	Reading West	6.19	2997	Con
32	Oldham East & Saddleworth	6.26	3389	LD
33	Finchley & Golders Green	6.34	3189	Con
34	Thanet South	6.40	2878	Con
35	Ilford North	6.60	3224	Con
36	Hemel Hempstead	6.60	3636	Con
37	The Wrekin	6.68	3025	Con
38	Upminster	6.70	2770	Con
39	Putney	6.76	2976	Con
40	Selby	6.81	3836	Con
41	Croydon Central	6.98	3897	Con
42	Bexleyheath & Crayford	7.08	3415	Con
43	Hammersmith & Fulham	7.11	3842	Con
44	Gedling	7.29	3802	Con
45	Reading East	7.56	3795	Con
46	Aberdeen South	7.64	3365	LD
47	Brighton Kemptown	7.66	3534	Con
48	Leeds North West	7.79	3844	Con
49	Hove	8.23	3959	Con
50	Carmarthen East & Dinefwr	8.27	3450	PC
51	Dartford	8.32	4328	Con
52	Stafford	8.33	4314	Con
53	Bradford West	8.51	3877	Con
54	Monmouth	8.52	4178	Con
55	Colne Valley	8.58	4840	Con
56	Wansdyke	8.77	4799	Con
57	St Albans	8.78	4459	Con
58	Glasgow Govan	9.04	2914	SNP
59	Ribble South	9.20	5084	Con
60	Scarborough & Whitby	9.43	5124	Con
61	Rochdale	9.45	4545	LD
62	Portsmouth North	9.55	4323	Con
63	Broxtowe	9.59	5575	Con
64	Birmingham Edgbaston	9.99	4842	Con
65	Wolverhampton S. W.	10.46	5118	Con
66	Watford	10.49	5792	Con
67	Brent North	10.53	4019	Con
68	Welwyn Hatfield	10.56	5595	Con
69	Ochil	10.62	4652	SNP
70	Edinburgh Pentlands	10.63	4862	Con
71	Gravesham	10.85	5779	Con
72	Loughborough	10.91	5712	Con
73	Swindon South	11.03	5645	Con
74	Calder Valley	11.08	6255	Con
75	Chesterfield	11.24	5775	LD
76	Battersea	11.31	5360	Con
77	Stourbridge	11.36	5645	Con
78	Burton	11.61	6330	Con
79	Pudsey	11.77	6207	Con
80	Medway	11.97	5354	Con
81	Morecambe & Lunesdale	12.11	5965	Con
82	Hendon	12.30	6155	Con
83	Wyre Forest	12.62	6946	Con
84	Forest of Dean	12.64	6343	Con
85	Hornchurch	12.93	5680	Con
86	Batley & Spen	13.08	6141	Con
87	Brigg & Goole	13.65	6389	Con
88	Redditch	13.69	6125	Con
89	Keighley	13.85	7132	Con
90	Birmingham Yardley	14.07	5315	LD
91	Gloucester	14.26	8259	Con
92	Bury North	14.29	7866	Con
93	Enfield North	14.31	6822	Con
94	Worcester	14.38	7425	Con
95	Bolton West	14.39	7072	Con
96	Wirral South	14.56	7004	Con
97	Ayr	14.62	6543	Con
98	Stirling	14.92	6411	Con
99	Tamworth	15.04	7496	Con
100	Peterborough	15.12	7323	Con
101	Erewash	15.14	9135	Con
102	Leeds North East	15.29	6959	Con
103	Kilmarnock & Loudoun	15.31	7256	SNP
104	High Peak	15.38	8791	Con
105	Swindon North	15.93	7688	Con
106	Elmet	16.23	8779	Con
107	Crosby	16.27	7182	Con
108	Ealing North	16.44	9160	Con
109	Blackpool N. & Fleetwood	16.64	8946	Con
110	Cardiff North	16.76	8126	Con
111	Bedford	16.96	8300	Con
112	Harrow East	17.08	9734	Con
113	Chorley	17.10	9870	Con
114	Norwich North	17.20	9470	Con
115	Great Yarmouth	17.73	8668	Con
116	Cleethorpes	18.18	9176	Con
117	Cardiff Central	18.75	7923	LD
118	City of Chester	18.76	10553	Con
119	Derby North	18.91	10615	Con
120	Exeter	18.92	11705	Con
121	Dewsbury	19.32	8323	Con
122	Northampton North	19.34	10000	Con
123	Dumfries	19.47	9643	Con
124	Vale of Glamorgan	19.53	10532	Con

125	Warrington South	19.62	10807	Con	176	Edinburgh North & Leith	26.81	10978	SNP
126	Staffordshire Moorlands	19.66	10049	Con	177	Cunninghame North	26.84	11039	Con
127	Dudley North	19.78	9457	Con	178	Brighton Pavilion	26.93	13181	Con
128	Middlesbrough S. & Cleveland E.	19.79	10607	Con	179	Dudley South	27.20	13027	Con
129	Plymouth Sutton	19.81	9440	Con	180	Warwickshire North	27.23	14767	Con
130	Renfrewshire West	20.05	7979	SNP	181	Linlithgow	27.33	10838	SNP
131	Birmingham Hall Green	20.13	8420	Con	182	Slough	27.38	13071	Con
132	Milton Keynes S. W.	20.28	10292	Con	183	Livingston	27.42	11747	SNP
133	Luton North	20.34	9626	Con	184	Cambridge	27.54	14137	Con
134	Preseli Pembrokeshire	20.60	8736	Con	185	Nottingham South	27.54	13364	Con
135	Bristol North West	20.60	11382	Con	186	Cannock Chase	27.65	14478	Con
136	Halesowen & Rowley Regis	21.20	10337	Con	187	Weaver Vale	27.84	13448	Con
137	Amber Valley	21.20	11613	Con	188	Birmingham Selly Oak	27.87	14088	Con
138	Rossendale & Darwen	21.38	10949	Con	189	Midlothian	28.00	9870	SNP
139	Waveney	21.50	12093	Con	190	Stretford & Urmston	28.01	13640	Con
140	Ipswich	21.58	10436	Con	191	Norwich South	28.03	14239	Con
141	Dover	21.66	11739	Con	192	Ilford South	28.39	14200	Con
142	Coventry South	21.85	10953	Con	193	Carlisle	28.41	12390	Con
143	Corby	21.98	11860	Con	194	Mitcham & Morden	28.66	13741	Con
144	Harlow	21.99	10514	Con	195	Bradford South	28.71	12936	Con
145	Tynemouth	22.04	11273	Con	196	Wakefield	28.93	14604	Con
146	Halifax	22.18	11212	Con	197	Copeland	28.98	11996	Con
147	Western Isles	22.20	3576	SNP	198	Walsall North	29.07	12588	Con
148	Stockton South	22.23	11585	Con	199	Birmingham Northfield	29.46	11443	Con
149	Stevenage	22.54	11582	Con	200	Glasgow Kelvin	29.60	9665	SNP
150	Carmarthen W. & P'brokeshire S.	22.56	9621	Con	201	Sherwood	29.74	16812	Con
151	Blackpool South	22.63	11616	Con	202	Gower	30.01	13007	Con
152	Vale of Clwyd	22.88	8955	Con	203	Edmonton	30.05	13472	Con
153	Pendle	23.01	10824	Con	204	Barrow & Furness	30.06	14497	Con
154	Crawley	23.22	11707	Con	205	Hampstead & Highgate	30.17	13284	Con
155	Derbyshire South	23.29	13967	Con	206	Aberdeen Central	30.33	10801	Con
156	Eltham	23.45	10182	Con	207	Clydesdale	30.41	13809	SNP
157	Luton South	23.49	11319	Con	208	Telford	30.42	11290	Con
158	Hyndburn	23.72	11448	Con	209	Blackburn	30.43	14451	Con
159	Kingswood	23.80	14253	Con	210	Bradford North	30.48	12770	Con
160	Lincoln	23.91	11130	Con	211	Ellesmere Port & Neston	30.51	16035	Con
161	Bury South	24.58	12381	Con	212	Dundee West	30.56	11859	SNP
162	Dundee East	24.58	9961	SNP	213	Coventry North West	30.56	16601	Con
163	Basildon	25.02	13280	Con	214	Kirkcaldy	30.62	10710	SNP
164	Bethnal Green & Bow	25.26	11285	Con	215	Cumbernauld & Kilsyth	30.89	11128	SNP
165	Nuneaton	25.30	13540	Con	216	Regent's Park & Kensington N.	30.96	14657	Con
166	Leicestershire N. W.	25.41	13219	Con	217	Sheffield Hillsborough	31.03	16451	LD
167	Edinburgh South	25.54	11452	Con	218	Derby South	31.08	16106	Con
168	Brentford & Isleworth	25.70	14424	Con	219	Delyn	31.15	12693	Con
169	Bolton North East	25.75	12669	Con	220	Crewe & Nantwich	31.22	15798	Con
170	Edinburgh Central	25.90	11070	Con	221	Lancashire West	31.28	17119	Con
171	Aberdeen North	26.06	10010	SNP	222	Birmingham Erdington	31.32	12657	Con
172	Southampton Test	26.09	13684	Con	223	Wolverhampton N. E.	31.37	12987	Con
173	Walsall South	26.16	11312	Con	224	Leicester West	31.44	12864	Con
174	Dumbarton	26.37	10883	SNP	225	Morley & Rothwell	32.14	14750	Con
175	Southampton Itchen	26.43	14229	Con	226	Falkirk East	32.18	13385	SNP

227	Wrexham	32.29 11762 Con
228	Lewisham East	32.42 12127 Con
229	Tooting	32.56 15011 Con
230	Ealing Acton & Shepherd's Bush	32.56 15650 Con
231	Cardiff South & Penarth	32.68 13861 Con
232	West Bromwich East	32.74 13584 Con
233	East Lothian	32.74 14221 Con
234	Feltham & Heston	32.76 15273 Con
235	Strathkelvin & Bearsden	32.77 16292 Con
236	Wythenshawe & Sale E.	32.98 15019 Con
237	Darlington	33.27 16025 Con
238	Bristol East	33.52 16159 Con
239	Fife Central	33.64 13713 SNP
240	Don Valley	33.65 14659 Con
241	Dunfermline West	33.91 12354 SNP
242	Clydebank & Milngavie	34.08 13320 SNP
243	Scunthorpe	34.09 14173 Con
244	Paisley South	34.14 12750 SNP
245	Leicester South	34.28 16493 Con
246	Stalybridge & Hyde	34.37 14806 Con
247	Edinburgh E. & Musselburgh	34.50 14530 SNP
248	Heywood & Middleton	34.70 17542 Con
249	Hayes & Harlington	34.78 14291 Con
250	Oxford East	34.81 16665 Con
251	Motherwell & Wishaw	34.93 12791 SNP
252	Croydon North	35.00 18398 Con
253	Newcastle-under-Lyme	35.02 17206 Con
254	Clwyd South	35.07 13810 Con
255	York	35.18 20523 Con
256	Bridgend	35.25 15248 Con
257	Derbyshire North E.	35.25 18321 Con
258	Oldham West & Royton	35.42 16201 Con
259	Huddersfield	35.57 15848 Con
260	East Kilbride	35.63 17384 SNP
261	Swansea West	35.73 14459 Con
262	Newcastle upon Tyne Central	35.76 16480 Con
263	Falkirk West	35.92 13783 SNP
264	Bassetlaw	36.14 17348 Con
265	Blaydon	36.16 16605 LD
266	Newport West	36.16 14537 Con
267	Newport East	36.30 13523 Con
268	Thurrock	36.55 17256 Con
269	Plymouth Devonport	36.69 19067 Con
270	Dulwich & West Norwood	36.76 16769 Con
271	Normanton	36.96 15893 Con
272	Airdrie & Shotts	37.43 15412 SNP
273	Paisley North	37.54 12814 SNP
274	Greenock & Inverclyde	37.59 13040 SNP
275	Great Grimsby	37.69 16244 Con
276	Burnley	37.71 17062 Con
277	Worsley	37.92 17741 Con

278	Warrington North	38.10 19527 Con
279	Lewisham West	38.11 14317 Con
280	Leyton & Wanstead	38.62 15186 Con
281	Bristol South	38.77 19328 Con
282	Nottingham East	38.80 15419 Con
283	Cardiff West	38.80 15628 Con
284	Glasgow Cathcart	38.83 12965 SNP
285	Preston	38.86 18680 Con
286	Llanelli	38.92 16039 PC
287	Alyn & Deeside	39.10 16403 Con
288	Ealing Southall	39.21 21423 Con
289	Hartlepool	39.39 17508 Con
290	Sheffield Heeley	39.47 17078 LD
291	Stoke-on-Trent S.	39.59 18303 Con
292	Warley	39.73 15451 Con
293	Workington	39.81 19656 Con
294	Hornsey & Wood Green	39.81 20499 Con
295	Hull West & Hessle	40.48 15525 LD
296	Stockport	40.52 18912 Con
297	Wallasey	40.72 19074 Con
298	Barnsley West & Penistone	40.91 17267 Con
299	Streatham	41.04 18423 Con
300	Doncaster Central	41.10 17856 Con
301	Islington South & Finsbury	41.24 14563 LD
302	Birmingham Perry Barr	41.31 18957 Con
303	Leicester East	41.49 18422 Con
304	Birmingham Hodge Hill	41.58 14200 Con
305	Blyth Valley	41.75 17736 LD
306	Erith & Thamesmead	41.90 17424 Con
307	Cunninghame South	41.95 14869 SNP
308	Glasgow Pollok	42.04 13791 SNP
309	Manchester Withington	42.20 18581 Con
310	Glasgow Rutherglen	42.25 15007 SNP
311	Liverpool Garston	42.36 18417 LD
312	Newcastle upon Tyne N.	42.74 19332 Con
313	Walthamstow	42.81 17149 Con
314	Carrick, Cumnock & Doon Valley	42.83 21062 Con
315	Liverpool Wavertree	42.90 19701 LD
316	Mansfield	43.26 20518 Con
317	Wolverhampton S. E.	43.59 15182 Con
318	Denton & Reddish	44.07 20311 Con
319	Redcar	44.25 21667 Con
320	Hackney South & Shoreditch	44.40 14990 LD
321	Glasgow Anniesland	44.73 15154 SNP
322	Greenwich & Woolwich	44.87 18128 Con
323	Ashfield	44.91 22728 Con
324	Hamilton North & Bellshill	44.91 17067 SNP
325	Stoke-on-Trent N.	44.98 17392 Con
326	Brent East	45.03 15882 Con
327	Nottingham North	45.41 18801 Con
328	Bishop Auckland	45.74 21064 Con

329	City of Durham	45.80	22504	Con			
330	Sheffield Central	46.42	16906	LD			
331	Glasgow Baillieston	46.59	14840	SNP			
332	Birm'ham Sparkbrook & Small Heath	46.75	19526	Con			
333	Coventry North East	46.94	22569	Con			
334	Holborn & St Pancras	47.11	17903	Con			
335	Dagenham	47.16	17054	Con			
336	St Helens North	47.57	23417	Con			
337	Manchester Gorton	47.76	17342	LD			
338	Vauxhall	47.77	18660	LD			
339	Eccles	47.97	21916	Con			
340	Hamilton South	47.98	15878	SNP			
341	Glasgow Maryhill	47.99	14264	SNP			
342	Stockton North	48.02	21357	Con			
343	Poplar & Canning Town	48.17	18915	Con			
344	Barking	48.22	15896	Con			
345	Hackney N. & Stoke Newington	48.26	15627	Con			
346	East Ham	48.53	19358	Con			
347	Ashton under Lyne	48.57	22965	Con			
348	Leeds East	48.80	17466	Con			
349	Leeds West	49.16	19771	Con			
350	Bolton South East	49.16	21311	Con			
351	Sunderland South	49.19	19638	Con			
352	Sheffield Attercliffe	49.23	21818	Con			
353	Stoke-on-Trent C.	49.51	19924	Con			
354	Wansbeck	49.52	22367	LD			
355	Jarrow	49.91	21933	Con			
356	Pontypridd	50.44	23129	LD			
357	Hull North	50.79	19705	Con			
358	Rother Valley	50.88	23485	Con			
359	Dunfermline East	51.26	18751	SNP			
360	Coatbridge & Chryston	51.30	19292	SNP			
361	Salford	51.53	17069	Con			
362	Sunderland North	51.55	19697	Con			
363	Wigan	51.67	22643	Con			
364	Knowsley N. & Sefton E.	52.61	26147	Con			
365	Hemsworth	52.76	23992	Con			
366	Halton	53.22	23650	Con			
367	Leigh	53.34	24496	Con			
368	Sedgefield	53.36	25143	Con			
369	Durham North West	53.44	24754	Con			
370	Tottenham	53.58	20200	Con			
371	St Helens South	53.64	23739	Con			
372	Middlesbrough	54.27	25018	Con			
373	Manchester Blackley	54.78	19588	Con			
374	Glasgow Springburn	54.87	17326	SNP			
375	Doncaster North	55.00	21937	Con			
376	Birkenhead	55.55	21843	Con			
377	Islington North	55.65	19955	LD			
378	Durham North	55.76	26299	Con			
379	Leeds Central	55.90	20689	Con			
380	Lewisham Deptford	56.11	18878	Con
381	Torfaen	56.74	24536	Con
382	South Shields	56.83	22153	Con
383	Rotherham	57.02	21469	Con
384	Brent South	57.08	19691	Con
385	Caerphilly	57.08	25839	Con
386	Liverpool Riverside	57.16	21799	LD
387	Newcastle upon Tyne E. & Wallsend	57.25	23811	Con
388	Bolsover	57.26	27149	Con
389	Wentworth	57.34	23959	Con
390	Hull East	57.60	23318	Con
391	West Ham	57.91	19494	Con
392	Gateshead E. & Washington W.	57.91	24950	Con
393	Camberwell & Peckham	57.98	16451	Con
394	Makerfield	58.15	26177	Con
395	Manchester Central	58.69	19682	LD
396	Sheffield Brightside	58.92	19954	LD
397	Tyneside North	59.05	26643	Con
398	Cynon Valley	59.11	19755	PC
399	Glasgow Shettleston	59.18	15868	SNP
400	Aberavon	59.98	21571	LD
401	Birmingham Ladywood	60.78	23082	Con
402	Rhondda	61.09	24931	PC
403	Barnsley E. & Mexborough	61.76	26763	Con
404	Liverpool West Derby	62.14	26197	LD
405	Pontefract & Castleford	62.14	25725	Con
406	Houghton & Washington E.	63.49	26555	Con
407	Ogmore	64.22	24447	Con
408	Knowsley South	64.53	30708	Con
409	Neath	64.84	26741	Con
410	Tyne Bridge	65.73	22906	Con
411	Islwyn	65.74	23931	LD
412	Swansea East	66.11	25569	Con
413	Barnsley Central	67.15	24501	Con
414	Liverpool Walton	67.25	27038	LD
415	Merthyr Tydfil & Rhymney	69.20	27086	LD
416	Blaenau Gwent	70.74	28035	LD
417	Easington	71.64	30012	Con
418	Bootle	74.36	28421	Con

Liberal Democrat seats

		%maj	vote	2nd
1	Winchester	0.00	2	Con
2	Torbay	0.02	12	Con
3	Kingston & Surbiton	0.10	56	Con
4	Somerton & Frome	0.23	130	Con
5	Eastleigh	1.36	754	Con
6	Weston-Super-Mare	2.39	1274	Con
7	Lewes	2.64	1300	Con
8	Colchester	3.04	1581	Con
9	Devon West & Torridge	3.31	1957	Con
10	Northavon	3.42	2137	Con
11	Tweeddale, Ettrick & Lauderdale	3.82	1489	Lab
12	Taunton	4.00	2443	Con
13	Sutton & Cheam	4.45	2097	Con
14	Carshalton & Wallington	4.68	2267	Con
15	Richmond Park	5.19	2951	Con
16	Aberdeenshire W & Kincardine	6.16	2662	Con
17	Twickenham	7.36	4281	Con
18	Caithness, Sutherland & Easter Ross	7.74	2259	Lab
19	Southwark N. & Bermondsey	8.30	3387	Lab
20	Portsmouth South	8.37	4327	Con
21	Isle of Wight	8.76	6406	Con
22	Ross, Skye & Inverness W.	10.06	4019	Lab
23	Oxford West & Abingdon	10.27	6285	Con
24	Devon North	11.28	6181	Con
25	Cornwall South East	11.28	6480	Con
26	Brecon & Radnorshire	11.89	5097	Con
27	Southport	12.17	6160	Con
28	Hereford	12.65	6648	Con
29	Harrogate & Knaresborough	13.09	6236	Con
30	Cheltenham	13.21	6645	Con
31	St Ives	13.30	7170	Con
32	Newbury	15.08	8517	Con
33	Edinburgh West	15.23	7253	Con
34	Gordon	16.56	6997	Con
35	Argyll & Bute	17.02	6081	SNP
36	Bath	17.26	9319	Con
37	Sheffield Hallam	18.19	8271	Con
38	Berwick-upon-Tweed	19.24	8042	Lab
39	Montgomeryshire	19.74	6303	Con
40	Yeovil	21.10	11403	Con
41	Truro & St Austell	22.03	12501	Con
42	Roxburgh & Berwickshire	22.63	7906	Con
43	Cornwall North	23.67	13847	Con
44	Hazel Grove	23.94	11814	Con
45	Fife North East	24.75	10356	Con
46	Orkney & Shetland	33.72	6968	Lab

Scottish Nationalist seats

		%maj	vote	2nd
1	Perth	7.05	3141	Con
2	Tayside North	9.12	4160	Con
3	Galloway & Upper Nithsdale	13.38	5624	Con
4	Moray	14.00	5566	Con
5	Angus	23.65	10189	Con
6	Banff & Buchan	31.97	12845	Con

Plaid Cymru seats

		%maj	vote	2nd
1	Ynys Mon	6.21	2481	Lab
2	Ceredigion	17.32	6961	Lab
3	Caernarfon	21.59	7449	Lab
4	Meirionnydd Nant Conwy	27.69	6805	Lab

Independent seat

		%maj	vote	2nd
1	Tatton	22.70	11077	Con

Ulster Unionist seats

		%maj	vote	2nd
1	Tyrone West	2.51	1161	SDLP
2	Londonderry East	9.96	3794	DUP
3	Belfast South	11.65	4600	SDLP
4	Strangford	14.06	5852	DUP
5	Antrim East	18.60	6389	APNI
6	Upper Bann	19.36	9252	SDLP
7	Fermanagh & South Tyrone	28.35	13688	SF
8	Belfast North	31.42	13024	SDLP
9	Lagan Valley	38.20	16925	APNI
10	Antrim South	41.33	16611	SDLP

Democratic Unionist seats

		%maj	vote	2nd
1	Belfast East	17.31	6754	UU
2	Antrim North	22.89	10574	UU

SDLP seats

		%maj	vote	2nd
1	Newry and Armagh	9.18	4889	UU
2	Down South	20.07	9933	UU
3	Foyle	28.58	13664	SF

Sinn Fein seats

		%maj	vote	2nd
1	Ulster Mid	3.72	1883	DUP
2	Belfast West	17.24	7909	SDLP

UKU seat

		%maj	vote	2nd
1	Down North	3.96	1449	UU

	Table 7: Conservative change of vote share 1992/97 and winning party		
		%ch	lst
1	Bethnal Green & Bow	4.66	Lab
2	Greenwich & Woolwich	0.34	Lab
3	Bradford West	-0.76	Lab
4	Linlithgow	-1.19	Lab
5	Liverpool Riverside	-1.35	Lab
6	Liverpool Wavertree	-1.72	Lab
7	Western Isles	-1.85	Lab
8	Glasgow Pollok	-2.14	Lab
9	Glasgow Baillieston	-2.15	Lab
10	Blyth Valley	-2.29	Lab
11	Glasgow Kelvin	-2.32	Lab
12	Dundee East	-2.65	Lab
13	Blaenau Gwent	-3.23	Lab
14	Aberdeen North	-3.63	Lab
15	Glasgow Maryhill	-3.76	Lab
16	Rhondda	-4.01	Lab
17	Glasgow Anniesland	-4.19	Lab
18	Cumbernauld & Kilsyth	-4.50	Lab
19	Motherwell & Wishaw	-4.62	Lab
20	Ayr	-4.63	Lab
21	Merthyr Tydfil & Rhymney	-4.66	Lab
22	Huntingdon	-4.72	Con
23	Hamilton North & Bellshill	-4.84	Lab
24	Glasgow Springburn	-4.87	Lab
25	Llanelli	-4.89	Lab
26	Sheffield Hillsborough	-4.96	Lab
27	Southwark North & Bermondsey	-5.04	LD
28	Ogmore	-5.35	Lab
29	Forest of Dean	-5.46	Lab
30	Bootle	-5.62	Lab
31	Dundee West	-5.69	Lab
32	Telford	-5.89	Lab
33	Ribble Valley	-5.91	Con
34	Liverpool West Derby	-5.94	Lab
35	Barnsley East & Mexborough	-5.95	Lab
36	Airdrie & Shotts	-5.99	Lab
37	Inverness East, Nairn & Lochaber	-5.99	Lab
38	Aberavon	-6.01	Lab
39	Cynon Valley	-6.11	Lab
40	Paisley North	-6.11	Lab
41	Staffordshire Moorlands	-6.11	Lab
42	City of Durham	-6.17	Lab
43	Liverpool Walton	-6.17	Lab
44	Falkirk East	-6.22	Lab
45	Cunninghame South	-6.25	Lab
46	Devon North	-6.25	LD
47	Dunfermline East	-6.30	Lab
48	Macclesfield	-6.39	Con
49	Neath	-6.56	Lab
50	Bradford North	-6.58	Lab
51	Montgomeryshire	-6.60	LD
52	East Kilbride	-6.63	Lab
53	Stirling	-6.66	Lab
54	Midlothian	-6.66	Lab
55	Glasgow Shettleston	-6.69	Lab
56	Paisley South	-6.70	Lab
57	Falkirk West	-6.76	Lab
58	Sheffield Central	-6.78	Lab
59	Wentworth	-6.83	Lab
60	Caernarfon	-6.92	PC
61	Bromsgrove	-6.95	Con
62	Coatbridge & Chryston	-6.97	Lab
63	Edinburgh North & Leith	-6.98	Lab
64	Islwyn	-6.99	Lab
65	Swindon North	-7.06	Lab
66	Clydesdale	-7.10	Lab
67	Birmingham Ladywood	-7.11	Lab
68	Brecon & Radnorshire	-7.13	LD
69	Clwyd South	-7.16	Lab
70	Weaver Vale	-7.16	Lab
71	Aldridge - Brownhills	-7.18	Con
72	Congleton	-7.26	Con
73	Taunton	-7.32	LD
74	Pudsey	-7.34	Lab
75	Pontefract & Castleford	-7.37	Lab
76	Pontypridd	-7.41	Lab
77	Caerphilly	-7.42	Lab
78	Hamilton South	-7.45	Lab
79	Doncaster North	-7.50	Lab
80	The Wrekin	-7.54	Lab
81	Worcestershire Mid	-7.54	Con
82	Bury St Edmunds	-7.57	Con
83	Manchester Central	-7.59	Lab
84	Chesterfield	-7.67	Lab
85	South Holland & The Deepings	-7.76	Con
86	Manchester Gorton	-7.76	Lab
87	Edinburgh Pentlands	-7.81	Lab
88	Worsley	-7.88	Lab
89	Cheltenham	-7.92	LD
90	Knowsley South	-7.93	Lab
91	Swansea East	-7.95	Lab
92	Yorkshire East	-7.95	Con
93	Torfaen	-7.96	Lab
94	Hemsworth	-7.98	Lab
95	Cotswold	-8.03	Con
96	Monmouth	-8.04	Lab
97	Falmouth & Camborne	-8.05	Lab
98	Tewkesbury	-8.06	Con
99	Windsor	-8.08	Con

100	Birmingham Sparkbrook & Small Heath	-8.09	Lab
101	Newcastle-under-Lyme	-8.11	Lab
102	Somerton & Frome	-8.11	LD
103	Easington	-8.15	Lab
104	Edinburgh Central	-8.16	Lab
105	Kilmarnock & Loudoun	-8.22	Lab
106	Carmarthen East & Dinefwr	-8.27	Lab
107	Batley & Spen	-8.30	Lab
108	Stroud	-8.33	Lab
109	Sheffield Brightside	-8.35	Lab
110	Boston & Skegness	-8.39	Con
111	Wigan	-8.43	Lab
112	Kirkcaldy	-8.43	Lab
113	Fife Central	-8.45	Lab
114	Jarrow	-8.50	Lab
115	Hull North	-8.55	Lab
116	Wrexham	-8.56	Lab
117	Heywood & Middleton	-8.57	Lab
118	Tweeddale, Ettrick & Lauderdale	-8.57	LD
119	Bolsover	-8.58	Lab
120	Newcastle upon Tyne E. & Wallsend	-8.59	Lab
121	Devon West & Torridge	-8.59	LD
122	Edinburgh East & Musselburgh	-8.62	Lab
123	Leeds West	-8.63	Lab
124	Leeds Central	-8.65	Lab
125	Leyton & Wanstead	-8.66	Lab
126	Barnsley Central	-8.69	Lab
127	Carrick, Cumnock & Doon Valley	-8.71	Lab
128	Coventry North East	-8.71	Lab
129	Livingston	-8.71	Lab
130	Berwick-upon-Tweed	-8.71	LD
131	Argyll & Bute	-8.76	LD
132	Glasgow Cathcart	-8.81	Lab
133	Burton	-8.82	Lab
134	Houghton & Washington East	-8.83	Lab
135	Stafford	-8.88	Lab
136	Woodspring	-8.89	Con
137	Carmarthen W. & Pembrokeshire S.	-8.92	Lab
138	Clydebank & Milngavie	-8.95	Lab
139	Bolton South East	-8.97	Lab
140	Birmingham Erdington	-8.99	Lab
141	Makerfield	-9.00	Lab
142	Salford	-9.04	Lab
143	Salisbury	-9.06	Con
144	Ceredigion	-9.08	PC
145	Loughborough	-9.09	Lab
146	Staffordshire South	-9.15	Con
147	Devon East	-9.16	Con
148	Stone	-9.16	Con
149	Ludlow	-9.20	Con
150	Renfrewshire West	-9.21	Lab
151	Louth & Horncastle	-9.27	Con
152	Yeovil	-9.28	LD
153	Aberdeen Central	-9.29	Lab
154	Colne Valley	-9.30	Lab
155	Liverpool Garston	-9.33	Lab
156	Wolverhampton South West	-9.36	Lab
157	Ochil	-9.40	Lab
158	Dorset Mid & Poole North	-9.43	Con
159	Rotherham	-9.45	Lab
160	Bristol North West	-9.45	Lab
161	Conwy	-9.46	Lab
162	Knowsley North & Sefton E.	-9.49	Lab
163	St Helens South	-9.50	Lab
164	Wellingborough	-9.57	Lab
165	Greenock & Inverclyde	-9.61	Lab
166	Winchester	-9.62	LD
167	Leeds East	-9.64	Lab
168	Scunthorpe	-9.64	Lab
169	Wansbeck	-9.65	Lab
170	Leicester East	-9.66	Lab
171	Blackpool South	-9.66	Lab
172	Barnsley West & Penistone	-9.68	Lab
173	Dorset West	-9.70	Con
174	Arundel & South Downs	-9.71	Con
175	Worcestershire West	-9.71	Con
176	Kettering	-9.76	Lab
177	Worcester	-9.79	Lab
178	Orkney & Shetland	-9.79	LD
179	Wythenshawe & Sale East	-9.80	Lab
180	Ashton under Lyne	-9.81	Lab
181	Tunbridge Wells	-9.81	Con
182	Gloucester	-9.81	Lab
183	Bridgwater	-9.82	Con
184	Chorley	-9.86	Lab
185	Glasgow Rutherglen	-9.90	Lab
186	Birkenhead	-9.90	Lab
187	Hertfordshire North East	-9.92	Con
188	Tiverton & Honiton	-9.94	Con
189	Dewsbury	-9.95	Lab
190	Moray	-9.97	SNP
191	Vale of Glamorgan	-9.98	Lab
192	Pendle	-9.99	Lab
193	Hackney N. & Stoke Newington	-10.01	Lab
194	Newport East	-10.02	Lab
195	Rushcliffe	-10.03	Con
196	Hull East	-10.06	Lab
197	Bassetlaw	-10.11	Lab
198	New Forest East	-10.13	Con
199	Devizes	-10.14	Con
200	Walsall South	-10.15	Lab
201	New Forest West	-10.15	Con

202	Rugby & Kenilworth	-10.16	Lab
203	Wells	-10.16	Con
204	Eddisbury	-10.18	Con
205	Rother Valley	-10.18	Lab
206	Basingstoke	-10.18	Con
207	Warley	-10.19	Lab
208	Edinburgh West	-10.23	LD
209	Aberdeenshire W & Kincardine	-10.24	LD
210	East Lothian	-10.24	Lab
211	Sheffield Attercliffe	-10.27	Lab
212	Sedgefield	-10.28	Lab
213	Gainsborough	-10.28	Con
214	Rochford & Southend East	-10.28	Con
215	Roxburgh & Berwickshire	-10.29	LD
216	Holborn & St Pancras	-10.29	Lab
217	Sheffield Heeley	-10.30	Lab
218	Stretford & Urmston	-10.32	Lab
219	Torbay	-10.34	LD
220	Durham North	-10.34	Lab
221	Weston-Super-Mare	-10.35	LD
222	Bradford South	-10.35	Lab
223	Calder Valley	-10.37	Lab
224	Burnley	-10.38	Lab
225	Dunfermline West	-10.39	Lab
226	Preston	-10.44	Lab
227	Sunderland South	-10.44	Lab
228	Braintree	-10.45	Lab
229	Cambridgeshire North East	-10.48	Con
230	Halifax	-10.50	Lab
231	City of Chester	-10.51	Lab
232	High Peak	-10.51	Lab
233	Meirionnydd Nant Conwy	-10.53	PC
234	Stratford-on-Avon	-10.55	Con
235	Morley & Rothwell	-10.57	Lab
236	Norfolk North West	-10.59	Lab
237	Dartford	-10.60	Lab
238	Shropshire North	-10.60	Con
239	Tayside North	-10.64	SNP
240	Coventry North West	-10.64	Lab
241	Erewash	-10.65	Lab
242	Birmingham Edgbaston	-10.66	Lab
243	Cunninghame North	-10.66	Lab
244	Keighley	-10.68	Lab
245	Colchester	-10.69	LD
246	Warwick & Leamington	-10.69	Lab
247	Poplar & Canning Town	-10.74	Lab
248	Islington North	-10.75	Lab
249	Manchester Blackley	-10.75	Lab
250	Gravesham	-10.76	Lab
251	Lewes	-10.77	LD
252	Hemel Hempstead	-10.77	Lab
253	Coventry South	-10.78	Lab
254	Caithness, Sutherland & Easter Ross	-10.79	LD
255	Bournemouth West	-10.84	Con
256	Esher & Walton	-10.85	Con
257	Warrington North	-10.85	Lab
258	Middlesbrough S. & Cleveland E.	-10.86	Lab
259	Edinburgh South	-10.88	Lab
260	Glasgow Govan	-10.88	Lab
261	Eastbourne	-10.89	Con
262	Leicester South	-10.89	Lab
263	Worthing East & Shoreham	-10.90	Con
264	Swansea West	-10.90	Lab
265	Redcar	-10.91	Lab
266	Harborough	-10.91	Con
267	Banff & Buchan	-10.92	SNP
268	Leeds North West	-10.92	Lab
269	Ross, Skye & Inverness W.	-10.93	LD
270	Surrey East	-10.94	Con
271	Battersea	-10.95	Lab
272	Blaby	-10.96	Con
273	Aberdeen South	-10.99	Lab
274	Newark	-10.99	Lab
275	Cannock Chase	-11.00	Lab
276	Redditch	-11.01	Lab
277	Bosworth	-11.02	Con
278	Welwyn Hatfield	-11.02	Lab
279	Tyne Bridge	-11.03	Lab
280	Teignbridge	-11.05	Con
281	Leominster	-11.07	Con
282	Corby	-11.09	Lab
283	Stevenage	-11.10	Lab
284	Southport	-11.10	LD
285	Sunderland North	-11.11	Lab
286	Penrith & The Border	-11.12	Con
287	St Helens North	-11.12	Lab
288	Perth	-11.13	SNP
289	Stoke-on-Trent Central	-11.21	Lab
290	Rossendale & Darwen	-11.22	Lab
291	Saffron Walden	-11.25	Con
292	Dover	-11.28	Lab
293	Gower	-11.30	Lab
294	Altrincham & Sale West	-11.32	Con
295	Hyndburn	-11.32	Lab
296	Skipton & Ripon	-11.33	Con
297	Wyre Forest	-11.34	Lab
298	Elmet	-11.35	Lab
299	Cardiff West	-11.35	Lab
300	Portsmouth South	-11.36	LD
301	Fylde	-11.36	Con
302	Rayleigh	-11.37	Con
303	Vauxhall	-11.40	Lab

304	Stalybridge & Hyde	-11.43	Lab	355	Dumbarton	-12.10	Lab
305	Erith & Thamesmead	-11.43	Lab	356	Nuneaton	-12.10	Lab
306	Daventry	-11.44	Con	357	Regent's Park & Kensington N.	-12.10	Lab
307	Plymouth Devonport	-11.45	Lab	358	Derbyshire West	-12.11	Con
308	Cardiff North	-11.45	Lab	359	Selby	-12.13	Lab
309	Plymouth Sutton	-11.46	Lab	360	Bury North	-12.13	Lab
310	Galloway & Upper Nithsdale	-11.47	SNP	361	Surrey Heath	-12.14	Con
311	Leeds North East	-11.52	Lab	362	Crawley	-12.14	Lab
312	Oxford East	-11.53	Lab	363	Don Valley	-12.15	Lab
313	Horsham	-11.55	Con	364	Bexhill & Battle	-12.16	Con
314	Wolverhampton South East	-11.55	Lab	365	Ipswich	-12.16	Lab
315	Lancaster & Wyre	-11.56	Lab	366	Newcastle upon Tyne C.	-12.17	Lab
316	Richmond (Yorks)	-11.56	Con	367	Hull West & Hessle	-12.18	Lab
317	Ryedale	-11.61	Con	368	Bolton West	-12.19	Lab
318	Newport West	-11.64	Lab	369	Norfolk South	-12.20	Con
319	Westbury	-11.64	Con	370	Dorset North	-12.21	Con
320	Bolton North East	-11.67	Lab	371	Sevenoaks	-12.22	Con
321	Wokingham	-11.67	Con	372	Brentwood & Ongar	-12.22	Con
322	Leigh	-11.68	Lab	373	Bath	-12.23	LD
323	Islington South & Finsbury	-11.69	Lab	374	Camberwell & Peckham	-12.23	Lab
324	Hereford	-11.71	LD	375	Ribble South	-12.24	Lab
325	Norwich North	-11.71	Lab	376	Carlisle	-12.26	Lab
326	Norfolk North	-11.74	Con	377	Bristol West	-12.30	Lab
327	Canterbury	-11.75	Con	378	Great Yarmouth	-12.30	Lab
328	Maidenhead	-11.76	Con	379	Birmingham Hodge Hill	-12.30	Lab
329	St Ives	-11.77	LD	380	Tyneside North	-12.35	Lab
330	Bedford	-11.77	Lab	381	Dudley North	-12.35	Lab
331	Preseli Pembrokeshire	-11.80	Lab	382	Richmond Park	-12.36	LD
332	Twickenham	-11.81	LD	383	Ashfield	-12.37	Lab
333	Truro & St Austell	-11.82	LD	384	Southampton Test	-12.37	Lab
334	Shrewsbury & Atcham	-11.82	Lab	385	Newcastle upon Tyne N.	-12.38	Lab
335	Walsall North	-11.85	Lab	386	Wiltshire North	-12.40	Con
336	Halesowen & Rowley Regis	-11.87	Lab	387	Eccles	-12.41	Lab
337	Crewe & Nantwich	-11.88	Lab	388	Northampton North	-12.41	Lab
338	Wansdyke	-11.90	Lab	389	Sittingbourne & Sheppey	-12.42	Lab
339	Mansfield	-11.90	Lab	390	St Albans	-12.43	Lab
340	Manchester Withington	-11.91	Lab	391	Hertford & Stortford	-12.47	Con
341	Banbury	-11.95	Con	392	Strathkelvin & Bearsden	-12.47	Lab
342	Maidstone & The Weald	-11.95	Con	393	Dudley South	-12.48	Lab
343	Thanet South	-11.95	Con	394	Morecambe & Lunesdale	-12.48	Lab
344	Wealden	-11.96	Con	395	Warwickshire North	-12.48	Lab
345	Normanton	-11.97	Lab	396	Doncaster Central	-12.50	Lab
346	Hammersmith & Fulham	-11.98	Lab	397	Buckingham	-12.51	Con
347	Stockton South	-11.99	Lab	398	Waveney	-12.53	Lab
348	Durham North West	-11.99	Lab	399	Exeter	-12.55	Lab
349	Wakefield	-12.00	Lab	400	Denton & Reddish	-12.55	Lab
350	Bristol South	-12.01	Lab	401	Hampshire East	-12.58	Con
351	Workington	-12.02	Lab	402	Hove	-12.60	Lab
352	Fife North East	-12.04	LD	403	Shipley	-12.60	Lab
353	Cities of London & Westminster	-12.05	Con	404	Tamworth	-12.61	Lab
354	South Shields	-12.06	Lab	405	Cambridge	-12.62	Lab

406	Ruislip Northwood	-12.62 Con	457	Folkestone & Hythe	-13.30 Con
407	Halton	-12.63 Lab	458	Harrogate & Knaresborough	-13.32 LD
408	Bognor Regis & Littlehampton	-12.64 Con	459	Wycombe	-13.32 Con
409	Milton Keynes North East	-12.64 Lab	460	Putney	-13.32 Lab
410	Bishop Auckland	-12.64 Lab	461	Beverley & Holderness	-13.33 Con
411	Birmingham Hall Green	-12.72 Lab	462	Mole Valley	-13.34 Con
412	Norfolk South West	-12.74 Con	463	Broxbourne	-13.41 Con
413	Middlesbrough	-12.77 Lab	464	Reading West	-13.44 Lab
414	Eltham	-12.78 Lab	465	West Bromwich East	-13.45 Lab
415	Tonbridge & Malling	-12.79 Con	466	Angus	-13.47 SNP
416	Runnymede & Weybridge	-12.81 Con	467	Blaydon	-13.50 Lab
417	Northavon	-12.83 LD	468	Hartlepool	-13.53 Lab
418	Hampshire North West	-12.84 Con	469	Stoke-on-Trent North	-13.54 Lab
419	Uxbridge	-12.84 Con	470	Hertsmere	-13.54 Con
420	Guildford	-12.84 Con	471	Wolverhampton North East	-13.54 Lab
421	Chichester	-12.86 Con	472	Broxtowe	-13.54 Lab
422	Blackburn	-12.87 Lab	473	Hampstead & Highgate	-13.54 Lab
423	Cardiff South & Penarth	-12.88 Lab	474	Chipping Barnet	-13.55 Con
424	Lewisham Deptford	-12.90 Lab	475	Scarborough & Whitby	-13.56 Lab
425	Bridgend	-12.91 Lab	476	Ealing Acton & Shepherd's Bush	-13.57 Lab
426	Luton South	-12.91 Lab	477	Gateshead E. & Washington W.	-13.58 Lab
427	Sutton Coldfield	-12.93 Con	478	Henley	-13.59 Con
428	Suffolk West	-12.93 Con	479	Oxford West & Abingdon	-13.59 LD
429	Nottingham East	-12.94 Lab	480	Delyn	-13.60 Lab
430	Poole	-12.97 Con	481	Spelthorne	-13.66 Con
431	Huddersfield	-12.97 Lab	482	Hexham	-13.67 Con
432	Tooting	-12.99 Lab	483	Bury South	-13.67 Lab
433	Chesham & Amersham	-12.99 Con	484	Reigate	-13.68 Con
434	Derbyshire North East	-13.00 Lab	485	Wirral West	-13.68 Lab
435	Stourbridge	-13.01 Lab	486	Gedling	-13.71 Lab
436	Amber Valley	-13.01 Lab	487	Southampton Itchen	-13.78 Lab
437	Ellesmere Port & Neston	-13.01 Lab	488	Essex North	-13.80 Con
438	Bracknell	-13.04 Con	489	Fareham	-13.81 Con
439	Eastwood	-13.08 Lab	490	Chatham & Aylesford	-13.83 Lab
440	Meriden	-13.09 Con	491	Cardiff Central	-13.86 Lab
441	Ynys Mon	-13.09 PC	492	Suffolk Coastal	-13.86 Con
442	Hampshire North East	-13.10 Con	493	Brentford & Isleworth	-13.86 Lab
443	Milton Keynes South West	-13.10 Lab	494	Harlow	-13.86 Lab
444	Thanet North	-13.11 Con	495	Brighton Kemptown	-13.88 Lab
445	Havant	-13.12 Con	496	Cheadle	-13.92 Lab
446	Portsmouth North	-13.13 Lab	497	Crosby	-13.93 Lab
447	Aylesbury	-13.14 Con	498	Isle of Wight	-13.93 LD
448	Warrington South	-13.16 Lab	499	Surrey South West	-13.93 Con
449	Ashford	-13.18 Con	500	Vale of Clwyd	-13.93 Lab
450	Swindon South	-13.18 Lab	501	Chingford & Woodford Green	-13.94 Con
451	Lincoln	-13.18 Lab	502	Reading East	-13.95 Lab
452	Suffolk Central & Ipswich N.	-13.24 Con	503	Suffolk South	-13.98 Con
453	Hertfordshire South West	-13.25 Con	504	Bournemouth East	-14.04 Con
454	Lancashire West	-13.26 Lab	505	Tottenham	-14.06 Lab
455	Brigg & Goole	-13.29 Lab	506	Nottingham South	-14.07 Lab
456	Watford	-13.30 Lab	507	Alyn & Deeside	-14.08 Lab

508	Charnwood	-14.08	Con		559	West Ham	-14.99	Lab
509	Barrow & Furness	-14.08	Lab		560	Finchley & Golders Green	-15.01	Lab
510	Sherwood	-14.10	Lab		561	Bedfordshire North East	-15.05	Con
511	Stockton North	-14.11	Lab		562	Grantham & Stamford	-15.06	Con
512	Lichfield	-14.13	Con		563	Dumfries	-15.06	Lab
513	Great Grimsby	-14.14	Lab		564	Cornwall South East	-15.15	LD
514	Derby North	-14.16	Lab		565	Harwich	-15.17	Lab
515	Copeland	-14.17	Lab		566	Maldon & Chelmsford East	-15.18	Con
516	Ealing North	-14.18	Lab		567	Brent South	-15.22	Lab
517	Bristol East	-14.20	Lab		568	Haltemprice & Howden	-15.28	Con
518	Blackpool North & Fleetwood	-14.22	Lab		569	Tynemouth	-15.31	Lab
519	Old Bexley & Sidcup	-14.23	Con		570	Epsom & Ewell	-15.44	Con
520	Chelmsford West	-14.24	Con		571	Aldershot	-15.45	Con
521	Cambridgeshire North West	-14.24	Con		572	Sussex Mid	-15.45	Con
522	Basildon	-14.25	Lab		573	Bedfordshire South West	-15.45	Con
523	Brent East	-14.26	Lab		574	Medway	-15.46	Lab
524	Epping Forest	-14.26	Con		575	Ealing Southall	-15.50	Lab
525	Hazel Grove	-14.27	LD		576	Castle Point	-15.52	Lab
526	Peterborough	-14.29	Lab		577	Stockport	-15.54	Lab
527	Totnes	-14.30	Con		578	Hitchin & Harpenden	-15.58	Con
528	Wantage	-14.31	Con		579	Worthing West	-15.61	Con
529	Croydon South	-14.33	Con		580	Bromley & Chislehurst	-15.64	Con
530	Stoke-on-Trent South	-14.36	Lab		581	Rutland & Melton	-15.64	Con
531	Rochdale	-14.42	Lab		582	Birmingham Perry Barr	-15.64	Lab
532	Wirral South	-14.45	Lab		583	Hackney South & Shoreditch	-15.67	Lab
533	Leicestershire North West	-14.46	Lab		584	Oldham East & Saddleworth	-15.67	Lab
534	Norwich South	-14.47	Lab		585	Derby South	-15.71	Lab
535	York	-14.51	Lab		586	Bexleyheath & Crayford	-15.75	Lab
536	Sleaford & North Hykeham	-14.51	Con		587	Kingswood	-15.86	Lab
537	Cleethorpes	-14.52	Lab		588	East Ham	-15.87	Lab
538	Birmingham Selly Oak	-14.52	Lab		589	Vale of York	-15.89	Con
539	Beaconsfield	-14.52	Con		590	Derbyshire South	-15.92	Lab
540	Cambridgeshire South East	-14.53	Con		591	Southend West	-15.93	Con
541	Birmingham Northfield	-14.54	Lab		592	Feltham & Heston	-15.94	Lab
542	Gosport	-14.54	Con		593	Clwyd West	-16.00	Lab
543	Kensington & Chelsea	-14.56	Con		594	Harrow West	-16.02	Lab
544	Northampton South	-14.56	Lab		595	Gillingham	-16.03	Lab
545	Westmorland & Lonsdale	-14.64	Con		596	Edmonton	-16.04	Lab
546	Upminster	-14.67	Lab		597	Hornchurch	-16.17	Lab
547	Orpington	-14.68	Con		598	Solihull	-16.19	Con
548	Darlington	-14.70	Lab		599	Carshalton & Wallington	-16.24	LD
549	Devon South West	-14.72	Lab		600	Barking	-16.26	Lab
550	Oldham West & Royton	-14.72	Lab		601	Bedfordshire Mid	-16.37	Con
551	Witney	-14.76	Con		602	Wimbledon	-16.42	Lab
552	Faversham & Kent Mid	-14.77	Con		603	Romford	-16.46	Lab
553	Leicester West	-14.79	Lab		604	Sheffield Hallam	-16.46	LD
554	Slough	-14.79	Lab		605	Kingston & Surbiton	-16.48	LD
555	Dorset South	-14.81	Con		606	Cambridgeshire South	-16.49	Con
556	Nottingham North	-14.84	Lab		607	Enfield North	-16.55	Lab
557	Cornwall North	-14.85	LD		608	Hendon	-16.60	Lab
558	Norfolk Mid	-14.97	Con		609	Birmingham Yardley	-16.65	Lab

610	Streatham	-16.66	Lab
611	Mitcham & Morden	-16.77	Lab
612	Ilford South	-16.79	Lab
613	Enfield Southgate	-16.81	Lab
614	Lewisham East	-16.86	Lab
615	Walthamstow	-16.90	Lab
616	Croydon Central	-16.91	Lab
617	Thurrock	-16.92	Lab
618	Luton North	-16.94	Lab
619	Ilford North	-17.07	Lab
620	Eastleigh	-17.16	LD
621	Romsey	-17.24	Con
622	Hornsey & Wood Green	-17.25	Lab
623	Brent North	-17.29	Lab
624	Sutton & Cheam	-17.33	LD
625	Christchurch	-17.35	Con
626	Harrow East	-17.51	Lab
627	Croydon North	-17.51	Lab
628	Brighton Pavilion	-17.57	Lab
629	Beckenham	-17.71	Con
630	Hayes & Harlington	-17.72	Lab
631	Billericay	-17.88	Con
632	Wallasey	-18.02	Lab
633	Newbury	-18.05	LD
634	Dagenham	-18.32	Lab
635	Hastings & Rye	-18.40	Lab
636	Dulwich & West Norwood	-18.60	Lab
637	Lewisham West	-18.98	Lab
638	Woking	-20.70	Con
639	Gordon	-21.92	LD
640	Tatton	-24.72	Ind
641	West Bromwich West	-37.57	Spkr

Table 8: Labour change of vote share 1992/97 and winning party

		%ch	lst
1	Liverpool Wavertree	23.14	Lab
2	Crosby	22.38	Lab
3	Brent North	20.36	Lab
4	Cambridgeshire North East	20.22	Con
5	Hove	20.12	Lab
6	Stockton South	19.68	Lab
7	Wimbledon	19.48	Lab
8	Morecambe & Lunesdale	19.43	Lab
9	Erith & Thamesmead	19.07	Lab
10	Pudsey	19.02	Lab
11	Harrow West	19.01	Lab
12	Walthamstow	18.85	Lab
13	Greenwich & Woolwich	18.84	Lab
14	Beverley & Holderness	18.78	Con
15	Harrow East	18.67	Lab
16	Hastings & Rye	18.65	Lab
17	Castle Point	18.42	Lab
18	Bishop Auckland	18.29	Lab
19	Thanet South	18.03	Lab
20	Enfield Southgate	17.99	Lab
21	Dumfries	17.91	Lab
22	Ealing North	17.85	Lab
23	Croydon North	17.77	Lab
24	Wyre Forest	17.53	Lab
25	Ilford North	17.47	Lab
26	Thurrock	17.47	Lab
27	Luton North	17.44	Lab
28	Billericay	17.27	Con
29	Hayes & Harlington	17.16	Lab
30	Gosport	17.06	Con
31	St Albans	16.97	Lab
32	Wansdyke	16.82	Lab
33	Stevenage	16.76	Lab
34	Coventry North East	16.62	Lab
35	Sittingbourne & Sheppey	16.61	Lab
36	Reading West	16.48	Lab
37	Ilford South	16.41	Lab
38	Hertsmere	16.39	Con
39	Chatham & Aylesford	16.37	Lab
40	Wirral South	16.36	Lab
41	Milton Keynes South West	16.34	Lab
42	Richmond (Yorks)	16.26	Con
43	Waveney	16.23	Lab
44	Coventry South	16.17	Lab
45	Tewkesbury	16.13	Con
46	Upminster	16.08	Lab
47	Gillingham	16.02	Lab
48	Louth & Horncastle	15.97	Con

49	Maldon & Chelmsford East	15.97	Con	100	Bexleyheath & Crayford	14.24	Lab
50	Swindon South	15.96	Lab	101	Bedford	14.22	Lab
51	Canterbury	15.94	Con	102	Feltham & Heston	14.19	Lab
52	Hendon	15.82	Lab	103	Essex North	14.14	Con
53	Scarborough & Whitby	15.78	Lab	104	Gateshead E. & Washington W.	14.11	Lab
54	Milton Keynes North East	15.73	Lab	105	Northampton North	14.10	Lab
55	Hornchurch	15.73	Lab	106	Rayleigh	14.06	Con
56	Enfield North	15.71	Lab	107	Hexham	14.06	Con
57	Cleethorpes	15.69	Lab	108	Harwich	14.05	Lab
58	Wallasey	15.67	Lab	109	Croydon Central	14.05	Lab
59	Eastwood	15.60	Lab	110	Dagenham	14.03	Lab
60	Knowsley North & Sefton E.	15.50	Lab	111	Basingstoke	14.03	Con
61	Great Yarmouth	15.41	Lab	112	Newcastle upon Tyne E. & Wallsend	13.98	Lab
62	Brent South	15.36	Lab	113	Old Bexley & Sidcup	13.97	Con
63	Vale of York	15.36	Con	114	Brighton Kemptown	13.96	Lab
64	Mitcham & Morden	15.28	Lab	115	Wycombe	13.96	Con
65	Hitchin & Harpenden	15.27	Con	116	Vale of Clwyd	13.93	Lab
66	Braintree	15.27	Lab	117	Portsmouth North	13.93	Lab
67	Spelthorne	15.26	Con	118	Caernarfon	13.93	PC
68	Edmonton	15.25	Lab	119	Wirral West	13.87	Lab
69	Birmingham Hall Green	15.21	Lab	120	Reading East	13.84	Lab
70	Finchley & Golders Green	15.19	Lab	121	Plymouth Devonport	13.83	Lab
71	Suffolk Central & Ipswich N.	15.18	Con	122	Altrincham & Sale West	13.81	Con
72	Basildon	15.14	Lab	123	Cambridge	13.77	Lab
73	Dorset South	15.11	Con	124	Redcar	13.77	Lab
74	Leyton & Wanstead	15.03	Lab	125	Maidstone & The Weald	13.76	Con
75	The Wrekin	15.01	Lab	126	Chingford & Woodford Green	13.68	Con
76	Bognor Regis & Littlehampton	15.00	Con	127	Blackpool South	13.64	Lab
77	Thanet North	14.99	Con	128	Barking	13.59	Lab
78	Shipley	14.97	Lab	129	Erewash	13.51	Lab
79	Lewisham West	14.97	Lab	130	Darlington	13.50	Lab
80	West Ham	14.94	Lab	131	Runnymede & Weybridge	13.48	Con
81	Romford	14.84	Lab	132	Streatham	13.39	Lab
82	Stockport	14.82	Lab	133	Broxbourne	13.31	Con
83	Bedfordshire South West	14.74	Con	134	Rutland & Melton	13.30	Con
84	Crawley	14.73	Lab	135	Hornsey & Wood Green	13.28	Lab
85	Ealing Southall	14.73	Lab	136	Stroud	13.27	Lab
86	Chipping Barnet	14.68	Con	137	Warwick & Leamington	13.27	Lab
87	Brentford & Isleworth	14.67	Lab	138	Gloucester	13.15	Lab
88	Dulwich & West Norwood	14.62	Lab	139	Hemel Hempstead	13.15	Lab
89	Bolton South East	14.57	Lab	140	Kingswood	13.12	Lab
90	Hertford & Stortford	14.56	Con	141	Suffolk West	13.09	Con
91	Blackpool North & Fleetwood	14.56	Lab	142	Tynemouth	13.07	Lab
92	Hertfordshire North East	14.54	Con	143	Fylde	13.07	Con
93	Brigg & Goole	14.51	Lab	144	Devon South West	13.06	Con
94	Eltham	14.50	Lab	145	Rushcliffe	13.04	Con
95	Brent East	14.50	Lab	146	Epping Forest	13.02	Con
96	Brighton Pavilion	14.42	Lab	147	Ruislip Northwood	12.99	Con
97	Charnwood	14.38	Con	148	Faversham & Kent Mid	12.99	Con
98	Blyth Valley	14.32	Lab	149	Lewisham East	12.96	Lab
99	Medway	14.25	Lab	150	High Peak	12.91	Lab

151	Harborough	12.85	Con	202	Islington North	11.81	Lab
152	Stockton North	12.83	Lab	203	Tyneside North	11.77	Lab
153	Tottenham	12.81	Lab	204	Rochdale	11.74	Lab
154	Uxbridge	12.80	Con	205	Ashford	11.73	Con
155	Aberdeen North	12.78	Lab	206	Ellesmere Port & Neston	11.73	Lab
156	Boston & Skegness	12.78	Con	207	Bury St Edmunds	11.70	Con
157	Newcastle upon Tyne North	12.77	Lab	208	Derbyshire North East	11.65	Lab
158	Folkestone & Hythe	12.75	Con	209	Grantham & Stamford	11.61	Con
159	Bedfordshire Mid	12.73	Con	210	Luton South	11.61	Lab
160	Bristol South	12.69	Lab	211	Perth	11.58	SNP
161	Leeds North West	12.63	Lab	212	Regent's Park & Kensington N.	11.57	Lab
162	Bedfordshire North East	12.60	Con	213	Leeds West	11.55	Lab
163	Tamworth	12.60	Lab	214	Dunfermline West	11.55	Lab
164	Stafford	12.60	Lab	215	Tooting	11.53	Lab
165	Leicestershire North West	12.54	Lab	216	Cardiff North	11.53	Lab
166	Peterborough	12.53	Lab	217	Birmingham Northfield	11.52	Lab
167	Slough	12.52	Lab	218	Colne Valley	11.51	Lab
168	Witney	12.46	Con	219	Corby	11.50	Lab
169	Denton & Reddish	12.43	Lab	220	Oldham East & Saddleworth	11.47	Lab
170	Dartford	12.40	Lab	221	Middlesbrough S. & Cleveland E.	11.42	Lab
171	City of Chester	12.37	Lab	222	Chorley	11.41	Lab
172	Sleaford & North Hykeham	12.37	Con	223	Aberdeen South	11.38	Lab
173	Leeds North East	12.35	Lab	224	Kettering	11.37	Lab
174	Warwickshire North	12.32	Lab	225	Warrington South	11.35	Lab
175	Gedling	12.32	Lab	226	Staffordshire Moorlands	11.34	Lab
176	Bosworth	12.30	Con	227	Islington South & Finsbury	11.32	Lab
177	Derby North	12.29	Lab	228	Watford	11.30	Lab
178	Broxtowe	12.26	Lab	229	Kensington & Chelsea	11.30	Con
179	Havant	12.26	Con	230	Harlow	11.28	Lab
180	Bury South	12.25	Lab	231	Exeter	11.28	Lab
181	Devizes	12.24	Con	232	Worcestershire Mid	11.26	Con
182	Beckenham	12.23	Con	233	Halton	11.25	Lab
183	Caithness, Sutherland & Easter Ross	12.21	LD	234	Chelmsford West	11.25	Con
184	Northampton South	12.20	Lab	235	Heywood & Middleton	11.24	Lab
185	Stoke-on-Trent South	12.19	Lab	236	Brentwood & Ongar	11.22	Con
186	Birmingham Yardley	12.19	Lab	237	Hampstead & Highgate	11.19	Lab
187	Rochford & Southend East	12.17	Con	238	Derbyshire West	11.17	Con
188	Carlisle	12.14	Lab	239	Norfolk Mid	11.16	Con
189	Fareham	12.13	Con	240	Birmingham Perry Barr	11.14	Lab
190	New Forest East	12.08	Con	241	Welwyn Hatfield	11.07	Lab
191	Ealing Acton & Shepherd's Bush	12.01	Lab	242	Rugby & Kenilworth	11.06	Lab
192	Edinburgh North & Leith	12.00	Lab	243	Hampshire North West	11.03	Con
193	Blaby	12.00	Con	244	Cities of London & Westminster	11.01	Con
194	Ribble South	11.97	Lab	245	Sherwood	10.99	Lab
195	Birmingham Hodge Hill	11.97	Lab	246	Alyn & Deeside	10.99	Lab
196	Falkirk East	11.96	Lab	247	Tweeddale, Ettrick & Lauderdale	10.99	LD
197	Poplar & Canning Town	11.93	Lab	248	Shrewsbury & Atcham	10.98	Lab
198	Dover	11.87	Lab	249	Lancashire West	10.93	Lab
199	Bristol West	11.86	Lab	250	Halifax	10.85	Lab
200	Edinburgh Pentlands	11.84	Lab	251	Southampton Itchen	10.81	Lab
201	Cotswold	11.83	Con	252	York	10.78	Lab

253	Macclesfield	10.78	Con
254	Norfolk South West	10.76	Con
255	Holborn & St Pancras	10.76	Lab
256	Stone	10.75	Con
257	Warley	10.74	Lab
258	Durham North West	10.72	Lab
259	Inverness East, Nairn & Lochaber	10.72	Lab
260	Sheffield Hillsborough	10.69	Lab
261	Surrey East	10.68	Con
262	Portsmouth South	10.67	LD
263	East Ham	10.66	Lab
264	Crewe & Nantwich	10.63	Lab
265	Worthing East & Shoreham	10.60	Con
266	Carmarthen W. & Pembrokeshire S.	10.60	Lab
267	Sunderland South	10.59	Lab
268	Penrith & The Border	10.57	Con
269	Wolverhampton South West	10.53	Lab
270	Ashton under Lyne	10.52	Lab
271	Southend West	10.50	Con
272	Westbury	10.50	Con
273	Daventry	10.48	Con
274	Elmet	10.48	Lab
275	Nuneaton	10.46	Lab
276	Derbyshire South	10.45	Lab
277	Hertfordshire South West	10.44	Con
278	Bolton West	10.42	Lab
279	Durham North	10.40	Lab
280	Stoke-on-Trent North	10.35	Lab
281	Plymouth Sutton	10.35	Lab
282	Delyn	10.33	Lab
283	Middlesbrough	10.32	Lab
284	South Shields	10.30	Lab
285	Ashfield	10.30	Lab
286	Wellingborough	10.29	Lab
287	Amber Valley	10.29	Lab
288	Aldershot	10.29	Con
289	Reigate	10.27	Con
290	Wolverhampton North East	10.26	Lab
291	Norfolk North West	10.24	Lab
292	Bury North	10.24	Lab
293	Makerfield	10.23	Lab
294	Liverpool Garston	10.22	Lab
295	Lewisham Deptford	10.21	Lab
296	Worcester	10.19	Lab
297	Preseli Pembrokeshire	10.18	Lab
298	Selby	10.15	Lab
299	Tonbridge & Malling	10.15	Con
300	Rossendale & Darwen	10.08	Lab
301	Mansfield	10.07	Lab
302	Glasgow Pollok	10.06	Lab
303	Meriden	10.06	Con
304	Tyne Bridge	10.04	Lab
305	Workington	10.02	Lab
306	City of Durham	10.02	Lab
307	Nottingham North	9.96	Lab
308	Hull North	9.93	Lab
309	Poole	9.91	Con
310	Walsall North	9.89	Lab
311	Salford	9.86	Lab
312	Shropshire North	9.81	Con
313	Ross, Skye & Inverness West	9.80	LD
314	Cunninghame South	9.79	Lab
315	Burton	9.79	Lab
316	Cambridgeshire South	9.78	Con
317	Leeds East	9.77	Lab
318	Surrey Heath	9.75	Con
319	Keighley	9.73	Lab
320	Ynys Mon	9.73	PC
321	Nottingham East	9.73	Lab
322	Lancaster & Wyre	9.72	Lab
323	Oldham West & Royton	9.71	Lab
324	Walsall South	9.66	Lab
325	Bristol East	9.63	Lab
326	Birmingham Selly Oak	9.62	Lab
327	Leigh	9.62	Lab
328	Dudley South	9.59	Lab
329	Vale of Glamorgan	9.59	Lab
330	Halesowen & Rowley Regis	9.56	Lab
331	Wantage	9.55	Con
332	Stretford & Urmston	9.55	Lab
333	Barrow & Furness	9.54	Lab
334	Bracknell	9.54	Con
335	Suffolk Coastal	9.52	Con
336	Maidenhead	9.49	Con
337	Copeland	9.49	Lab
338	Battersea	9.48	Lab
339	Bolsover	9.46	Lab
340	Normanton	9.45	Lab
341	Redditch	9.43	Lab
342	Norwich North	9.41	Lab
343	Houghton & Washington East	9.38	Lab
344	Newark	9.37	Lab
345	Yorkshire East	9.36	Con
346	Cunninghame North	9.32	Lab
347	Epsom & Ewell	9.28	Con
348	Conwy	9.28	Lab
349	Birmingham Edgbaston	9.27	Lab
350	Gravesham	9.26	Lab
351	Chesham & Amersham	9.25	Con
352	West Bromwich East	9.25	Lab
353	South Holland & The Deepings	9.23	Con
354	Camberwell & Peckham	9.18	Lab

355	Leicester East	9.16	Lab
356	East Kilbride	9.16	Lab
357	Wakefield	9.15	Lab
358	Bradford South	9.08	Lab
359	Eccles	9.08	Lab
360	Eddisbury	9.05	Con
361	Pendle	9.04	Lab
362	Putney	9.04	Lab
363	Livingston	9.04	Lab
364	Croydon South	8.99	Con
365	Morley & Rothwell	8.98	Lab
366	Huntingdon	8.97	Con
367	Staffordshire South	8.95	Con
368	Arundel & South Downs	8.93	Con
369	Sedgefield	8.93	Lab
370	Warrington North	8.93	Lab
371	Stourbridge	8.92	Lab
372	Manchester Withington	8.89	Lab
373	Sutton Coldfield	8.88	Con
374	Hartlepool	8.87	Lab
375	Edinburgh East & Musselburgh	8.87	Lab
376	Lincoln	8.87	Lab
377	Stirling	8.82	Lab
378	Loughborough	8.80	Lab
379	Ipswich	8.79	Lab
380	Great Grimsby	8.77	Lab
381	Glasgow Anniesland	8.77	Lab
382	Hyndburn	8.73	Lab
383	Aylesbury	8.73	Con
384	Bexhill & Battle	8.72	Con
385	Calder Valley	8.69	Lab
386	Southampton Test	8.68	Lab
387	Bolton North East	8.67	Lab
388	Buckingham	8.66	Con
389	Hamilton South	8.65	Lab
390	Sunderland North	8.62	Lab
391	Edinburgh Central	8.56	Lab
392	Wythenshawe & Sale East	8.56	Lab
393	Salisbury	8.55	Con
394	Newcastle-under-Lyme	8.53	Lab
395	Sevenoaks	8.44	Con
396	Aldridge - Brownhills	8.43	Con
397	Leicester West	8.41	Lab
398	Hull East	8.40	Lab
399	Greenock & Inverclyde	8.39	Lab
400	Congleton	8.37	Con
401	Clwyd South	8.36	Lab
402	Worsley	8.35	Lab
403	Woodspring	8.31	Con
404	Bournemouth East	8.30	Con
405	Haltemprice & Howden	8.29	Con
406	Bradford North	8.24	Lab
407	Stoke-on-Trent Central	8.24	Lab
408	Bath	8.17	LD
409	Hammersmith & Fulham	8.13	Lab
410	Glasgow Cathcart	8.03	Lab
411	Sussex Mid	8.01	Con
412	Bromley & Chislehurst	7.99	Con
413	Wealden	7.99	Con
414	Derby South	7.98	Lab
415	Kirkcaldy	7.98	Lab
416	Clydesdale	7.95	Lab
417	Moray	7.95	SNP
418	Fife Central	7.94	Lab
419	Wigan	7.93	Lab
420	Gainsborough	7.92	Con
421	Henley	7.92	Con
422	Falkirk West	7.90	Lab
423	Banbury	7.89	Con
424	Manchester Blackley	7.86	Lab
425	Eastbourne	7.81	Con
426	Sheffield Attercliffe	7.80	Lab
427	Western Isles	7.79	Lab
428	Huddersfield	7.75	Lab
429	Doncaster Central	7.72	Lab
430	Vauxhall	7.69	Lab
431	Bassetlaw	7.68	Lab
432	Don Valley	7.68	Lab
433	Preston	7.66	Lab
434	Hampshire East	7.66	Con
435	Glasgow Shettleston	7.66	Lab
436	Norfolk South	7.66	Con
437	Weaver Vale	7.65	Lab
438	Woking	7.64	Con
439	Solihull	7.63	Con
440	St Helens South	7.59	Lab
441	Nottingham South	7.59	Lab
442	Paisley North	7.59	Lab
443	Knowsley South	7.57	Lab
444	Skipton & Ripon	7.57	Con
445	Worthing West	7.55	Con
446	Easington	7.52	Lab
447	Wells	7.49	Con
448	Suffolk South	7.46	Con
449	Newcastle upon Tyne C.	7.46	Lab
450	Newport West	7.41	Lab
451	Rotherham	7.37	Lab
452	Eastleigh	7.37	LD
453	Hackney N. & Stoke Newington	7.35	Lab
454	Blaydon	7.29	Lab
455	Stalybridge & Hyde	7.26	Lab
456	East Lothian	7.22	Lab

457	Bromsgrove	7.18	Con
458	Isle of Wight	7.18	LD
459	Saffron Walden	7.16	Con
460	Birkenhead	7.13	Lab
461	Cardiff West	7.13	Lab
462	Hull West & Hessle	7.11	Lab
463	Stratford-on-Avon	7.10	Con
464	Swindon North	7.10	Lab
465	Rother Valley	7.08	Lab
466	Cambridgeshire South East	7.02	Con
467	Ribble Valley	7.02	Con
468	Wolverhampton South East	7.01	Lab
469	St Helens North	6.98	Lab
470	Hampshire North East	6.85	Con
471	Bridgend	6.78	Lab
472	Dundee East	6.78	Lab
473	Monmouth	6.77	Lab
474	Strathkelvin & Bearsden	6.77	Lab
475	Hemsworth	6.76	Lab
476	Horsham	6.76	Con
477	Aberdeen Central	6.74	Lab
478	Paisley South	6.71	Lab
479	Montgomeryshire	6.69	LD
480	Blackburn	6.60	Lab
481	Oxford East	6.59	Lab
482	Liverpool West Derby	6.59	Lab
483	Coatbridge & Chryston	6.54	Lab
484	Weston-Super-Mare	6.50	LD
485	Colchester	6.46	LD
486	Glasgow Springburn	6.45	Lab
487	Batley & Spen	6.44	Lab
488	Beaconsfield	6.35	Con
489	Cambridgeshire North West	6.33	Con
490	Bootle	6.31	Lab
491	Barnsley Central	6.24	Lab
492	Roxburgh & Berwickshire	6.21	LD
493	Wrexham	6.20	Lab
494	Clwyd West	6.19	Lab
495	Carshalton & Wallington	6.19	LD
496	Scunthorpe	6.13	Lab
497	Dundee West	6.13	Lab
498	Guildford	6.10	Con
499	New Forest West	6.07	Con
500	Hackney South & Shoreditch	6.02	Lab
501	Liverpool Walton	5.98	Lab
502	Dumbarton	5.97	Lab
503	Leeds Central	5.94	Lab
504	Somerton & Frome	5.93	LD
505	Windsor	5.88	Con
506	Chichester	5.86	Con
507	Pontefract & Castleford	5.83	Lab
508	Cannock Chase	5.82	Lab
509	Ayr	5.81	Lab
510	Lichfield	5.80	Con
511	Southwark North & Bermondsey	5.79	LD
512	Forest of Dean	5.78	Lab
513	Wansbeck	5.75	Lab
514	Norwich South	5.73	Lab
515	Carrick, Cumnock & Doon Valley	5.73	Lab
516	Tunbridge Wells	5.73	Con
517	Ceredigion	5.73	PC
518	Hamilton North & Bellshill	5.72	Lab
519	Leicester South	5.71	Lab
520	Dudley North	5.68	Lab
521	Swansea East	5.67	Lab
522	Romsey	5.67	Con
523	Coventry North West	5.64	Lab
524	Sutton & Cheam	5.54	LD
525	Devon East	5.53	Con
526	Birmingham Erdington	5.52	Lab
527	Neath	5.52	Lab
528	Wokingham	5.51	Con
529	Truro & St Austell	5.50	LD
530	Westmorland & Lonsdale	5.49	Con
531	Mole Valley	5.42	Con
532	Esher & Walton	5.40	Con
533	Doncaster North	5.36	Lab
534	Midlothian	5.35	Lab
535	Edinburgh South	5.30	Lab
536	Yeovil	5.28	LD
537	Torbay	5.27	LD
538	Twickenham	5.23	LD
539	Leominster	5.17	Con
540	Merthyr Tydfil & Rhymney	5.12	Lab
541	Bournemouth West	5.07	Con
542	Telford	5.06	Lab
543	Sheffield Heeley	5.05	Lab
544	Kilmarnock & Loudoun	5.05	Lab
545	Teignbridge	5.02	Con
546	Clydebank & Milngavie	4.96	Lab
547	Linlithgow	4.95	Lab
548	Torfaen	4.94	Lab
549	Burnley	4.93	Lab
550	Dorset West	4.75	Con
551	Fife North East	4.70	LD
552	Bristol North West	4.67	Lab
553	Cumbernauld & Kilsyth	4.67	Lab
554	Falmouth & Camborne	4.67	Lab
555	Tayside North	4.32	SNP
556	Totnes	4.26	Con
557	Aberavon	4.25	Lab
558	Dorset North	4.18	Con

559	Meirionnydd Nant Conwy	4.18	PC	610	Southport	1.94	LD
560	Caerphilly	4.16	Lab	611	Tiverton & Honiton	1.90	Con
561	Glasgow Rutherglen	4.14	Lab	612	Worcestershire West	1.89	Con
562	Glasgow Kelvin	4.11	Lab	613	Norfolk North	1.88	Con
563	Wiltshire North	4.07	Con	614	Manchester Central	1.84	Lab
564	Oxford West & Abingdon	4.06	LD	615	Cardiff Central	1.72	Lab
565	Gordon	4.03	LD	616	Edinburgh West	1.42	LD
566	Sheffield Central	4.02	Lab	617	Carmarthen East & Dinefwr	1.40	Lab
567	Ludlow	3.95	Con	618	Birmingham Sparkbrook & Small Heath	1.19	Lab
568	Dunfermline East	3.95	Lab	619	Glasgow Govan	1.04	Lab
569	Devon North	3.90	LD	620	Barnsley West & Penistone	1.02	Lab
570	Dorset Mid & Poole North	3.86	Con	621	Motherwell & Wishaw	0.87	Lab
571	Wentworth	3.80	Lab	622	Taunton	0.83	LD
572	Richmond Park	3.79	LD	623	Cynon Valley	0.64	Lab
573	Renfrewshire West	3.70	Lab	624	Blaenau Gwent	0.49	Lab
574	Gower	3.67	Lab	625	Brecon & Radnorshire	0.36	LD
575	Cornwall South East	3.58	LD	626	Barnsley East & Mexborough	0.24	Lab
576	Northavon	3.54	LD	627	Hazel Grove	0.22	LD
577	Chesterfield	3.53	Lab	628	Rhondda	-0.10	Lab
578	Cheltenham	3.44	LD	629	Islwyn	-0.16	Lab
579	Llanelli	3.39	Lab	630	Newbury	-0.59	LD
580	Berwick-upon-Tweed	3.37	LD	631	Airdrie & Shotts	-0.67	Lab
581	Galloway & Upper Nithsdale	3.37	SNP	632	St Ives	-0.82	LD
582	Kingston & Surbiton	3.37	LD	633	Orkney & Shetland	-1.58	LD
583	Ryedale	3.31	Con	634	Cardiff South & Penarth	-2.16	Lab
584	Cheadle	3.29	Con	635	Harrogate & Knaresborough	-4.83	LD
585	Banff & Buchan	3.23	SNP	636	Sheffield Hallam	-4.93	LD
586	Swansea West	3.22	Lab	637	Christchurch	-5.18	Con
587	Sheffield Brightside	3.12	Lab	638	Bethnal Green & Bow	-7.19	Lab
588	Orpington	3.09	Con	639	Bradford West	-11.67	Lab
589	Pontypridd	3.08	Lab	640	Tatton	-19.04	Ind
590	Surrey South West	3.03	Con	641	West Bromwich West	-50.63	Spkr
591	Bridgwater	3.02	Con				
592	Winchester	3.02	LD				
593	Manchester Gorton	2.95	Lab				
594	Cornwall North	2.89	LD				
595	Devon West & Torridge	2.86	LD				
596	Angus	2.69	SNP				
597	Birmingham Ladywood	2.68	Lab				
598	Newport East	2.65	Lab				
599	Glasgow Baillieston	2.47	Lab				
600	Lewes	2.41	LD				
601	Jarrow	2.36	Lab				
602	Glasgow Maryhill	2.34	Lab				
603	Aberdeenshire W & Kincardine	2.27	LD				
604	Ogmore	2.25	Lab				
605	Dewsbury	2.14	Lab				
606	Argyll & Bute	2.11	LD				
607	Liverpool Riverside	1.99	Lab				
608	Hereford	1.96	LD				
609	Ochil	1.95	Lab				

Table 9: Liberal Democrat change of vote share 1992/97 and winning party		
	%ch	lst
1 Sheffield Hallam	20.60	LD
2 Christchurch	19.21	Con
3 Harrogate & Knaresborough	18.18	LD
4 Newbury	15.81	LD
5 Gordon	15.42	LD
6 Edinburgh West	13.31	LD
7 Hazel Grove	11.37	LD
8 Kingston & Surbiton	10.73	LD
9 Cornwall South East	8.98	LD
10 Sutton & Cheam	8.54	LD
11 Cheadle	8.08	Con
12 Worcestershire West	7.97	Con
13 Northavon	7.91	LD
14 Orpington	7.36	Con
15 Carshalton & Wallington	7.29	LD
16 Oxford West & Abingdon	7.09	LD
17 Richmond Park	7.03	LD
18 Norfolk North	6.89	Con
19 Tiverton & Honiton	6.85	Con
20 Hereford	6.60	LD
21 Southport	6.60	LD
22 Cambridgeshire North West	6.41	Con
23 Aberdeenshire W & Kincardine	6.39	LD
24 Barnsley West & Penistone	6.35	Lab
25 Romsey	6.34	Con
26 Surrey South West	6.32	Con
27 Wiltshire North	6.26	Con
28 Bromley & Chislehurst	5.93	Con
29 Westmorland & Lonsdale	5.88	Con
30 Twickenham	5.78	LD
31 Cornwall North	5.76	LD
32 Wokingham	5.74	Con
33 Orkney & Shetland	5.56	LD
34 Lichfield	5.54	Con
35 Great Grimsby	5.37	Lab
36 Eastleigh	5.36	LD
37 Argyll & Bute	5.29	LD
38 Winchester	5.15	LD
39 Brecon & Radnorshire	5.05	LD
40 Pontypridd	4.89	Lab
41 Fife North East	4.82	LD
42 Norwich South	4.54	Lab
43 Edinburgh South	4.45	Lab
44 St Ives	4.41	LD
45 Solihull	4.31	Con
46 Bradford West	4.26	Lab
47 Lewes	4.09	LD
48 Ludlow	4.05	Con
49 Aldershot	4.05	Con
50 Swansea West	3.97	Lab
51 Bridgwater	3.96	Con
52 Cambridgeshire South East	3.85	Con
53 Buckingham	3.78	Con
54 Chesterfield	3.75	Lab
55 Haltemprice & Howden	3.68	Con
56 Devon North	3.66	LD
57 Worthing West	3.64	Con
58 Teignbridge	3.62	Con
59 Cardiff Central	3.58	Lab
60 Streatham	3.57	Lab
61 Derby South	3.53	Lab
62 Manchester Gorton	3.49	Lab
63 Ryedale	3.42	Con
64 Cynon Valley	3.33	Lab
65 Denton & Reddish	3.32	Lab
66 Blaydon	3.14	Lab
67 Gower	3.04	Lab
68 Stalybridge & Hyde	2.98	Lab
69 Moray	2.96	SNP
70 Nottingham South	2.90	Lab
71 Glasgow Rutherglen	2.89	Lab
72 Sheffield Heeley	2.87	Lab
73 Birmingham Yardley	2.77	Lab
74 Islwyn	2.76	Lab
75 Aberdeen Central	2.68	Lab
76 Stourbridge	2.55	Lab
77 Sussex Mid	2.41	Con
78 Ogmore	2.40	Lab
79 Chichester	2.38	Con
80 Gainsborough	2.35	Con
81 Blaenau Gwent	2.34	Lab
82 Nottingham East	2.32	Lab
83 Newcastle upon Tyne C.	2.30	Lab
84 Southend West	2.27	Con
85 Ealing Southall	2.26	Lab
86 Sheffield Brightside	2.14	Lab
87 Kensington & Chelsea	2.13	Con
88 Leicester South	2.09	Lab
89 Lincoln	2.05	Lab
90 Rochdale	2.04	Lab
91 Devon East	2.03	Con
92 Tooting	1.98	Lab
93 Horsham	1.98	Con
94 Beaconsfield	1.94	Con
95 Taunton	1.88	LD
96 Birmingham Selly Oak	1.83	Lab
97 Cheltenham	1.83	LD

98	Aylesbury	1.79	Con	149	Oxford East	0.71	Lab
99	Manchester Central	1.78	Lab	150	Wansbeck	0.66	Lab
100	Colchester	1.70	LD	151	Angus	0.65	SNP
101	Dorset North	1.63	Con	152	Mole Valley	0.62	Con
102	West Bromwich East	1.62	Lab	153	Hampshire East	0.62	Con
103	Vauxhall	1.59	Lab	154	Arundel & South Downs	0.62	Con
104	Bath	1.58	LD	155	Wallasey	0.62	Lab
105	Weston-Super-Mare	1.58	LD	156	Barnsley East & Mexborough	0.61	Lab
106	Copeland	1.57	Lab	157	York	0.59	Lab
107	Wantage	1.56	Con	158	Medway	0.59	Lab
108	Cardiff South & Penarth	1.54	Lab	159	Regent's Park & Kensington N.	0.59	Lab
109	Dorset West	1.53	Con	160	Workington	0.58	Lab
110	Poole	1.47	Con	161	Loughborough	0.56	Lab
111	Strathkelvin & Bearsden	1.46	Lab	162	Southampton Test	0.56	Lab
112	Suffolk South	1.45	Con	163	Hammersmith & Fulham	0.50	Lab
113	Beckenham	1.42	Con	164	Paisley South	0.48	Lab
114	Hampstead & Highgate	1.41	Lab	165	Glasgow Maryhill	0.47	Lab
115	Peterborough	1.37	Lab	166	Oldham West & Royton	0.44	Lab
116	Norfolk South	1.36	Con	167	Wells	0.41	Con
117	Dorset Mid & Poole North	1.36	Con	168	Dewsbury	0.41	Lab
118	Birmingham Sparkbrook & Small Heath	1.36	Lab	169	Bournemouth East	0.36	Con
119	Derbyshire North East	1.35	Lab	170	Glasgow Govan	0.36	Lab
120	Edinburgh North & Leith	1.32	Lab	171	Rhondda	0.36	Lab
121	Hornsey & Wood Green	1.30	Lab	172	Bournemouth West	0.34	Con
122	Guildford	1.26	Con	173	Motherwell & Wishaw	0.30	Lab
123	Huddersfield	1.25	Lab	174	Battersea	0.29	Lab
124	Bridgend	1.23	Lab	175	Newport West	0.27	Lab
125	Putney	1.16	Lab	176	Tayside North	0.26	SNP
126	Chingford & Woodford Green	1.15	Con	177	Hitchin & Harpenden	0.26	Con
127	Berwick-upon-Tweed	1.09	LD	178	Lancashire West	0.24	Lab
128	Eccles	1.09	Lab	179	Stoke-on-Trent North	0.24	Lab
129	Sheffield Attercliffe	1.07	Lab	180	Chelmsford West	0.23	Con
130	Bedfordshire Mid	1.03	Con	181	Tunbridge Wells	0.22	Con
131	Burnley	1.01	Lab	182	Woking	0.18	Con
132	Oldham East & Saddleworth	1.00	Lab	183	Slough	0.17	Lab
133	Aberdeen South	0.98	Lab	184	Dundee West	0.16	Lab
134	Cambridgeshire South	0.96	Con	185	Devon West & Torridge	0.13	LD
135	Dulwich & West Norwood	0.96	Lab	186	Clydesdale	0.12	Lab
136	Clydebank & Milngavie	0.92	Lab	187	Banff & Buchan	0.11	SNP
137	Worsley	0.92	Lab	188	Carrick, Cumnock & Doon Valley	0.11	Lab
138	Leicester West	0.90	Lab	189	Leeds West	0.10	Lab
139	Neath	0.87	Lab	190	Warrington South	0.06	Lab
140	Hull West & Hessle	0.84	Lab	191	Bristol East	0.05	Lab
141	Henley	0.83	Con	192	Ross, Skye & Inverness West	0.04	LD
142	Preston	0.82	Lab	193	Sutton Coldfield	0.04	Con
143	Hartlepool	0.79	Lab	194	Roxburgh & Berwickshire	0.04	LD
144	Ipswich	0.76	Lab	195	Watford	0.03	Lab
145	Scunthorpe	0.74	Lab	196	Hackney South & Shoreditch	0.02	Lab
146	Derbyshire South	0.74	Lab	197	Leominster	-0.02	Con
147	Preseli Pembrokeshire	0.73	Lab	198	Manchester Blackley	-0.02	Lab
148	Tynemouth	0.71	Lab	199	Alyn & Deeside	-0.02	Lab

200	Coventry South	-0.03 Lab	251	Nottingham North	-0.62 Lab
201	Wolverhampton South East	-0.03 Lab	252	Telford	-0.63 Lab
202	Ellesmere Port & Neston	-0.04 Lab	253	Birkenhead	-0.64 Lab
203	Birmingham Erdington	-0.05 Lab	254	Tottenham	-0.64 Lab
204	Glasgow Springburn	-0.06 Lab	255	Chesham & Amersham	-0.66 Con
205	Vale of Glamorgan	-0.06 Lab	256	Totnes	-0.68 Con
206	Greenock & Inverclyde	-0.07 Lab	257	Birmingham Hodge Hill	-0.69 Lab
207	Wakefield	-0.08 Lab	258	Redditch	-0.72 Lab
208	Stratford-on-Avon	-0.11 Con	259	Knowsley South	-0.73 Lab
209	Cardiff West	-0.11 Lab	260	Keighley	-0.73 Lab
210	Lewisham West	-0.13 Lab	261	Bootle	-0.74 Lab
211	Dumbarton	-0.14 Lab	262	Delyn	-0.76 Lab
212	Dundee East	-0.17 Lab	263	Crewe & Nantwich	-0.76 Lab
213	Dudley South	-0.18 Lab	264	Somerton & Frome	-0.76 LD
214	Conwy	-0.18 Lab	265	Halifax	-0.76 Lab
215	Dunfermline East	-0.19 Lab	266	Renfrewshire West	-0.77 Lab
216	Bolton North East	-0.22 Lab	267	Paisley North	-0.77 Lab
217	Hertfordshire South West	-0.23 Con	268	Kingswood	-0.78 Lab
218	Torbay	-0.23 LD	269	Midlothian	-0.81 Lab
219	Birmingham Ladywood	-0.23 Lab	270	Hendon	-0.82 Lab
220	Lewisham East	-0.24 Lab	271	Edinburgh East & Musselburgh	-0.82 Lab
221	Bury North	-0.26 Lab	272	Makerfield	-0.86 Lab
222	Wolverhampton South West	-0.28 Lab	273	Normanton	-0.87 Lab
223	Sunderland South	-0.29 Lab	274	Liverpool Walton	-0.87 Lab
224	Caerphilly	-0.30 Lab	275	Glasgow Pollok	-0.87 Lab
225	Glasgow Cathcart	-0.31 Lab	276	Bolsover	-0.88 Lab
226	Airdrie & Shotts	-0.34 Lab	277	Birmingham Perry Barr	-0.90 Lab
227	St Helens North	-0.37 Lab	278	Caernarfon	-0.90 PC
228	Western Isles	-0.37 Lab	279	Torfaen	-0.91 Lab
229	Wentworth	-0.38 Lab	280	Warrington North	-0.96 Lab
230	Epsom & Ewell	-0.39 Con	281	Sherwood	-0.98 Lab
231	Ruislip Northwood	-0.42 Con	282	Hyndburn	-0.99 Lab
232	Windsor	-0.44 Con	283	Rugby & Kenilworth	-1.00 Lab
233	Middlesbrough	-0.44 Lab	284	Meriden	-1.01 Con
234	Birmingham Edgbaston	-0.46 Lab	285	Blackburn	-1.01 Lab
235	Fife Central	-0.49 Lab	286	Falkirk West	-1.03 Lab
236	Sevenoaks	-0.49 Con	287	Kirkcaldy	-1.03 Lab
237	Coatbridge & Chryston	-0.49 Lab	288	Selby	-1.04 Lab
238	Glasgow Baillieston	-0.50 Lab	289	Luton North	-1.05 Lab
239	Croydon South	-0.50 Con	290	Birmingham Northfield	-1.05 Lab
240	Stirling	-0.51 Lab	291	Brent East	-1.06 Lab
241	St Helens South	-0.52 Lab	292	Linlithgow	-1.07 Lab
242	Derby North	-0.54 Lab	293	Darlington	-1.07 Lab
243	Ynys Mon	-0.54 PC	294	Stretford & Urmston	-1.07 Lab
244	East Lothian	-0.54 Lab	295	Rother Valley	-1.08 Lab
245	Sunderland North	-0.55 Lab	296	Leicester East	-1.11 Lab
246	Worcester	-0.56 Lab	297	Banbury	-1.11 Con
247	Bury South	-0.56 Lab	298	Aberavon	-1.13 Lab
248	Manchester Withington	-0.56 Lab	299	Gravesham	-1.14 Lab
249	Swansea East	-0.60 Lab	300	New Forest East	-1.14 Con
250	Dumfries	-0.60 Lab	301	Stockton North	-1.15 Lab

302	Cunninghame North	-1.16	Lab	353	Swindon North	-1.72	Lab
303	Bristol West	-1.16	Lab	354	Edinburgh Central	-1.72	Lab
304	Barnsley Central	-1.18	Lab	355	Clwyd South	-1.73	Lab
305	Leigh	-1.19	Lab	356	Ochil	-1.73	Lab
306	Rossendale & Darwen	-1.21	Lab	357	Leicestershire North West	-1.74	Lab
307	Aldridge - Brownhills	-1.24	Con	358	Brent South	-1.75	Lab
308	Suffolk Central & Ipswich N.	-1.27	Con	359	Harlow	-1.77	Lab
309	Woodspring	-1.28	Con	360	Bolton South East	-1.81	Lab
310	Hackney N. & Stoke Newington	-1.30	Lab	361	Saffron Walden	-1.81	Con
311	Suffolk Coastal	-1.31	Con	362	Devon South West	-1.82	Con
312	Coventry North West	-1.32	Lab	363	Pontefract & Castleford	-1.84	Lab
313	Wealden	-1.32	Con	364	Broxtowe	-1.84	Lab
314	Surrey Heath	-1.32	Con	365	Cities of London & Westminster	-1.85	Con
315	Ealing Acton & Shepherd's Bush	-1.34	Lab	366	Brentford & Isleworth	-1.86	Lab
316	Holborn & St Pancras	-1.36	Lab	367	Tamworth	-1.86	Lab
317	Halesowen & Rowley Regis	-1.36	Lab	368	Morley & Rothwell	-1.88	Lab
318	Monmouth	-1.36	Lab	369	Elmet	-1.88	Lab
319	Calder Valley	-1.37	Lab	370	Wirral West	-1.89	Lab
320	Don Valley	-1.37	Lab	371	Reading East	-1.89	Lab
321	Thurrock	-1.38	Lab	372	Rotherham	-1.90	Lab
322	Bassetlaw	-1.40	Lab	373	Edmonton	-1.91	Lab
323	Exeter	-1.40	Lab	374	Islington South & Finsbury	-1.92	Lab
324	Amber Valley	-1.45	Lab	375	Meirionnydd Nant Conwy	-1.93	PC
325	Dudley North	-1.46	Lab	376	Ilford North	-1.94	Lab
326	Sleaford & North Hykeham	-1.47	Con	377	Bromsgrove	-1.95	Con
327	Halton	-1.49	Lab	378	Congleton	-1.96	Con
328	Tonbridge & Malling	-1.49	Con	379	Cumbernauld & Kilsyth	-1.96	Lab
329	Newport East	-1.50	Lab	380	Shrewsbury & Atcham	-1.99	Lab
330	Kilmarnock & Loudoun	-1.50	Lab	381	Dunfermline West	-1.99	Lab
331	Hamilton South	-1.52	Lab	382	Norwich North	-2.00	Lab
332	Newark	-1.52	Lab	383	Walsall South	-2.02	Lab
333	Mansfield	-1.52	Lab	384	Truro & St Austell	-2.03	LD
334	Finchley & Golders Green	-1.52	Lab	385	Wolverhampton North East	-2.03	Lab
335	Stone	-1.53	Con	386	Burton	-2.07	Lab
336	Islington North	-1.54	Lab	387	Walthamstow	-2.08	Lab
337	Hemsworth	-1.55	Lab	388	Wythenshawe & Sale East	-2.09	Lab
338	Esher & Walton	-1.56	Con	389	Falkirk East	-2.10	Lab
339	Carmarthen East & Dinefwr	-1.58	Lab	390	Barrow & Furness	-2.10	Lab
340	Mitcham & Morden	-1.58	Lab	391	Croydon Central	-2.11	Lab
341	Rutland & Melton	-1.59	Con	392	Enfield North	-2.13	Lab
342	Luton South	-1.62	Lab	393	Skipton & Ripon	-2.15	Con
343	Eddisbury	-1.63	Con	394	Gedling	-2.16	Lab
344	Uxbridge	-1.64	Con	395	Glasgow Shettleston	-2.16	Lab
345	Stoke-on-Trent Central	-1.65	Lab	396	Weaver Vale	-2.17	Lab
346	Cunninghame South	-1.66	Lab	397	Galloway & Upper Nithsdale	-2.17	SNP
347	Wigan	-1.67	Lab	398	Rayleigh	-2.18	Con
348	Bristol North West	-1.67	Lab	399	Southampton Itchen	-2.19	Lab
349	Sheffield Central	-1.68	Lab	400	Ashton under Lyne	-2.20	Lab
350	Hamilton North & Bellshill	-1.69	Lab	401	Stockport	-2.20	Lab
351	Wrexham	-1.71	Lab	402	West Ham	-2.24	Lab
352	Warley	-1.71	Lab	403	Salford	-2.32	Lab

404	Penrith & The Border	-2.34	Con
405	Bedfordshire South West	-2.34	Con
406	Hampshire North East	-2.35	Con
407	Rochford & Southend East	-2.36	Con
408	Livingston	-2.37	Lab
409	Bolton West	-2.39	Lab
410	Nuneaton	-2.40	Lab
411	Bradford South	-2.40	Lab
412	Lancaster & Wyre	-2.41	Lab
413	Doncaster Central	-2.42	Lab
414	Feltham & Heston	-2.45	Lab
415	Coventry North East	-2.47	Lab
416	Brent North	-2.47	Lab
417	Tyneside North	-2.48	Lab
418	Northampton North	-2.48	Lab
419	Plymouth Devonport	-2.49	Lab
420	Welwyn Hatfield	-2.50	Lab
421	Carlisle	-2.52	Lab
422	Batley & Spen	-2.54	Lab
423	Portsmouth South	-2.54	LD
424	Plymouth Sutton	-2.55	Lab
425	Great Yarmouth	-2.57	Lab
426	Milton Keynes South West	-2.58	Lab
427	Harrow East	-2.59	Lab
428	Carmarthen W. & Pembrokeshire S.	-2.61	Lab
429	Montgomeryshire	-2.62	LD
430	Shropshire North	-2.63	Con
431	Wirral South	-2.64	Lab
432	Essex North	-2.64	Con
433	Maldon & Chelmsford East	-2.65	Con
434	Witney	-2.67	Con
435	Cardiff North	-2.67	Lab
436	Liverpool Garston	-2.67	Lab
437	Daventry	-2.67	Con
438	Edinburgh Pentlands	-2.68	Lab
439	Leeds Central	-2.71	Lab
440	Bognor Regis & Littlehampton	-2.71	Con
441	Corby	-2.73	Lab
442	Ayr	-2.74	Lab
443	New Forest West	-2.76	Con
444	Southwark North & Bermondsey	-2.77	LD
445	Stoke-on-Trent South	-2.77	Lab
446	Dartford	-2.78	Lab
447	Leeds North East	-2.83	Lab
448	Warwickshire North	-2.84	Lab
449	Lewisham Deptford	-2.84	Lab
450	Hull East	-2.85	Lab
451	Ashfield	-2.85	Lab
452	Brighton Pavilion	-2.86	Lab
453	Eastbourne	-2.86	Con
454	Redcar	-2.86	Lab
455	Dover	-2.87	Lab
456	Isle of Wight	-2.88	LD
457	Hayes & Harlington	-2.88	Lab
458	Clwyd West	-2.92	Lab
459	Bosworth	-2.92	Con
460	Yeovil	-2.94	LD
461	Jarrow	-3.00	Lab
462	Hemel Hempstead	-3.03	Lab
463	Northampton South	-3.08	Lab
464	Worthing East & Shoreham	-3.13	Con
465	Tyne Bridge	-3.14	Lab
466	East Kilbride	-3.16	Lab
467	Bexleyheath & Crayford	-3.17	Lab
468	Ribble Valley	-3.17	Con
469	Croydon North	-3.21	Lab
470	Sedgefield	-3.23	Lab
471	South Holland & The Deepings	-3.27	Con
472	Hornchurch	-3.27	Lab
473	Cleethorpes	-3.30	Lab
474	Walsall North	-3.35	Lab
475	Basingstoke	-3.35	Con
476	Epping Forest	-3.37	Con
477	Wellingborough	-3.37	Lab
478	Spelthorne	-3.37	Con
479	Easington	-3.39	Lab
480	Blackpool North & Fleetwood	-3.40	Lab
481	Bexhill & Battle	-3.40	Con
482	Pendle	-3.41	Lab
483	Middlesbrough S. & Cleveland E.	-3.46	Lab
484	South Shields	-3.46	Lab
485	Chorley	-3.47	Lab
486	Cannock Chase	-3.53	Lab
487	Grantham & Stamford	-3.55	Con
488	High Peak	-3.56	Lab
489	Llanelli	-3.57	Lab
490	Blackpool South	-3.58	Lab
491	Maidenhead	-3.58	Con
492	Gateshead E. & Washington W.	-3.58	Lab
493	Houghton & Washington E.	-3.61	Lab
494	Fareham	-3.63	Con
495	Leeds East	-3.67	Lab
496	Vale of Clwyd	-3.68	Lab
497	Staffordshire South	-3.71	Con
498	Chipping Barnet	-3.72	Con
499	Cambridge	-3.73	Lab
500	Havant	-3.73	Con
501	Enfield Southgate	-3.76	Lab
502	Ealing North	-3.79	Lab
503	Merthyr Tydfil & Rhymney	-3.80	Lab
504	Tweeddale, Ettrick & Lauderdale	-3.82	LD
505	Camberwell & Peckham	-3.82	Lab

506	Waveney	-3.83	Lab	557	Doncaster North	-4.81	Lab
507	Forest of Dean	-3.84	Lab	558	Shipley	-4.87	Lab
508	Durham North West	-3.85	Lab	559	Harborough	-4.93	Con
509	Hampshire North West	-3.90	Con	560	Charnwood	-4.98	Con
510	Perth	-3.91	SNP	561	Erewash	-5.00	Lab
511	Bracknell	-3.92	Con	562	Salisbury	-5.05	Con
512	Macclesfield	-3.97	Con	563	Reading West	-5.05	Lab
513	Dagenham	-3.99	Lab	564	Blaby	-5.13	Con
514	Norfolk Mid	-4.01	Con	565	Liverpool Riverside	-5.16	Lab
515	Westbury	-4.06	Con	566	Warwick & Leamington	-5.26	Lab
516	Vale of York	-4.06	Con	567	Staffordshire Moorlands	-5.34	Lab
517	Bedford	-4.07	Lab	568	Hull North	-5.35	Lab
518	City of Chester	-4.11	Lab	569	Leyton & Wanstead	-5.45	Lab
519	Ribble South	-4.11	Lab	570	Basildon	-5.52	Lab
520	Bradford North	-4.13	Lab	571	Milton Keynes North East	-5.63	Lab
521	Reigate	-4.14	Con	572	Rushcliffe	-5.74	Con
522	Ilford South	-4.14	Lab	573	Altrincham & Sale West	-5.80	Con
523	Brentwood & Ongar	-4.16	Con	574	Devizes	-5.92	Con
524	Leeds North West	-4.17	Lab	575	Stafford	-5.94	Lab
525	Brighton Kemptown	-4.18	Lab	576	Derbyshire West	-5.98	Con
526	Norfolk North West	-4.19	Lab	577	Birmingham Hall Green	-5.98	Lab
527	Durham North	-4.21	Lab	578	Falmouth & Camborne	-5.99	Lab
528	Newcastle upon Tyne North	-4.23	Lab	579	Fylde	-6.07	Con
529	Bedfordshire North East	-4.28	Con	580	Stroud	-6.14	Lab
530	Hexham	-4.29	Con	581	City of Durham	-6.20	Lab
531	Swindon South	-4.30	Lab	582	Chatham & Aylesford	-6.24	Lab
532	Norfolk South West	-4.30	Con	583	Upminster	-6.25	Lab
533	Heywood & Middleton	-4.32	Lab	584	Liverpool West Derby	-6.26	Lab
534	Yorkshire East	-4.34	Con	585	Crawley	-6.27	Lab
535	Ashford	-4.34	Con	586	Thanet North	-6.33	Con
536	Surrey East	-4.38	Con	587	Dorset South	-6.38	Con
537	Boston & Skegness	-4.38	Con	588	The Wrekin	-6.46	Lab
538	Colne Valley	-4.40	Lab	589	Glasgow Anniesland	-6.47	Lab
539	Barking	-4.42	Lab	590	Billericay	-6.51	Con
540	Gillingham	-4.44	Lab	591	Thanet South	-6.63	Lab
541	Brigg & Goole	-4.45	Lab	592	Huntingdon	-6.65	Con
542	Romford	-4.47	Lab	593	Wansdyke	-6.77	Lab
543	Portsmouth North	-4.48	Lab	594	Hertsmere	-6.85	Con
544	Knowsley North & Sefton E.	-4.50	Lab	595	Beverley & Holderness	-6.87	Con
545	Wycombe	-4.51	Con	596	St Albans	-6.93	Lab
546	Bristol South	-4.54	Lab	597	Eltham	-7.02	Lab
547	Faversham & Kent Mid	-4.65	Con	598	Tewkesbury	-7.14	Con
548	Kettering	-4.67	Lab	599	Gloucester	-7.17	Lab
549	Harrow West	-4.69	Lab	600	Louth & Horncastle	-7.25	Con
550	Broxbourne	-4.69	Con	601	Hastings & Rye	-7.26	Lab
551	Wimbledon	-4.70	Lab	602	Suffolk West	-7.31	Con
552	Glasgow Kelvin	-4.73	Lab	603	Worcestershire Mid	-7.49	Con
553	Eastwood	-4.74	Lab	604	East Ham	-7.55	Lab
554	Scarborough & Whitby	-4.76	Lab	605	Morecambe & Lunesdale	-7.66	Lab
555	Old Bexley & Sidcup	-4.79	Con	606	Hertford & Stortford	-7.75	Con
556	Runnymede & Weybridge	-4.81	Con	607	Maidstone & The Weald	-7.89	Con

608	Newcastle-under-Lyme	-7.96	Lab
609	Gosport	-8.03	Con
610	Newcastle upon Tyne E. & Wallsend	-8.04	Lab
611	Hertfordshire North East	-8.15	Con
612	Stevenage	-8.18	Lab
613	Crosby	-8.46	Lab
614	Folkestone & Hythe	-8.47	Con
615	Sittingbourne & Sheppey	-8.49	Lab
616	Sheffield Hillsborough	-8.50	Lab
617	Bury St Edmunds	-8.73	Con
618	Richmond (Yorks)	-8.77	Con
619	Caithness, Sutherland & Easter Ross	-8.83	LD
620	Canterbury	-8.83	Con
621	Poplar & Canning Town	-9.18	Lab
622	Inverness East, Nairn & Lochaber	-9.18	Lab
623	Braintree	-9.23	Lab
624	Aberdeen North	-9.71	Lab
625	Hove	-9.73	Lab
626	Castle Point	-9.94	Lab
627	Ceredigion	-10.03	PC
628	Harwich	-10.04	Lab
629	Bishop Auckland	-10.22	Lab
630	Stockton South	-10.38	Lab
631	Cotswold	-10.41	Con
632	Blyth Valley	-11.08	Lab
633	West Bromwich West	-11.80	Spkr
634	Pudsey	-12.42	Lab
635	Liverpool Wavertree	-13.19	Lab
636	Wyre Forest	-13.34	Lab
637	Erith & Thamesmead	-13.38	Lab
638	Bethnal Green & Bow	-13.79	Lab
639	Cambridgeshire North East	-14.55	Con
640	Tatton	-18.11	Ind
641	Greenwich & Woolwich	-22.57	Lab

Table 10: SNP change of vote share 1992/97 and winning party

		%ch	1st
1	Angus	9.11	SNP
2	Ochil	8.32	Lab
3	Galloway & Upper Nithsdale	7.46	SNP
4	Glasgow Govan	7.42	Lab
5	Airdrie & Shotts	6.28	Lab
6	Tayside North	6.06	SNP
7	Renfrewshire West	5.89	Lab
8	Banff & Buchan	4.94	SNP
9	Dumbarton	4.82	Lab
10	Caithness, Sutherland & Easter Ross	4.63	LD
11	Inverness East, Nairn & Lochaber	3.90	Lab
12	Kilmarnock & Loudoun	3.81	Lab
13	Strathkelvin & Bearsden	3.42	Lab
14	Clydebank & Milngavie	2.68	Lab
15	East Lothian	2.43	Lab
16	Midlothian	2.28	Lab
17	Fife North East	2.27	LD
18	Glasgow Kelvin	2.09	Lab
19	Perth	2.00	SNP
20	Carrick, Cumnock & Doon Valley	1.57	Lab
21	Orkney & Shetland	1.54	LD
22	Livingston	1.52	Lab
23	Ayr	1.40	Lab
24	Gordon	1.38	LD
25	Greenock & Inverclyde	1.30	Lab
26	Edinburgh East & Musselburgh	1.14	Lab
27	Motherwell & Wishaw	1.04	Lab
28	Dunfermline East	0.82	Lab
29	Ross, Skye & Inverness West	0.76	LD
30	Roxburgh & Berwickshire	0.71	LD
31	Aberdeenshire W & Kincardine	0.61	LD
32	Edinburgh Central	0.57	Lab
33	Eastwood	0.55	Lab
34	Kirkcaldy	0.31	Lab
35	Coatbridge & Chryston	0.26	Lab
36	Cunninghame North	0.21	Lab
37	Glasgow Anniesland	0.10	Lab
38	Fife Central	0.08	Lab
39	Edinburgh South	0.03	Lab
40	Tweeddale, Ettrick & Lauderdale	-0.06	LD
41	Falkirk West	-0.11	Lab
42	Edinburgh North & Leith	-0.23	Lab
43	Glasgow Rutherglen	-0.31	Lab
44	Glasgow Cathcart	-0.55	Lab
45	Argyll & Bute	-0.64	LD

46	Hamilton North & Bellshill	-0.65	Lab
47	Aberdeen North	-0.65	Lab
48	Dunfermline West	-0.66	Lab
49	Clydesdale	-0.95	Lab
50	Stirling	-1.11	Lab
51	Cumbernauld & Kilsyth	-1.15	Lab
52	Paisley South	-1.18	Lab
53	Dundee West	-1.32	Lab
54	Aberdeen Central	-1.38	Lab
55	Paisley North	-1.59	Lab
56	Glasgow Shettleston	-2.18	Lab
57	Aberdeen South	-2.33	Lab
58	Glasgow Maryhill	-2.48	Lab
59	Edinburgh Pentlands	-2.66	Lab
60	East Kilbride	-2.70	Lab
61	Hamilton South	-2.71	Lab
62	Dumfries	-2.72	Lab
63	Moray	-3.05	SNP
64	Linlithgow	-3.34	Lab
65	Glasgow Springburn	-3.39	Lab
66	Cunninghame South	-3.44	Lab
67	Glasgow Baillieston	-3.47	Lab
68	Edinburgh West	-3.70	LD
69	Western Isles	-3.79	Lab
70	Falkirk East	-4.43	Lab
71	Dundee East	-5.54	Lab
72	Glasgow Pollok	-7.11	Lab

Table 11: Plaid Cymru change of vote share 1992/97 and winning party

		%ch	Ist
1	Ceredigion	10.67	PC
2	Clwyd West	8.88	Lab
3	Meirionnydd Nant Conwy	6.77	PC
4	Carmarthen East & Dinefwr	5.58	Lab
5	Llanelli	3.23	Lab
6	Swansea West	2.81	Lab
7	Islwyn	2.38	Lab
8	Ynys Mon	2.34	PC
9	Cardiff West	2.26	Lab
10	Newport East	1.94	Lab
11	Cardiff Central	1.82	Lab
12	Gower	1.64	Lab
13	Newport West	1.61	Lab
14	Cardiff South & Penarth	1.56	Lab
15	Rhondda	1.54	Lab
16	Delyn	1.29	Lab
17	Vale of Clwyd	1.09	Lab
18	Monmouth	1.05	Lab
19	Bridgend	1.05	Lab
20	Aberavon	1.02	Lab
21	Ogmore	0.70	Lab
22	Alyn & Deeside	0.62	Lab
23	Cardiff North	0.56	Lab
24	Wrexham	0.55	Lab
25	Brecon & Radnorshire	0.51	LD
26	Vale of Glamorgan	0.46	Lab
27	Blaenau Gwent	0.40	Lab
28	Montgomeryshire	0.25	LD
29	Caerphilly	0.01	Lab
30	Merthyr Tydfil & Rhymney	-0.11	Lab
31	Torfaen	-0.15	Lab
32	Swansea East	-0.21	Lab
33	Cynon Valley	-0.39	Lab
34	Conwy	-0.51	Lab
35	Clwyd South	-1.61	Lab
36	Preseli Pembrokeshire	-2.30	Lab
37	Carmarthen W. & Pembrokeshire S.	-2.43	Lab
38	Pontypridd	-2.61	Lab
39	Neath	-3.21	Lab
40	Caernarfon	-7.99	PC

Table 12: Highest Conservative share of the vote	

		%share
1	Huntingdon	55.30
2	Kensington & Chelsea	53.62
3	Arundel & South Downs	53.08
4	Sutton Coldfield	52.24
5	Surrey Heath	51.59
6	Hampshire North East	50.90
7	Horsham	50.76
8	New Forest West	50.55
9	Chesham & Amersham	50.38
10	Ruislip Northwood	50.24
11	Surrey East	50.11
12	Wokingham	50.06
13	Staffordshire South	50.02
14	Esher & Walton	49.84
15	Maidenhead	49.80
16	Buckingham	49.79
17	Wealden	49.78
18	Rayleigh	49.73
19	Macclesfield	49.61
20	South Holland & The Deepings	49.25
21	Beaconsfield	49.22
22	Fylde	48.87
23	Richmond (Yorks)	48.86
24	Broxbourne	48.86
25	Rochford & Southend East	48.74
26	Maldon & Chelmsford East	48.67
27	Runnymede & Weybridge	48.59
28	Stratford-on-Avon	48.26
29	Windsor	48.20
30	Cambridgeshire North West	48.11
31	Bexhill & Battle	48.11
32	Hampshire East	48.04
33	Tonbridge & Malling	48.02
34	Mole Valley	48.01
35	Penrith & The Border	47.59
36	Chingford & Woodford Green	47.49
37	Worcestershire Mid	47.41
38	Bracknell	47.36
39	Croydon South	47.32
40	Cities of London & Westminster	47.27
41	Aldridge - Brownhills	47.13
42	Bromsgrove	47.11
43	Stone	46.84
44	Fareham	46.83
45	Ribble Valley	46.66
46	Skipton & Ripon	46.54
47	Charnwood	46.48
48	Christchurch	46.43
49	Chichester	46.42
50	Henley	46.38

Table 13: Highest Labour share of the vote	

		%share
1	Bootle	82.85
2	Easington	80.20
3	Blaenau Gwent	79.47
4	Liverpool Walton	78.38
5	Knowsley South	77.11
6	Barnsley Central	76.99
7	Tyne Bridge	76.81
8	Merthyr Tydfil & Rhymney	76.68
9	Houghton & Washington East	76.38
10	Pontefract & Castleford	75.71
11	Swansea East	75.38
12	Rhondda	74.45
13	Islwyn	74.15
14	Birmingham Ladywood	74.08
15	Ogmore	73.98
16	Bolsover	73.97
17	Makerfield	73.57
18	Sheffield Brightside	73.53
19	Neath	73.53
20	Glasgow Shettleston	73.16
21	Barnsley East & Mexborough	73.15
22	Brent South	72.99
23	West Ham	72.88
24	Tyneside North	72.72
25	Wentworth	72.34
26	Gateshead E. & Washington W.	72.07
27	Middlesbrough	71.43
28	South Shields	71.41
29	Glasgow Springburn	71.36
30	Aberavon	71.32
31	Rotherham	71.32
32	Hull East	71.31
33	Newcastle upon Tyne E. & Wallsend	71.19
34	Liverpool West Derby	71.17
35	Sedgefield	71.16
36	Manchester Central	70.98
37	Halton	70.88
38	Lewisham Deptford	70.82
39	Birkenhead	70.76
40	Hemsworth	70.56
41	Liverpool Riverside	70.43
42	Durham North	70.26
43	Manchester Blackley	70.04
44	Knowsley North & Sefton East	69.91
45	Doncaster North	69.80
46	Cynon Valley	69.74
47	Leeds Central	69.62
48	Camberwell & Peckham	69.55
49	Tottenham	69.28
50	Islington North	69.25

Table 14: Highest Liberal Democrat share of the vote		
	%share	lst
1 Hazel Grove	54.49	LD
2 Cornwall North	53.17	LD
3 Newbury	52.92	LD
4 Orkney & Shetland	51.99	LD
5 Harrogate & Knaresborough	51.54	LD
6 Sheffield Hallam	51.33	LD
7 Fife North East	51.22	LD
8 Devon North	50.76	LD
9 Cheltenham	49.45	LD
10 Yeovil	48.75	LD
11 Southwark North & Bermondsey	48.61	LD
12 Bath	48.47	LD
13 Truro & St Austell	48.46	LD
14 Southport	48.11	LD
15 Hereford	47.95	LD
16 Cornwall South East	47.09	LD
17 Roxburgh & Berwickshire	46.50	LD
18 Montgomeryshire	45.88	LD
19 Berwick-upon-Tweed	45.47	LD
20 Twickenham	45.12	LD
21 Richmond Park	44.66	LD
22 St Ives	44.46	LD
23 Lewes	43.22	LD
24 Edinburgh West	43.20	LD
25 Oxford West & Abingdon	42.92	LD
26 Isle of Wight	42.75	LD
27 Taunton	42.72	LD
28 Gordon	42.61	LD
29 Christchurch	42.58	Con
30 Northavon	42.38	LD
31 Sutton & Cheam	42.30	LD
32 Winchester	42.06	LD
33 Devon West & Torridge	41.84	LD
34 Aberdeenshire W & Kincardine	41.07	LD
35 Brecon & Radnorshire	40.85	LD
36 Argyll & Bute	40.20	LD
37 Weston-Super-Mare	40.11	LD
38 Rochdale	39.96	Lab
39 Surrey South West	39.80	Con
40 Chesterfield	39.56	Lab
41 Torbay	39.56	LD
42 Somerton & Frome	39.52	LD
43 Portsmouth South	39.50	LD
44 Dorset Mid & Poole North	39.33	Con
45 Dorset North	39.07	Con
46 Teignbridge	38.76	Con
47 Ross, Skye & Inverness West	38.72	LD
48 Tiverton & Honiton	38.53	Con
49 Wells	38.45	Con
50 Eastbourne	38.33	Con

Table 15: Highest SNP share of the vote		
	%share	lst
1 Banff & Buchan	55.77	SNP
2 Angus	48.27	SNP
3 Tayside North	44.85	SNP
4 Galloway & Upper Nithsdale	43.91	SNP
5 Moray	41.57	SNP
6 Perth	36.38	SNP
7 Glasgow Govan	35.05	Lab
8 Kilmarnock & Loudoun	34.52	Lab
9 Ochil	34.38	Lab
10 Western Isles	33.40	Lab
11 Inverness East, Nairn & Lochaber	28.99	Lab
12 Cumbernauld & Kilsyth	27.80	Lab
13 Livingston	27.46	Lab
14 Linlithgow	26.81	Lab
15 Dundee East	26.54	Lab
16 Renfrewshire West	26.51	Lab
17 Midlothian	25.51	Lab
18 Fife Central	25.02	Lab
19 Airdrie & Shotts	24.40	Lab
20 Falkirk East	23.94	Lab
21 Falkirk West	23.43	Lab
22 Paisley South	23.38	Lab
23 Dumbarton	23.23	Lab
24 Dundee West	23.23	Lab
25 Argyll & Bute	23.17	LD
26 Caithness, Sutherland & Easter Ross	23.00	LD
27 Kirkcaldy	22.93	Lab
28 Motherwell & Wishaw	22.47	Lab
29 Clydesdale	22.13	Lab
30 Paisley North	21.92	Lab
31 Aberdeen North	21.81	Lab
32 Glasgow Kelvin	21.37	Lab
33 Clydebank & Milngavie	21.14	Lab
34 East Kilbride	20.90	Lab
35 Cunninghame South	20.78	Lab
36 Edinburgh North & Leith	20.10	Lab
37 Gordon	19.97	LD
38 Ross, Skye & Inverness W.	19.57	LD
39 Dunfermline West	19.17	Lab
40 Glasgow Baillieston	19.10	Lab
41 Hamilton North & Bellshill	19.09	Lab
42 Edinburgh East & Musselburgh	19.07	Lab
43 Greenock & Inverclyde	18.57	Lab
44 Glasgow Cathcart	18.55	Lab
45 Cunninghame North	18.44	Lab
46 Glasgow Pollok	17.87	Lab
47 Hamilton South	17.62	Lab
48 Glasgow Anniesland	17.11	Lab
49 Tweeddale, Ettrick & Lauderdale	17.10	LD
50 Coatbridge & Chryston	17.02	Lab

Britain Votes 6

Table 16: Highest Plaid Cymru share of the vote		
	%share	lst
1 Caernarfon	51.05	PC
2 Meirionnydd Nant Conwy	50.72	PC
3 Ceredigion	41.63	PC
4 Ynys Mon	39.46	PC
5 Carmarthen East & Dinefwr	34.64	Lab
6 Llanelli	18.96	Lab
7 Clwyd West	13.47	Lab
8 Rhondda	13.36	Lab
9 Carmarthen W. & Pembrokeshire S.	12.67	Lab
10 Cynon Valley	10.63	Lab
11 Caerphilly	9.68	Lab
12 Neath	8.11	Lab
13 Ogmore	7.04	Lab
14 Conwy	6.84	Lab
15 Swansea West	6.61	Lab
16 Pontypridd	6.49	Lab
17 Clwyd South	6.35	Lab
18 Preseli Pembrokeshire	6.33	Lab
19 Islwyn	6.24	Lab
20 Merthyr Tydfil & Rhymney	5.99	Lab

Table 17: Highest Green share of the vote		
	%share	lst
1 Hackney N. & Stoke Newington	4.31	Lab
2 Islington North	4.23	Lab
3 Stroud	3.94	Lab
4 Tottenham	2.81	Lab
5 Sheffield Central	2.62	Lab
6 Brighton Pavilion	2.55	Lab
7 Louth & Horncastle	2.50	Con
8 Hornsey & Wood Green	2.36	Lab
9 Birmingham Sparkbrook & Small Heath	2.30	Lab
10 Leeds West	2.23	Lab
11 Vauxhall	2.21	Lab
12 Norfolk Mid	2.18	Con
13 Leominster	2.15	Con
14 Wansbeck	2.12	Lab
15 Huddersfield	2.11	Lab
16 Worcestershire West	2.04	Con
17 Oxford East	2.04	Lab
18 Bradford West	1.89	Lab
19 Manchester Gorton	1.88	Lab
20 Bethnal Green & Bow	1.82	Lab

Table 18: Highest Referendum share of the vote	
	%share
1 Harwich	9.20
2 Folkestone & Hythe	8.05
3 Suffolk West	7.59
4 Reigate	6.96
5 St Ives	6.89
6 Bexhill & Battle	6.74
7 Cotswold	6.64
8 Yeovil	6.61
9 Falmouth & Camborne	6.59
10 Truro & St Austell	6.49
11 Isle of Wight	6.47
12 Norfolk South West	6.28
13 Cornwall North	6.22
14 Cambridgeshire South	6.15
15 Devon East	6.09
16 Suffolk Coastal	6.07
17 Wealden	5.97
18 Chichester	5.95
19 Skipton & Ripon	5.91
20 Sussex Mid	5.88
21 Ashford	5.79
22 Dorset South	5.67
23 Norfolk Mid	5.62
24 Fareham	5.58
25 Leominster	5.57
26 Castle Point	5.56
27 Sleaford & North Hykeham	5.53
28 Huntingdon	5.47
29 Esher & Walton	5.41
30 Bury St Edmunds	5.29
31 Suffolk South	5.27
32 Gosport	5.25
33 Brentwood & Ongar	5.24
34 Thanet North	5.18
35 Eastbourne	5.17
36 Grantham & Stamford	5.14
37 Durham North West	5.12
38 Hastings & Rye	5.12
39 Norfolk North West	5.07
40 Lewes	5.05
41 Devizes	5.03
42 Surrey South West	5.01
43 Cambridgeshire South East	5.00
44 Tiverton & Honiton	4.99
45 Richmond (Yorks)	4.96
46 Havant	4.96
47 Bedfordshire North East	4.94
48 Dorset North	4.88
49 Surrey East	4.86
50 Croydon South	4.85

Table 19: Highest U.K. Independent share of the vote

		%share
1	Salisbury	5.72
2	Torbay	3.68
3	Romsey	3.52
4	Bognor Regis & Littlehampton	3.31
5	Devon West & Torridge	3.11
6	New Forest West	3.10
7	Dorset West	2.97
8	Arundel & South Downs	2.91
9	Hexham	2.56
10	Teignbridge	2.54
11	Hampshire North West	2.53
12	Cornwall South East	2.49
13	Essex North	2.35
14	Hertford & Stortford	2.26
15	Bromley & Chislehurst	2.23
16	Wellingborough	2.12
17	Northampton South	2.03
18	Worthing West	2.00
19	Birmingham Hodge Hill	1.93
20	Ryedale	1.88
21	Totnes	1.86
22	Maldon & Chelmsford East	1.86
23	Bournemouth East	1.82
24	Worthing East & Shoreham	1.79
25	Thurrock	1.76
26	Dorset South	1.75
27	Worcester	1.72
28	Bexhill & Battle	1.60
29	Rutland & Melton	1.56
30	Halifax	1.54
31	Sunderland South	1.53
32	Dorset North	1.52
33	Congleton	1.52
34	Aldershot	1.47
35	Isle of Wight	1.47
36	Kensington & Chelsea	1.46
37	Luton North	1.46
38	Chichester	1.43
39	Horsham	1.43
40	Thanet South	1.40
41	Southend West	1.37
42	Westbury	1.36
43	Witney	1.36
44	Beverley & Holderness	1.32
45	Worcestershire Mid	1.27
46	Ealing North	1.24
47	Runnymede & Weybridge	1.21
48	Surrey Heath	1.19
49	Lancaster & Wyre	1.19
50	Chesham & Amersham	1.18

Table 20: Highest Liberal share of the vote

		%share
1	Liverpool West Derby	9.58
2	Bethnal Green & Bow	6.63
3	Slough	3.84
4	Wolverhampton North East	3.77
5	Westbury	3.45
6	Exeter	3.33
7	Wyre Forest	3.03
8	Newcastle-under-Lyme	2.85
9	Romford	2.61
10	Devon East	2.59
11	Coventry North East	2.46
12	Torbay	2.18
13	Rochford & Southend East	2.16
14	Hastings & Rye	2.13
15	Ribble South	2.04
16	Wolverhampton South East	1.86
17	Maidenhead	1.76
18	Rayleigh	1.62
19	Birmingham Perry Barr	1.56
20	Camberwell & Peckham	1.56

Table 21: Highest Pro-Life share of the vote

		%share
1	East Kilbride	2.40
2	Hamilton South	2.07
3	Glasgow Cathcart	2.06
4	Cumbernauld & Kilsyth	1.69
5	Doncaster Central	1.60
6	Paisley North	1.56
7	Manchester Withington	1.39
8	Leyton & Wanstead	1.24
9	Glasgow Pollok	1.16
10	Glasgow Maryhill	1.16
11	Glasgow Anniesland	1.10
12	Solihull	1.06
13	Billericay	1.03
14	Rotherham	0.97
15	Copeland	0.94
16	Ealing Southall	0.87
17	Epsom & Ewell	0.86
18	Birmingham Selly Oak	0.82
19	Sheffield Central	0.77
20	Don Valley	0.76

	Table 22: Highest Natural Law Party share of the vote			Table 24: Highest National Democrat share of the vote	
		%share			%share
1	Glasgow Maryhill	2.19	1	West Bromwich West	11.39
2	Northampton South	0.95	2	Birmingham Ladywood	1.80
3	Buckingham	0.85	3	Blackburn	1.41
4	Lancashire West	0.82	4	Halesowen & Rowley Regis	1.21
5	Hull West & Hessle	0.81	5	Burton	1.11
6	Milton Keynes South West	0.77	6	Dudley North	0.98
7	Preston	0.72	7	Nottingham South	0.92
8	Peterborough	0.69	8	Wolverhampton North East	0.86
9	Ruislip Northwood	0.66	9	Yorkshire East	0.78
10	Waveney	0.57	10	East Ham	0.73
11	Orkney & Shetland	0.56	11	Leicester South	0.64
12	Hull North	0.55	12	Stoke-on-Trent South	0.62
13	Hitchin & Harpenden	0.55	13	Derby South	0.61
14	Oldham West & Royton	0.54	14	Dagenham	0.51
15	Brent North	0.53	15	Plymouth Devonport	0.46
16	Luton North	0.53	16	Leicester West	0.45
17	Wellingborough	0.53	17	Tiverton & Honiton	0.40
18	Redditch	0.51	18	Devon East	0.25
19	Reading East	0.51	19	Southwark North & Bermondsey	0.23
20	Antrim South	0.51	20	Londonderry East	0.21

	Table 23: Highest British National Party share of the vote			Table 25: Highest Socialist Labour share of the vote	
		%share			%share
1	Bethnal Green & Bow	7.50	1	East Ham	6.76
2	Poplar & Canning Town	7.26	2	Cardiff Central	5.28
3	Dewsbury	5.18	3	Newport East	5.24
4	West Ham	3.56	4	Dudley North	4.51
5	East Ham	3.15	5	Ealing Southall	3.86
6	Barking	2.71	6	Bradford West	3.40
7	Dagenham	2.49	7	Birkenhead	2.97
8	Chingford & Woodford Green	2.38	8	Lewisham Deptford	2.96
9	Bradford West	1.84	9	Oldham West & Royton	2.87
10	Southwark North & Bermondsey	1.75	10	Barnsley East & Mexborough	2.80
11	Erith & Thamesmead	1.73	11	Bolton West	2.79
12	Hackney South & Shoreditch	1.57	12	Vauxhall	2.52
13	Ilford North	1.55	13	Manchester Central	2.42
14	Stoke-on-Trent Central	1.51	14	Camberwell & Peckham	2.41
15	Feltham & Heston	1.46	15	Don Valley	2.35
16	Epping Forest	1.40	16	Newcastle-under-Lyme	2.20
17	Rochdale	1.36	17	Swansea West	2.19
18	Rossendale & Darwen	1.32	18	Motherwell & Wishaw	2.18
19	Broxbourne	1.30	19	Cannock Chase	2.14
20	Romford	1.24	20	Wythenshawe & Sale East	2.10

Table 26: Highest Socialist Party share of the vote

		%share
1	Coventry South	6.51
2	Liverpool Riverside	2.03
3	Nottingham North	1.54
4	Tyne Bridge	1.49
5	Sheffield Central	1.28
6	Easington	1.20
7	Liverpool Walton	1.10
8	Bootle	1.10
9	Jarrow	1.01
10	Uxbridge	0.96
11	Manchester Withington	0.85
12	Leeds Central	0.82
13	Camberwell & Peckham	0.82
14	Cardiff South & Penarth	0.81
15	Leicester West	0.80
16	Swansea East	0.75
17	Bristol South	0.71
18	Bradford West	0.54
19	Livingston	0.50
20	Hitchin & Harpenden	0.41

Table 27: Highest Scottish Socialist Alliance share of the vote

		%share
1	Glasgow Pollok	11.09
2	Glasgow Baillieston	3.05
3	Glasgow Govan	2.34
4	Glasgow Shettleston	1.80
5	Glasgow Maryhill	1.38
6	Glasgow Cathcart	1.37
7	Glasgow Springburn	1.29
8	Glasgow Kelvin	1.18
9	Dundee West	1.10
10	Cumbernauld & Kilsyth	0.96

Table 28: Highest Monster Raving Loony Party share of the vote

		%share
1	Wokingham	1.75
2	Sittingbourne & Sheppey	1.40
3	Sunderland North	1.07
4	Faversham & Kent Mid	1.03
5	Ashton under Lyne	0.97
6	Cannock Chase	0.95
7	West Ham	0.89
8	Bradford North	0.88
9	Cheltenham	0.75
10	Gillingham	0.60
11	Chipping Barnet	0.51
12	Birmingham Selly Oak	0.50
13	Winchester	0.49
14	Derbyshire West	0.49
15	Cardiff Central	0.48
16	Stafford	0.48
17	Stockport	0.46
18	Wansdyke	0.41
19	City of Chester	0.36
20	Richmond Park	0.36

Table 29: Highest Rainbow Alliance share of the vote

		%share
1	Esher & Walton	0.56
2	Hackney North & Stoke Newington	0.54
3	Brent North	0.52
4	Brent South	0.51
5	Holborn & St Pancras	0.41
6	Manchester Withington	0.41
7	Dulwich & West Norwood	0.38
8	Coventry North East	0.36
9	Coventry South	0.36
10	Regent's Park & Kensington North	0.35
11	West Ham	0.34
12	Brent East	0.34
13	St Albans	0.33
14	Coventry North West	0.32
15	Hampstead & Highgate	0.32

Table 30: Lowest share of the vote for the winning party				Table 31: Highest %Turnout and winning party		
		%share	Ist		%turnout	Ist
1	Tweeddale, Ettrick & Lauderdale	31.22	LD	1 Ulster Mid	85.75	SF
2	Falmouth & Camborne	33.84	Lab	2 Brecon & Radnorshire	82.24	LD
3	Inverness East, Nairn & Lochaber	33.89	Lab	3 Stirling	81.84	Lab
4	Hastings & Rye	34.37	Lab	4 Wirral South	81.08	Lab
5	Colchester	34.39	LD	5 Monmouth	80.54	Lab
6	Conwy	35.04	Lab	6 Cardiff North	80.19	Lab
7	Eastleigh	35.05	LD	7 Ayr	80.03	Lab
8	Bristol West	35.23	Lab	8 Vale of Glamorgan	79.98	Lab
9	Aberdeen South	35.27	Lab	9 Leicestershire North West	79.95	Lab
10	Caithness, Sutherland & Easter Ross	35.59	LD	10 Galloway & Upper Nithsdale	79.65	SNP
11	Dorset South	36.10	Con	11 Tyrone West	79.20	UU
12	Perth	36.38	SNP	12 Northavon	79.14	LD
13	Norfolk North	36.48	Con	13 Twickenham	79.03	LD
14	Totnes	36.52	Con	14 Richmond Park	79.02	LD
15	Kingston & Surbiton	36.67	LD	15 Wansdyke	79.00	Lab
16	Bridgwater	36.93	Con	16 Bedfordshire Mid	78.95	Con
17	Shrewsbury & Atcham	37.01	Lab	17 Dumfries	78.92	Lab
18	Clwyd West	37.06	Lab	18 High Peak	78.89	Lab
19	Suffolk South	37.33	Con	19 Dover	78.88	Lab
20	Carshalton & Wallington	38.18	LD	20 Strathkelvin & Bearsden	78.84	Lab
21	Bury St Edmunds	38.34	Con	21 Stroud	78.80	Lab
22	Woking	38.40	Con	22 Rushcliffe	78.77	Con
23	Suffolk Coastal	38.57	Con	23 Forest of Dean	78.74	Lab
24	Canterbury	38.65	Con	24 Welwyn Hatfield	78.59	Lab
25	Ross, Skye & Inverness W.	38.72	LD	25 Carmarthen East & Dinefwr	78.56	Lab
26	Harwich	38.76	Lab	26 Christchurch	78.53	Con
27	Hexham	38.76	Con	27 Buckingham	78.48	Con
28	Southend West	38.76	Con	28 Ribble Valley	78.47	Con
29	Folkestone & Hythe	39.03	Con	29 City of Chester	78.43	Lab
30	Teignbridge	39.21	Con	30 Woodspring	78.43	Con
31	Wells	39.39	Con	31 Mole Valley	78.42	Con
32	Milton Keynes North East	39.43	Lab	32 Norfolk South	78.37	Con
33	Ynys Mon	39.46	PC	33 Stone	78.33	Con
34	Portsmouth South	39.50	LD	34 Preseli Pembrokeshire	78.31	Lab
35	Somerton & Frome	39.52	LD	35 Broxtowe	78.28	Lab
36	Torbay	39.56	LD	36 Winchester	78.28	LD
37	Norfolk Mid	39.58	Con	37 Eastwood	78.26	Lab
38	Havant	39.74	Con	38 Derbyshire West	78.23	Con
39	Eastwood	39.74	Lab	39 Derbyshire South	78.21	Lab
40	Billericay	39.76	Con	40 Wantage	78.10	Con
41	Wantage	39.81	Con	41 Oxford West & Abingdon	78.03	LD
42	Gillingham	39.83	Lab	42 Hitchin & Harpenden	77.99	Con
43	Leeds North West	39.89	Lab	43 Erewash	77.95	Lab
44	Wycombe	39.93	Con	44 Edinburgh West	77.91	LD
45	Weston-Super-Mare	40.11	LD	45 Devon West & Torridge	77.91	LD
46	Norfolk South	40.15	Con	46 Maldon & Chelmsford East	77.90	Con
47	Argyll & Bute	40.20	LD	47 Exeter	77.90	Lab
48	Shropshire North	40.24	Con	48 Bury North	77.85	Lab
49	Worthing East & Shoreham	40.46	Con	49 Wells	77.84	Con
50	Sittingbourne & Sheppey	40.56	Lab	50 Ellesmere Port & Neston	77.79	Lab

Table 32: Lowest %Turnout and winning party		
	%turnout	1st
1 Liverpool Riverside	51.57	Lab
2 Manchester Central	51.74	Lab
3 Hackney North & Stoke Newington	51.97	Lab
4 Sheffield Central	53.04	Lab
5 Birmingham Ladywood	54.16	Lab
6 Leeds Central	54.18	Lab
7 Cities of London & Westminster	54.24	Con
8 West Bromwich West	54.35	Spkr
9 Hackney South & Shoreditch	54.45	Lab
10 Kensington & Chelsea	54.71	Con
11 Camberwell & Peckham	55.30	Lab
12 Vauxhall	55.47	Lab
13 Manchester Gorton	55.56	Lab
14 Glasgow Shettleston	55.74	Lab
15 Glasgow Kelvin	56.11	Lab
16 Salford	56.28	Lab
17 Glasgow Maryhill	56.40	Lab
18 Tottenham	56.91	Lab
19 Hull North	56.97	Lab
20 Birmingham Sparkbrook & Small Heath	57.04	Lab
21 Tyne Bridge	57.08	Lab
22 Manchester Blackley	57.23	Lab
23 Sheffield Brightside	57.47	Lab
24 Poplar & Canning Town	57.69	Lab
25 Antrim South	57.82	UU
26 Lewisham Deptford	57.87	Lab
27 Down North	57.93	UKU
28 Antrim East	58.18	UU
29 West Ham	58.45	Lab
30 Hull West & Hessle	58.69	Lab
31 Sunderland South	58.77	Lab
32 Glasgow Springburn	58.94	Lab
33 Sunderland North	59.05	Lab
34 Hull East	59.19	Lab
35 Strangford	59.39	UU
36 Liverpool Walton	59.47	Lab
37 Barnsley Central	59.66	Lab
38 Streatham	60.18	Lab
39 Bethnal Green & Bow	60.26	Lab
40 Holborn & St Pancras	60.29	Lab
41 East Ham	60.34	Lab
42 Southwark North & Bermondsey	60.39	LD
43 Nottingham East	60.54	Lab
44 Birmingham Erdington	60.83	Lab
45 Birmingham Hodge Hill	60.89	Lab
46 Liverpool West Derby	61.30	Lab
47 Barking	61.66	Lab
48 Belfast South	62.05	UU
49 Dagenham	62.10	Lab
50 Houghton & Washington East	62.10	Lab

Table 33: Largest Electorate and winning party		
	Electorate	1st
1 Isle of Wight	101680	LD
2 Bristol West	85275	Lab
3 Teignbridge	82098	Con
4 Ealing Southall	81704	Lab
5 Stratford-on-Avon	81542	Con
6 Portsmouth South	81014	LD
7 Daventry	80750	Con
8 Brentford & Isleworth	80722	Lab
9 Norfolk South West	80406	Con
10 Devizes	80383	Con
11 Wealden	80206	Con
12 Croydon Central	80152	Lab
13 Cornwall North	80076	LD
14 Harrow East	79981	Lab
15 Warwick & Leamington	79975	Lab
16 Taunton	79783	LD
17 York	79710	Lab
18 Northampton South	79672	Lab
19 Exeter	79418	Lab
20 Rugby & Kenilworth	79406	Lab
21 Bracknell	79292	Con
22 Winchester	79272	LD
23 Norfolk South	79239	Con
24 Salisbury	79099	Con
25 Aylesbury	79047	Con
26 Northavon	79011	LD
27 Solihull	78943	Con
28 Gloucester	78852	Lab
29 Rushcliffe	78849	Con
30 Orpington	78831	Con
31 Lancaster & Wyre	78684	Lab
32 Hammersmith & Fulham	78637	Lab
33 Oxford West & Abingdon	78425	LD
34 Ealing North	78144	Lab
35 Stroud	77856	Lab
36 Banbury	77797	Con
37 Wiltshire North	77440	Con
38 Erewash	77402	Lab
39 Norfolk North	77365	Con
40 Kingswood	77221	Lab
41 Norfolk North West	77083	Lab
42 Croydon North	77063	Lab
43 Basingstoke	77063	Con
44 Southampton Itchen	76910	Lab
45 Hampshire East	76890	Con
46 Coventry North West	76845	Lab
47 Derbyshire South	76672	Lab
48 Truro & St Austell	76634	LD
49 Aldershot	76499	Con
50 Cambridgeshire South East	76393	Con

Table 34: Smallest Electorate and winning party

		Electorate	Ist
1	Western Isles	22983	Lab
2	Orkney & Shetland	32325	LD
3	Meirionnydd Nant Conwy	32345	PC
4	Caithness, Sutherland & Easter Ross	41652	LD
5	Montgomeryshire	42753	LD
6	Hamilton South	46562	Lab
7	Caernarfon	46815	PC
8	Roxburgh & Berwickshire	47288	LD
9	Midlothian	47600	Lab
10	Cumbernauld & Kilsyth	48032	Lab
11	Glasgow Shettleston	48104	Lab
12	Cynon Valley	48286	Lab
13	Greenock & Inverclyde	48971	Lab
14	Argyll & Bute	48983	LD
15	Glasgow Pollok	49328	Lab
16	Glasgow Cathcart	49416	Lab
17	Cunninghame South	49543	Lab
18	Paisley North	49725	Lab
19	Glasgow Govan	49978	Lab
20	Aberavon	50031	Lab
21	Islwyn	50540	Lab
22	Glasgow Rutherglen	50673	Lab
23	Newport East	50676	Lab
24	Wrexham	50741	Lab
25	Tweeddale, Ettrick & Lauderdale	51114	LD
26	Glasgow Baillieston	51185	Lab
27	Camberwell & Peckham	51313	Lab
28	Coatbridge & Chryston	52024	Lab
29	Clydebank & Milngavie	52092	Lab
30	Dunfermline East	52133	Lab
31	Brecon & Radnorshire	52142	LD
32	Ogmore	52193	Lab
33	Motherwell & Wishaw	52252	Lab
34	Kirkcaldy	52266	Lab
35	Renfrewshire West	52348	Lab
36	Vale of Clwyd	52426	Lab
37	Stirling	52491	Lab
38	Dunfermline West	52538	Lab
39	Glasgow Maryhill	52693	Lab
40	Galloway & Upper Nithsdale	52751	SNP
41	Falkirk West	52850	Lab
42	Glasgow Anniesland	53112	Lab
43	Carmarthen East & Dinefwr	53121	Lab
44	Birmingham Yardley	53151	Lab
45	Ynys Mon	53294	PC
46	Barking	53458	Lab
47	Clwyd West	53467	Lab
48	Clwyd South	53495	Lab
49	Brent South	53505	Lab
50	Brent East	53548	Lab

Table 35: Gender of Candidates

	Female	%	Male	%
Con	69	10.6	579	89.4
Lab	157	24.6	482	75.4
LD	140	21.9	499	78.1
Grn	23	24.2	72	75.8
SNP	15	20.8	57	79.2
PC	7	17.5	33	82.5
Referendum	73	13.3	474	86.7
UK Ind	25	13.0	168	87.0
NLP	53	26.9	144	73.1
Other	110	16.8	544	83.2
Total	672	18.0	3052	82.0

Table 36: Gender of Winning Candidates

	Female	%	Male	%
Con	13	7.9	152	92.1
Lab	101	24.2	317	75.8
LD	3	6.5	43	93.5
SNP	2	33.3	4	66.7
PC	0	0.0	4	100.0
Other	1	5.0	19	95.0
Total	120	18.2	539	81.8

Table 37: Lost Deposits

Conservative	8
Labour	0
Liberal Democrat	13
Green	95
SNP	0
Plaid Cymru	15
Referendum	505
UK Independent	192
Natural Law Party	197
Other	568
Total	1593

INDEX TO GENERAL ELECTION CANDIDATES SHOWING PARTY
AFFILIATION AND CONSTITUENCY NUMBER

C

E

G

McIlwaine, S.P. (Con) 394
McIntosh, A.C.B. Ms. (Con) 600
McIntosh, G. (Con) 292
McIntyre, A.E.J. Ms. (Con) 473
McIntyre, M. (Con) 592
McIsaac, S. Ms. (Lab) 148
McIvor, E.R. Ms. (Grn) 579
McKay, G. Ms. (Ref) 265
McKee, J. (DUP) 13
McKenna, R. Ms. (Lab) 172
McKeon, R. Ms. (NLP) 202
McKerchar, J.E. (LD) 261
McKie, S.P. (UKI) 563
McKinlay, A. (LD) 92
McLaggan, J.H.N. (NLP) 97
McLaughlin, M. (SF) 258
McLean, I.R. (Ref) 231
McLeish, H.B. (Lab) 253
McLoughlin, P.A. (Con) 186
McManus, G. (Lab) 290
McMaster, G. (Lab) 452
McMinn, I.A. (Lab) 319
McMurdo, W. (UKI) 538
McNair, A. Ms. (Con) 33
McNamara, J.K. (Lab) 331
McNamee, P.D. (SF) 426
McNulty, A.J. (Lab) 302
McNulty, P.A. (Ref) 329
McPherson, D. (UKI) 224
McPhie, D.H. (Con) 269
McVey, P.J. (LD) 168
McVicar, C. Ms. (SSA) 273
McVicar, J. (SSA) 266
McWalter, T. (Lab) 310
McWhirter, I.C.H. (Ref) 110
McWhirter, R.A. (UKI) 285
McWilliam, J.D. (Lab) 69
Meacher, M.H. (Lab) 446
Mead, G.S. (NLP) 635
Mead, L.F. (Ref) 37
Mead, R.G.C. (UKI) 217
Meaden, G.J. (Grn) 122
Meads, H.S. (NLP) 60
Meads, J.D. (Lab) 495
Meads, L.P. Ms. (NLP) 605
Meakin, J.K. (Ind) 245
Meale, J.A. (Lab) 397
Mearns, D.F. (PL) 25
Mearns, V.P. Ms. (PL) 377
Mears, M.L. (NLP) 643
Meechan, H.L. (Ref) 134

Meeds, K.M. Ms. (Nat Dem) 288
Melding, D.R.M. (Con) 123
Melia, S.J. (LD) 458
Meling, M.M. Ms. (Lab) 454
Melling, J.M. (LD) 48
Mellor, A. (Ref) 114
Mellor, D.J. (Con) 468
Melton, K.M. (LD) 148
Merchant, P.R.G. (Con) 37
Merritt, S.L. (Lab) 480
Merron, G.J. Ms. (Lab) 373
Merton, C.R. (UKI) 147
Metcalfe, A. A. Ms. (LD) 29
Meyer, N.L. (LD) 484
Meynell, G. (Ind Grn) 186
Mian, A.K. (Ind) 371
Michael, A.E. (Lab) 125
Michael, V. Ms. (Grn) 162
Michie, B. (Lab) 513
Michie, R. Ms. (LD) 16
Micklem, A.C. Ms. (Lib) 544
Middleton, H. (Lib) 236
Middleton, J.P. (Con) 422
Middleton, M.J. (Nat Dem) 530
Midgley, J.A. (Con) 453
Mieklejohn, I.P.F. (Ref) 411
Miers, T.D.P.C. (Con) 113
Milburn, A. (Lab) 177
Miles, A.J. (Ref) 27
Miles, G.M. (LD) 243
Miles, J. Ms. (Ref) 28
Miles, S. Ms. (Grn) 313
Millar, L. (SNP) 404
Millen, P.W. (LD) 525
Miller, A.P. (Lab) 234
Miller, D.I. (Ref) 224
Miller, H.P.J. (UKI) 326
Miller, J.C.C. (LD) 626
Miller, K. (LD) 327
Miller, L. Ms. (BNP) 407
Miller, P.J. (NLP) 581
Miller, R. Ms. (Ref) 325
Miller, S.A. Ms. (PL) 548
Miller, T.P. (LD) 104
Milligan, A.H. (UKI) 265
Millington, A.J. (UKI) 654
Mills, D.B.L. Ms. (NLP) 436
Mills, D.C. (UKI) 91
Mills, P.L. (PL) 164
Mills, R.W. (Ref) 80
Millson, M.E. Ms. (LD) 326

Q

S

T